PRAISE FC

MW01195840

"A pastor and master storyteller, Shane unfurls the life of his father, Moon, a legendary, larger-than-life fisherman who left his family for Alaska's abundant streams and rivers. Under the surface, this story reveals a son both desperately seeking a father's love while also celebrating his adventurous life. Reminiscent of A *River Runs Through It, Moon and Sunn* weaves family and fishing into a rich narrative that brought tears of joy and sorrow to my eyes—I expect it will for you as well!"

—Joe Maxwell, Book editor and writer

"*Moon and Sunn* reveals the joys of a boy and his father in the outdoors and the painful and long-lasting effects of divorce into adulthood. As a product of both experiences, Sunn's memoir and its themes of forgiveness and healing hit home with me and served as a wonderful reminder of the beauty that can arise from the ashes of broken relationships."

—Brad Dye, Outdoor writer, syndicated columnist
(home paper—*The Meridian Star*)

Some men who live extraordinary lives become larger than life with each retelling of their experiences. Jimmy "Moon" Sunn's story resembles a modern-day *Jeremiah Johnson*, but with one exception: this unbelievable story is true. Shane intertwines childhood pain from his parents' divorce with exhilarating fishing adventures as he struggles to understand and love his father. The journey transformed the writer. *Moon and Sunn*, a page-turning memoir that reads like a novel, will keep you in your seat, except to go get the next good cup of coffee.

—Anthony Wood, author of *White & Black* and
winner of the Will Rogers Medallion Award

MOON

AND

SUNN

MEMOIR OF A FISHING LEGEND
AND HIS SON

SHANE SUNN

Moon and Sunn: Memoir of a Fishing Legend and His Son
Published by Sunn Author
Denver, Colorado

ISBN: 978-1-7369860-0-4

BIOGRAPHY & AUTOBIOGRAPHY / Personal Memoirs

Cover and Interior design by Victoria Wolf, wolfdesignandmarketing.com, copyright owned by Shane Sunn
Illustrations by John Moss Sunn.

For Jean, our children, our future grandchildren,
and stories yet to be told.

INTRODUCTION

THE BOOK YOU HOLD in your hands surprised me.

For years, locals insisted, "You must write a book about your daddy." According to them, James William "Moon" Sunn's story had to be told. Moon is a legend in my hometown of Ackerman, Mississippi, in all things out-of-doors, and a fading legend among the early bank fishermen on the Kenai River in Alaska. However, when I picked up the pen to tell his stories, I soon discovered the task wasn't an easy stroll in the park on a Sunday afternoon. Writing itself is difficult enough, but the difficulty I encountered was of a different origin.

When I was five, my parents, Moon and Farrah Sunn, divorced, which was a rarity in the mid-sixties, "Christ-haunted" South. Divorce was akin to Hawthorne's *The Scarlet Letter,* and I wore it as such. After the divorce, my time with Moon was relegated mainly to sporadic weekends and when he wasn't fishing in Alaska. Moon was everyone else's hero, but for me, as a kid, the designation was in question. Most days, I walked around with a real but indiscernible loneliness. I craved more meaningful time with him.

I naively thought I'd successfully dealt with my pain years before, but when I began to write, I discovered new depths, especially when delving into specific stories and events. So, I had a decision to make: to write or not to write? My choices seemed either to quit the book altogether or write and leave out the painful parts. The latter was a viable option because Moon's stories can easily stand on their own two feet. But how do you even write a story about your daddy without telling parts of your own? For me, the second option felt disingenuous, so I opted to take the plunge. Like anything worth doing, the process took time. I retraced significant events and contemplated buried pain, laughter, and tears. To my surprise, the experience was cathartic and healing. Pain can make you hard and lock you in the vault of bitterness or, if you stare it in the face and address it, transform you.

Like all legendary persons and their stories, Moon's stories have been told, retold, and embellished. Each time, the fish grew a little bit or a lot, and Moon's harrowing adventures increased in magnitude. However, I've tried to remain accurate in my descriptions of every detail. My readers might be tempted to think, "There's no way this actually happened." The truth is it actually did.

I've attempted to preserve Moon's voice and his method of storytelling. Jean, my wife, told me, "If you use Moon's voice, I'm afraid he will come across like an uneducated redneck. That's not who he is." I replied, "There are far worse designations in life!"

Moon is an armchair historian. He remembers everything. I interviewed and recorded Moon's recollections on numerous occasions. While writing, I attempted to research precise details related to history and geography. I was amazed at the accuracy of Moon's descriptions. Of course, I'm sure I failed at some junctures.

I have a vivid imagination. Listening to Moon's stories, especially the early ones surrounding Moon's memories of his dad, my granddad Mack, I took the liberty to imagine how things must have been and filled in the blanks. For example, the story of a Friday-night hoedown in Marked Tree, Arkansas, is the product of my imagination and a personal visit to the Lepanto Museum in Arkansas, where I discovered hoedowns occurred regularly in the area during the early part of the last century. Mack's time in a WWI field hospital and other stories are of similar origin.

Attempting honesty, I have avoided protecting most names, lives, and painful stories. Writer Anne Lamott, in an April 2017 TED Talk, said, "If people wanted you to write more warmly about them, they should have behaved better." However, I realize those shoes could easily be placed on my two feet. I appeal to Samuel Clemens, who said this about his attempt to write his autobiography: "I have been dictating this autobiography of mine daily for three months; I have thought of fifteen hundred or two thousand incidents in my life which I am ashamed of, but I have not gotten one of them to consent to go on paper yet."[1] I've attempted to remain honest about the glories and pain, others' and my own, but as Clemens articulates, that's not so easy to do, and it is never complete in this life.

To understand the subtleties of any story, one must pay attention to the nuances of *place*. By *place,* I mean more than a dot on McNally's highway atlas. I mean the soil, the smells, the trees, the rocks, the water, the fish, and the people past and present—their histories, their struggles, their hopes and aspirations. Stories don't just happen anywhere; they happen somewhere—in a particular place. And every minute detail cries out with meaning.

The significant dots on this story's map are Ackerman, Mississippi, and Soldotna, Alaska, but the story is really about the journey. I explore Moon's journeys back and forth to Alaska, attempting to reconcile a divorce and the untimely death of his dad, Mack. I explore my own journey to understand and come to terms with my often absent and always fishing dad. Like any

---

1   Mark Twain, *Autobiography of Mark Twain, Volume 1: The Complete Authoritative Edition*, Edited by Harriet Elinor Smith (Berkeley: The University of California Press, 2010), 57.

journey worth taking, it was not always easy. So, this story is also about the journey behind the fishing journeys—life's journey, Moon's and mine—the joys, the sorrows, and the important lessons learned along the way. It's really a story of our collective journeys East of Eden, of life, death, exhilaration, pain, meaning, and hope.

I moved away from the South in July 2000, unwittingly trading cypress swamps and mud for mountain vistas and dry. I prefer cypress swamps and mud. I love the fertile, fecund smell of methane gas bubbling to the water's surface from the disturbed decaying matter below, preferably with a 12-gauge or fishing utensil in hand. Writing this story was like wading in a cypress swamp, methane bubbling to the surface from fond and painful memories below, finally finding their release into the air. Not necessarily dry or humid air, just air. Like methane gas, some of it might smell strange, even bad, but for me, the smell is sweet.

In the end, it's a family fishing tale.

CHAPTER 1

Moon Sunn

1972 — Duck Hill, Mississippi

MOON SUNN HAS MADE a careful study of every watershed lake built in north Mississippi and has fished most. Many of these lakes are posted, but Moon believes they belong to the citizens because they were built with state and federal dollars, meaning his tax dollars. When I was eleven, I remember a trip to fish a lake near the small community of Duck Hill, Mississippi.

It was early spring in Mississippi and had been raining buckets for several days straight. We drove the old yellow Dodge down a lengthy logging road, spinning, swerving, and gunning it through mud holes, just barely avoiding getting stuck in the absolute middle of nowhere. Finally, we arrived at a locked gate. That's when you get your fishing stuff together and hike as far as necessary to get to the lake. That day the lake was muddy, the color of an orange milkshake. The fishing was going to be beyond challenging.

Moon disappeared, leaving me on the levee, where I cast in the same spot over and over, most likely hundreds of times. Yes, this was standard operating procedure when I was still too young to follow. Finally, I gave up and simply doodled in the mud to avoid worry and boredom.

He reappeared hours later, wet from head to toe, with a couple of nice bass tied to a nylon string on his side, and announced, "I've found some clearer water toward the back of the lake. Get on my back." The overgrowth around the lake was so substantial that walking there would've been like hacking through the Amazon jungle, so we took the easier route.

Away we went, my arms wrapped around his neck, Moon swimming with one hand and holding the rods out of the water with the other, the fish still tied to his side. Stopping, treading water to catch his breath, we angled for the other side. I held on for dear life. Finally feeling the mucky bottom, we waded out under a canopy of large oak trees, some still holding their brown leaves from last summer's growth. At the water's edge, we startled an enormous boar coon that quickly ran and scampered up one of the oak trees.

"Man, that's a big coon. Shane, how'd you like a coonskin cap?"

I don't know what came over him; he never stopped fishing to do these sorts of things. Although Moon still considered himself the reincarnation of *Jeremiah Johnson,* and I suppose a coonskin cap for his son was a good way to prove it. Or maybe he felt a bit guilty that we had exerted so much effort to get to the lake, and our chances of catching any more fish that day were slim.

"Yeah, I'd love one."

"Okay, stand right here, and I'll go get the .22 out of the car. Hold this stick, and whatever you do, don't let that coon come down that tree."

"All right."

I never once considered the implications of standing alone in the middle of nowhere or the fact this wasn't the standard operating procedure for most fathers and sons. Moon had to swim back across the lake, hike back to the car to get the .22, and then make it all the way back again. The coon stayed put, but the fear of being alone in the woods, holding a stick at the base of an oak tree, welled up inside. I pushed it down. Finally, more than an hour later, I was relieved to hear the "swish, swish" of water as Moon waded out, holding the .22.

"I got the gun, but I could only find three 'cot-treges.' Is that coon still up there?"

"Yeah, but he climbed higher."

I'd shot a BB gun since I was five, but a .22 only a few times at targets. We walked out a distance from the base of the tree to get a better shot. After all the trouble, I knew there wasn't a chance he'd perform the honors. In Moon's way of thinking, the perceived value of a coonskin cap increases proportionally to its owner's participation in animal sacrifice. I put the gun to my shoulder and leaned against a small sapling to steady my aim.

"Put it on his head, take a deep breath, let it halfway out, and then gently squeeze the trigger."

My first shot hit the coon in the stomach. The tip-tip sound of blood droplets falling from high above rattled the dry oak leaves in front of us. Nerves weakening, my next two shots were clean misses.

"Daddy, we don't have any more bullets. What do we do now?"

Moon believes with religious zeal that every animal is sacred. So there was nothing to do but finish what we started.

"Pick up your stick. That wounded coon is gonna try to come down that tree, and if he does, you hit him with it. I'll drive the car to the nearest town and buy some more .22 'cot-treges.' Whatever you do, don't let that coon out of that tree."

Now the situation was bordering on insanity, but real convictions exist for times like these. I should have protested but knew it would've been pointless. "Swish, swish," Moon waded out, beginning his fifth swim across the lake. I held my stick, trying to hold back tears. Late afternoon turned to darkness, and weird sounds filled the woods as water birds and other critters heading for roost all sounded like they'd love nothing better than a young, tender boy for dinner. Increasingly terrified, I thought, *If only I was a better marksman, this wouldn't be happening.*

Beginning his descent down the tree, the wounded coon let out hair-raising moans at repetitive intervals. Tightening my grip on the stick, I tried to muster any remaining vestiges of bravery, warm tears streaming down my face. Squinting to locate the coon in the moonlight, I circled and beat the base of the tree with my only friend, the stick. The loud whops intermingled with my own moaning and crying stopped the coon's advance. He stayed put on a large branch twelve feet above the ground.

It turned colder, hours passed, and every terrifying explanation for why Moon wasn't back wedged its way into my young mind. *He's stuck somewhere on the muddy road* at least offered some hope he'd return.

Darker explanations entered my mind in rapid succession. *He was killed in a car accident on the highway, and not one soul knows I'm out here alone. He cramped up and drowned from all the swims back and forth across the lake, and his lifeless body is floating somewhere out there in the darkness.* Feasible, since we hadn't eaten a bite since early that morning.

Between sobs, I screamed as loudly as possible, "Daddy! Daddy!" My voice reverberated through the timber and echoed back to me. I only stopped long enough to carefully listen for any far-off muffled reply. Nothing! My voice grew hoarser with every successive attempt. *Are my ears playing tricks on me?* Several times, I was convinced I heard the familiar "swish-swish" of Moon wading to shore.

I screamed again, "Is that you?" No reply, only the vacuous sound of the darkness. *Oh, maybe it's just a beaver busy at its nightly work or the two fish splashing that are still tied to a bush at the water's edge.*

Finally, I screamed again, listened, and thought I detected a distant faint reply. I waited a few minutes and tried again. This time, the reply was more audible, and I said to myself, aloud for reassurance, "That's him, that's him!"

Tears of fear became tears of joy when minutes later, I heard the reassuring sound of Moon wading ashore. I quickly wiped them away. He walked up to the tree carrying a six-volt flashlight and a box of .22 shorts he had managed to keep dry on the swim by putting them in his hat. Overjoyed, I propped my friend, the stick, against the tree.

"Sorry it took me so long. I had to drive all the way to Winona to find any rifle 'cot-treges.' Where's that coon?"

"He's right there on that limb."

He shined the flashlight upward, and the coon's two yellow eyes peered down at us.

"Let me get behind you with the light so you can see how to aim."

A bit shaky from the cold, the fuzzy lines between fathers and sons, life and death, even the raccoon's sacrifice all converged within me. I focused the rifle sights, inhaled, exhaled, and squeezed the trigger. With a loud plop, the coon hit the ground. We walked over, Moon scanning the light back and forth on the dead coon.

"Perfect shot. You hit him right between the eyes. That's a big coon. He'll make a fine hat. You hungry? I've got some food in the car."

Suddenly, I had never felt so hungry in my entire life. But we still had to swim the lake with a dead coon, a .22 rifle, two bass, a six-volt flashlight, and a box of .22 cartridges. Moon had wisely taken the fishing gear back to the car on one of his previous trips. We walked to the water's edge, and while I held the flashlight, Moon took out wads of string from his pockets.

"A man can never have too much rope or string."

He cut a section of string and tied a loop on each end. Securing the front and back legs, he made another loop and adjusted it so the coon fit snugly around his neck, resting on his shoulders. He wedged the rifle barrel in the flashlight's handle, pushed it down, and secured it with string. He put the box of .22 cartridges back in his hat. He tied the fish on his belt loop. Holding the rifle and attached light in his right hand high above the water, he waded chest-deep into the cold water.

"Shane, climb on."

Hesitantly wading into the frigid water, I wrapped my arms around Moon's neck, resting my chin on the dead coon's wet fur. Off we went, Moon swimming with one arm, holding the rifle in the other, kicking with both feet. I was shivering from head to toe when we reached the other side but felt warm inside.

"Walk fast and jog a little, Shane. It will help you warm up."

We made it to the gate and our mud-caked car. Moon started the engine and turned the heater and fan to high. As we bounced, swerved, and spun back down the muddy road, I felt the sensation of my cold extremities coming to life. We reached the pavement with the car still in motion and headed for Ackerman. We dined on cold fried chicken and potato logs smothered in ketchup. Food had never tasted so good. I was soon sound asleep. I don't even remember walking into my mom's house in the wee hours of the morning and crawling into bed.

During the following days, Moon kept me abreast of his progress on the coonskin cap. After school on certain afternoons, he'd stop on the street in front of our house in his yellow Dodge car and honk the horn. I'd run out and sit in the passenger's seat and receive all the updates. He meticulously skinned the coon and created a homemade paste out of who knows what in order to soften and tan the hide. One day, the horn honked, and he arrived, delivering a coonskin cap Daniel Boone and Jeremiah Johnson would've been proud of.

I regret I no longer have the cap. For several years, I wore it proudly, fighting furious battles between Indians and pioneers, the envy of all my neighborhood pals. We built a stick fort, and somehow during a tussle, my cap fell between the stick fort and a large log beside the fort. I searched and searched, finally becoming convinced one of my envious friends had lifted it.

Years later, when my attention had changed from Indians and pioneers to girls and football, Moon was off again to Alaska, looking for his dad. Me? Missing mine. I thought about the cap and the formative adventure we had together that produced it. I walked down to my old childhood play area, the remnants of the fort a rotten pile of sticks. I glanced over toward the old log, and laying there slightly underneath it was something white. I knelt and pulled up the decaying remains of the coonskin cap, completely ruined.

2017 — BERKELEY, CALIFORNIA

It was a warm mid-October day when I stopped in a small bookstore in Berkeley, California, to pick up a copy of Norman Maclean's *A River Runs*

Through It. My youngest son, Moss, had my copy at college in Lawrence, Kansas. While checking out and fumbling through my backpack for my wallet and debit card, the clerk mentioned it was the forty-year anniversary of its first publication, and this edition had a special foreword by Robert Redford. I was sixteen forty years earlier, and Moon was already deep into his fishing exploits in Alaska.

In 1991, Moon was fly-fishing in Montana. He sat in his truck, intensely studying road maps, his spectacles joined in the middle by duct tape lying crooked on the bridge of his wide nose, determined to find places where he could pull off and fish comfortably without being harassed by private landowners and "no trespassing" signs. As he eased back onto the highway, he spotted a roadside diner and decided to stop in for a cheeseburger. When he went to pay, he noticed a small placard by the register that read, "A River Runs Through It." So, he asked the cashier, "Which river?"

Of course, she looked puzzled, so he tried again. "A river runs through where?"

She chuckled. "Oh, you haven't heard about the movie?"

"No, what?"

"They're making a movie, and Robert Redford was just in here yesterday. In fact, he sat right where you did."

"Oh," Moon muttered, pulling out his map. "Could you tell me where this turnoff is?"

2020 — Ackerman, Mississippi

Norman Maclean was the son of a Presbyterian minister. I am the son of a fisherman. Norman's dad required his sons to study *The Shorter Catechism.* My dad required me to study absolutely nothing, but he did expect me to know how to fish. I'm a Presbyterian minister and, I might add, a fisherman.

In Maclean's family, "there was no clear line between religion and fly-fishing."[2] In my family, the same was true, but it happened backward. I learned to fish behind greatness, not knowing all the while I was learning how to be a minister.

Real fishermen and real clergymen both share the necessity of faith and the undying pursuit of beauty. This story is about Moon, an incredible fisherman whose unquenchable quest for the next fish was his attempt to reconcile the untimely death of his dad, my granddad. Unresolved pain drives many of us in ways we are unaware.

I inherited the joys and sorrows of this pain, like my children will from me. The sorrows have been my greatest teachers, and the joys have brushed eternity. So, this fishing story is also about life. Just like Moon always says about fishing lures, "Some are designed to catch fish; others are designed to catch men."

In February 2020, before the harsh reality of COVID-19 fully set in, Jean, my wife, and I spent three days in Ackerman interviewing Moon and recording his stories. Late afternoons, we visited other family members to get their perspectives on specific stories and events. On Day One, we slowly meandered the lazy streets of Ackerman in our rental car, Moon riding shotgun, Jean tending the iPhone resting on the console in record mode. We asked questions. Moon told continuous stories in his gravelly voice. I'd heard many of the stories before, but as we listened, somehow, this time his stories made more sense as they melded with my own life and experience.

That evening and for the next two days, Jean persistently asked, "Where were you and what were you doing when this or that happened?" Her question nudged me to travel back in time, remembering childhood experiences I'd forgotten—I realized, some selectively.

---

2   Norman Maclean, *A River Runs Through It* (Chicago: University of Chicago Press, 2017), 3.

CHAPTER 2

MACK SUNN

"Earth's crammed with heaven.
And every common bush afire with God;
But only he who sees, takes off his shoes,
The rest sit round it and pluck blackberries."

— Excerpt from *"Aurora Leigh"* by Elizabeth Browning, 1856

MOON'S STORY BEGINS LIKE THIS: "My granddaddy and his brother made their livins' cypress loggin' in the Arkansas delta. They called that place the 'sunken lands.' What they did was cut giant cypress trees in the swamps and then sawmill 'em. There were a lot more cypress trees in Arkansas than where they had come from in Kentucky. But Daddy was never too much inclined to work with his family in the loggin' business. I don't know exactly why, maybe the loggin', especially the way they did it back then, was too dangerous for a boy. But I think Daddy must have had different kinds of aspirations from the very start. His job was to gather all the food."

"Sunken lands" logging camp, Lepanto, Arkansas, 1910.

1811 — THE NEW MADRID EARTHQUAKES

I pulled the car into a local station to refuel and re-caffeinate. Jean paused the recorder and asked Moon if he wanted anything. He responded, "Thank you, no I'm fine."

We got back in the car, and Moon continued, "You know the 'sunken lands' were created by the New Madrid earthquakes that happened in about 1812. They say the mighty Mississippi flowed back-ards!"

The New Madrid earthquakes brought untold devastation and completely reconfigured the landscape for hundreds of miles on both sides of the Mississippi River. The quakes started in December 1811 and continued until April 1812.

On Monday, December 16, 1811, the earth began to convulse. At New Madrid, settlers were shaken from their beds at 2:15 a.m. They wandered into the streets in a panic, huddling together throughout the night as houses were leveled, trees toppled, and animals ran wild. The earth swayed, shook, and gaped open in giant fissures, swallowing anything in its path.

An early chronicler living in Poinsett County, Arkansas, near the St. Francis River, the future destination of Mack's family, described the earthquakes. "The ground moved like waves on the land, when suddenly the earth would burst, sending up huge volumes of water and sand, leaving great chasms where the earth had burst open. Great forests that stood moments before simply disappeared swallowed whole by the earth. Vast tracts of land sank as far as fifty feet into the earth. The St. Francis River between Lake City and Marked Tree, Arkansas, dropped six to eight feet during the quakes causing the river to form the geographical phenomena known as the 'sunken lands.'"[3]

Today, the Arkansas Game and Fish Commission conserves more than twenty-seven thousand acres of this land known as The St. Francis Sunken Lands Wildlife Management Area.

Cypress thrived for millennia in the fertile biosphere created by the annual flooding of the Mississippi River, but the quakes produced new vast acres of shallow water combined with decaying biomass, creating ideal conditions for new-growth cypress. A century later, a palatial canopy of old and new-growth cypress covered the sunken lands in every direction as far as the eye could see—the cypress Garden of Eden.

1907 — MARKED TREE, ARKANSAS

The wagons of the Son brothers, James and William, rolled off the steamboat Handy at the dock on the St. Francis River near Marked Tree, Arkansas, loaded with their families, domestic supplies, and as much tree

---

3   *The Encyclopedia of Arkansas History & Culture,* "New Madrid Earthquakes of 1811–1812," https://encyclopediaofarkansas.net/entries/new-madrid-earthquakes-of-1811-1812-2218/.

harvesting equipment as they could reasonably transport. Onboard and restless with excitement, ten-year-old George McClellan Son, born in 1895 near Sacramento, Kentucky, and known as "Mack," surveyed his new surroundings. It was seven years before the Great War, the American pioneer spirit still very much alive, always beckoning iron-willed settlers westward in search of new opportunities for prosperity and adventure. The brothers' ambitions centered on harvesting the vast stands of cypress timber, some trees protruding a hundred feet above the endless miles of swamps, sloughs, and bayous. Cypress lumber was highly treasured because its chemical composition made it far more resistant to decay than other species.

Turn-of-the-century logging camps weren't known for cleanliness, or decency, for that matter. Most certainly, an unsuitable place for women and children. The families, adaptable from the outset, utilized their wagons as temporary shelters until they were able to construct permanent dwellings near Lepanto, Arkansas, sometime during 1909.

James and William worked long and arduous days, swinging axes and pushing then pulling opposite ends of a crosscut saw. Chainsaws weren't developed until the 1920s, leading to an increase in timber production comparable to what occurred when the crosscut saw replaced the axe. The best technique for harvesting cypress was to take advantage of the annual river flooding. Sawmills were assembled adjacent to the flood plain so cut logs could be floated to the mill. Late winter through spring was the time for felling, cutting, and floating logs. Summer through fall was the time for sawing, stacking, and transporting lumber.

The grueling labor was so physically demanding the loggers needed large amounts of daily protein for enough energy to meet the challenge. It brings to mind the protein requirements of the Lewis and Clark expedition, according to the book *Undaunted Courage* by Stephen Ambrose, as quoted by Tori Avey in a PBS special.

"To understand how difficult and physically demanding the Corps of Discovery Expedition was, you need only look at the amount of food they consumed. On July 13, 1805, Clark wrote: 'We eat an emensity of meat; it requires 4 deer, or an elk and a deer, or one buffaloe to supply us plentifully 24 hours. When wild game was plentiful, each man consumed up to 9 pounds of meat in one day.' That's a lot of protein! Meat was vital to their diet; it helped to fill their hungry bellies and gave them the strength required to pull canoes and carry heavy loads. The types of meat that were eaten also served as a reflection of the season, terrain, and climate they encountered. Bison and deer were prominent during the crossing of the Great Plains, while salmon and a starchy tuber known as wapato kept them nourished as they entered territory west of the Rocky Mountains. *Fish* was eaten in abundance, a favorite being the eulachon, or candlefish, which Lewis claimed to be superior to any fish he had ever tasted. At Fort Clatsop, elk was in large supply. It was served boiled, dried and roasted for breakfast, lunch and dinner."[4]

FISHIN' PARADISE

Moon explained, "Man, Daddy was livin' in a huntin' and fishin' paradise!"

In the "sunken lands," the identical conditions that produced the abundant cypress growth created a rich ecosystem teeming with abundant wildlife: white-tailed deer, black bear, ducks, geese, and all sorts of fish—big healthy ones! The Sons had not only landed in the cypress Garden of Eden, but they also had landed in the hunting and fishing Garden of Eden.

While his family worked grueling days logging, Mack was free to roam the countryside. Like Adam set loose in paradise, he immersed himself in hunting and fishing. His preferred passion: water-fowling.

Due to the demand for a steady supply of protein, James finally conceded that Mack could do more for the family in the woods and water with hook, line, and shotgun than in the family business. There was a demand, and Mack was more than happy to provide the supply.

---

4   *What Lewis and Clark Ate*, Tori Avey, Rocky Mountain PBS, 2013, pbs.org.

As the sunken lands burst to life each new morning, Mack pushed off from shore, paddling his dugout boat through tupelo gums and cypress knobs, anticipating the telltale tugging of his lines. By midmorning, his boat was filled with catfish, crappie, and bass. Pausing long enough for a tin of sardines, a can of pork and beans, and some corn pone, it was off again to seine the shallows, catching enough live bait to reset his lines before dark. The day's work complete, eagerly anticipating the next, a long gray serpentine wake trailed as Mack slowly sculled toward home with the day's catch.

Most evenings, he encountered his cousin Larry, making the same trek. They communicated important details of the day's exploits using only signs and gestures. The tall cypress drew long black shadows across the water, the westward-facing trunks reflected the last rays of brilliant orange light, and an otherworldly peace filled Mack's soul; the world was right.

Season Change

"Daddy liked to fish more than any man I've ever been around, but do you know what his absolute favorite thing to do was, Shane?"

"No, what?"

"He loved to duck hunt. I don't remember exactly when it was, but Daddy won second place in the State of Arkansas duck-calling contest, usin' only his hand. He could call ducks on his hand makin' all the sounds different species of ducks make, even the mallard feed call. When I was a boy, he used to take me over to the Mississippi Delta, and you can't believe how good he was at duck huntin'."

I remembered stories of Mack calling ducks with his bare hand, but I also remembered the intriguing old duck calls I played with as a kid in the overstuffed junk drawer in the entry hall at Othermother's house. "Othermother," a nickname bestowed by her grandchildren, was Moon's mom, my grandmother.

In the fall, when the cypress boughs changed from emerald to burnt orange, Mack laid his shotgun and a box of shells beside him in the boat.

Filled with wonder over the seasonal transformations of the earth, he paddled to his favorite cypress hole, calling greenheads down through the timber using only his cupped hand.

In winter, when the river rose and the fishing slowed, Mack subsidized his daily provision of fish with waterfowl, gray squirrels, and sometimes a white-tailed deer or feral hog. Anything extra was gladly shared with the many poor and hungry families living in the area. His lifestyle closely resembled the frontiersmen preceding him a century before. Mack was living the outdoorsman's dream, not a care in the world.

ENTREPRENEUR

Moon continued, "Daddy was always thinkin' ahead. He built fish pens out of cypress strips and, I guess, chicken wire. He tied 'em to the pier at the steamboat dock on the St. Francis. On Tuesdays and Thursdays when the steamboat whistle blew, he'd be there waitin' to sell his fish. They weighed the fish and threw 'em on ice and sold 'em in St. Louis. I think they paid him by the pound. He used whatever money he made from sellin' the fish to do it better the next time."

Maybe it was the spirit of the times or maybe simply an endowment from the Creator, but young Mack was one of the rare individuals able to combine his outdoor skill with a strong entrepreneurial bent.

Able to spot potential business opportunities, Mack familiarized himself with the latest outdoor gear and gadgets.

"Daddy owned a Pflueger Supreme bait-castin' reel and steel rod. The first fiberglass rods came out in the mid-1940s. Those steel rods and old reels were archaic by today's standards. The reels were prone to backlash." [Moon was referring to what happens when the lure slows down after casting, but the spool does not, resulting in a tangled mess of line, also known as a "bird's nest."]

"They were spooled with an early form of braided line they called 'silk.' While everybody else was still fishin' for bass with cane poles and live minnows, Daddy mostly fished with rod and reel. He could cast like a magician. I couldn't do it when I was little; I always ended up with a backlash. Some of the reels back then, I don't think even had a level-wind," Moon explained, referring to the now-standard mechanism to wind line evenly on the spool.

"His favorite lures were the #7 Paw Paw Pearl Wobbler and an early version of the King Zig Zag. He continued trot-linin', but when he figured out he could catch more bass usin' the rod and reel, that's what he did. Besides, I think Daddy just loved the thrill of the catch."

As we listened, I remembered from my childhood Moon recapitulating, "Shane, the rod and reel enables the angler to feel and respect the power and fight of the fish."

What Moon means is: rod and reel in hand, feet firmly planted on "terra firma"—no boats and motors to assist in fighting the fish.

I thought, *Not only did Moon love and respect Mack immensely, but his most treasured values, some of them idiosyncratic, were inherited directly from Mack.*

I remembered Mack's old fishing lures that Aunt Patty had given me years before and his Remington Model 11 shotgun and worn duck call that I own. I thought, *Like a musician's instrument, a hunter and angler's gear is not only vital but meaningful in personal sorts of ways.*

As Moon continued to tell stories of Mack's teenage years, I thought about his hunting and fishing gear, relics from the past that I'd held and admired many times. Somehow that helped make the stories more concrete, connecting me to a grandfather I never knew.

BANISHMENT FROM THE GARDEN

"In the day of the good be mindful of the evil and
in the day of evil be mindful of the good."
— Martin Luther

For Mack, life in paradise was about to change—drastically change.

Moon continued, "The carefree days of fishin' and huntin' didn't last. I know a big thing was when Daddy lost his first cousin Larry. Back then the measure of a man was still determined by his ability in the woods and on the water."

My ears perked up. I thought, *back then?* It sure sounded like an apt description of motivational forces still operative in Moon's life.

"I always thought the best person paddling a boat I'd ever seen was Daddy, but he always told me the very best was his first cousin Larry. Uncle Luther told me the same thing. 'The only man who could paddle a boat better than your daddy was his cousin Larry. Your daddy and Larry were kinda inseparable.'"

Luther Spurgeon, "Uncle Luther," was Mack's brother-in-law and after Mack's death became Moon's hero and surrogate dad.

Moon explained, "Larry was born deaf and mute, and maybe that's why he was so good in the outdoors. They say he was real strong and tough as a pine knot. Daddy helped Larry sell his fish down at the pier because people made fun of him all the time. Daddy took up for Larry and loved him like a brother.

"One evenin', Larry failed to return home at the usual time. Daddy was only a teenager, but early the next mornin', he helped lead a search party. The first thing they found was Larry's dugout turned upside down. Daddy was very familiar with the fishin' grounds, and not far away from the overturned boat, he noticed a trotline slantin' down in the water at a funny angle. He paddled over there and could tell a fish was on the line. The line was so heavy he had to get the others to help him pull it up. When they got the line to the top, Larry was drowned between two big catfish still hooked on either side of his body. The fish were still fightin'. One of 'em was a giant flathead and the other, a big blue cat. Both fish weighed more than sixty pounds apiece. I think what happened was after boatin' the first fish, the other one surprised Larry and jerked the middle hook through his hand. He prob'ly tried to reach over with his other hand, and that's when the boat flipped. Larry was real strong, but he wouldn't that strong. I guess we all hope to die doin' what we love. Uncle Luther told me, 'Daddy took Larry's death real bad and never talked about it one bit, but he was never quite the same after that.'

"Uncle Luther also told me that not long after Larry's death, a terrible dispute broke out between Mack's dad and his brother (the Son brothers). I think it was over land, but I ain't sure because Daddy never talked about it when I was a kid. Whatever happened created a terrible conflict not only between my grandfather and great-uncle, but it also somehow alienated Daddy (Mack) from his family."

Moon's first cousin, genealogist Ruby Cockrell, writes, "I don't know why Uncle Mack changed his name. I was told that he and my dad had a disagreement, and he left. For a long time, I don't think they knew where Mack was. When he left, he told Grandma that she would never find him."

Moon continued, "After Larry died and the dispute broke out, Daddy just left. I'm not sure exactly what year it was or where he went, but he wasn't old enough to enlist in the army. But somehow, he went to another county in Arkansas and falsified his birth certificate, and they took him. He changed the spellin' of his last name. I'm not for sure if he changed the spellin' before or right after the war, but I think it was before. It used to be Son, S-O-N, but he changed it to Sunn, S-U-N-N. Daddy never talked about his daddy much when I was a boy, and he never went back to Arkansas except sometimes around his momma's birthday. I guess sometimes dire circumstances warrant a new outlook and a different approach."

The year before the US entered World War I, Congress passed the National Defense Act, which lowered the age to join without parental consent to eighteen. Enlistees between sixteen and eighteen needed parental consent. It is uncertain, but likely Mack falsified his birth certificate because he was seventeen and didn't have parental consent.

Listening, I wondered about the family conflict. *Why are the circumstances largely unknown, and why is it veiled in so much secrecy? Was it a land or business scandal or possibly marital infidelity?* Whatever it was, one thing is certain: Mack's idealistic childhood world was shattered. Devastated and disillusioned, Mack internalized his pain, placed the weight on his own shoulders, and wore it like a heavy wet coat. Like Adam's banishment from paradise, Mack carried his burden to the hellish world of WWI.

1917 — WWI

"I don't think Daddy really knew what he was gettin' himself into goin' over there," Moon explained.

I remembered the faded war photograph in the gray cardboard frame: Mack in full uniform. As a kid, I'd stared at it for what seemed like hours; it was in the overstuffed drawer with the old duck calls. It had probably been there since the day they moved things from the old house on Main Street by the railroad tracks.

"Daddy was hit by shrapnel from an explodin' shell, and he also got burned real bad by nerve gas."

My mind wandered to what I imagined Mack encountered "over there." Shells whined overhead and exploded with regularity, lighting up the night sky over Nancy, France. The survival skills learned in the "sunken lands" were soon to be put to the ultimate test. WWI proved to significantly shorten Mack's life.

Plans in place, the commanding officer gave the signal to advance forward out of the trenches toward the German lines. His heart racing, trying to avoid the barbed wire, Private Sunn trudged ahead in the calf-deep mud. Instantly, a shell exploded nearby, sending dirt and bodies skyward.

Shrapnel tore through his flesh, propelling him forward and slamming him face down in the cold muck. Black darkness engulfed Mack, an eerie yellow fog oozing up from the wet ground.

FIELD HOSPITAL

Bringing me back to the present, Moon interjected, "I don't know how long Daddy stayed in the field hospital, but I think it was two or three months."

I visualized Mack lying wounded in an overcrowded field hospital constructed of green canvas tents somewhere two miles from the front, fortunate to still be among the living. Vague shapes of white-uniformed nurses scurried back and forth among the wounded and dying, appearing and reappearing as Private Mack Sunn slowly emerged from his demonic dream. Ears ringing, head pounding, blinking his eyes to focus his blurry vision, Mack gradually regained consciousness.

Mack's body recoiled and stiffened when the nurse he hadn't noticed standing beside his bed said, "Here, drink this." Swallowing, the cool liquid penetrating his parched throat, Mack slipped back into dreamland. Over the following weeks, he began to recuperate.

Conscious, curious heads turned as the eyes of wounded patients carefully followed the path of the army sergeant and the head nurse, clipboards and papers in their hands. A premonition of their terminus, Mack quickly extinguished his cigarette and sat straight up in bed. The sergeant saluted; Private Sunn respectfully returned the gesture.

The nurse's smile broadened as she handed Mack the clipboard and pen. "You've made a steady recovery, but your wounds preclude you from further military service. Here's your discharge papers; sign all three copies."

Having anticipated this moment yet suddenly feeling disoriented, Mack hesitated. Blankly staring at the clipboard, he handed it back to the nurse. "Could I have a few days to think about it?"

"Of course, you can. We'll speak with you in a few days."

REASSIGNMENT

"I don't think Daddy really wanted to go home, plus he was always the kinda man who liked to finish whatever he started," Moon added, bringing me momentarily out of the unfolding scene I could see in my mind's eye. I smiled because Moon's description sounded very familiar, maybe too familiar.

That night, Mack tossed and turned as he thought about his future. *How can I leave so soon when there is still work to be done? How can I live with myself if I go home while my comrades continue to risk their lives in the field?*

Realizing the desperate need for more ambulance drivers, rather than punching his ticket home, Mack had an idea.

The sergeant listened as Mack suggested his plan. "I know I'm not capable of fighting, but I am well enough to drive an ambulance. Would you please consider reassignment, Sir?"

"Let us review your records, and I will have an answer in a few days."

"Thank you, Sir!"

Reassigned, Mack drove an ambulance until the war's end, transporting wounded soldiers from the front lines to field hospitals or the dead to receiving stations for transport home.

"Daddy never talked about the war very much, but when he did, he always talked about how bad the smells were drivin' that ambulance."

1918 — ARMISTICE DAY AND REENTRY

Revelers flooded the streets in Paris, London, Philadelphia, New York, and around the world as news of the armistice quickly spread. Never the same, Mack briefly returned to Poinsett County, Arkansas, suffering from what we today recognize as PTSD. He hoped to put his boat in the water, dust off his fishing gear, and put the war behind him. But as he and many others would soon discover, reentry into civilian life was far more complicated. As Mack recouped and tried to clear his head, he had already met his eventual killer in the unsanitary trenches of France: rheumatic fever, an autoimmune disorder that affected over ninety thousand soldiers in WWI.

Moon is a keen observer of cause and effect. He attributes the personal pain he endured by Mack's untimely death to WWI: "They didn't have penicillin back then, and strep would get in your bloodstream and damage your heart valves. It was just the same kinda strep throat you get today. Although Daddy always had heart trouble from the day he got back, he never complained about it. Sometimes I wondered how he kept goin.'"

Listening to Moon, I remembered as a young boy excitedly, but naively, imploring Othermother, "Tell me stories of Mack fighting in WWI!"

Somber, Othermother replied, "Until the day he died, Mack would wake up in the middle of the night with terrible nightmares. He'd sit straight up in bed, wringing wet with sweat, and just mumble a bunch of gibberish."

Her answer was not what I anticipated or hoped to hear. What I didn't understand then is this: War is hell, and the physical and psychological toll it takes on soldiers and their families lasts for generations after the conflict.

Aunt Ethelyn, Mack's eldest daughter whom I had the privilege of interviewing when she was ninety-seven, recalled, "Daddy always had a nervous energy about him I attributed to being 'shell-shocked' in France during WWI."

1917 — WILL AND MAMIE MOSS

Moon wanted us to know the circumstances surrounding how Mack and Othermother met, so he launched into a story about how, during WWI, Will and Mamie Moss (Othermother's parents, Moon's grandparents) left Ackerman for Arkansas. We knew we were about to hear a great love story with lots of details, maybe too many!

Moon continued, "During and after the war, jobs in Choctaw County [Ackerman is the county seat] were hard to come by. Papa [Will Moss] owned a one-mule farm on a five-acre red clay hilltop between Ackerman and Choctaw Lake. He'd plant cotton every year and a big garden. The big garden made more than the cotton did. One day, Papa saw an ad in the *Choctaw Plaindealer* [the Ackerman, Mississippi, local newspaper established in 1887 and still in publication today] for land for sale in Lepanto, Arkansas. That ad said, 'Get Rich Farmin' in the Arkansas Delta.' He fell for that ad in the paper. I don't know where he got the money because he never had very much. He bought the land in Arkansas, or made a down payment on it, and he'd never even seen it before! It was 160 acres. Papa and Mamie had six daughters: Pearl, *Momma*, Money, Rachel, Margaret, and Mildred, and one son, Uncle Byron. Margaret and Mildred were twins. He and Mamie [Addie Mabus Moss, Moon's maternal grandmother] loaded up all the kids and just struck out."

Once more, as Moon recounted the family history, I watched scenes play out from generations past.

It was the era of mules and Model T Fords. With a tired sigh, Will Moss opened the front door of his rented home in Lepanto, Arkansas, after another long day felling cypress timber. He really wished he were back in Ackerman behind his mule, plowing his red clay hillside.

The two eldest daughters, Pearl and Willie Lee (Othermother), were soon to meet their future husbands but not because things went as imagined in Arkansas. The Mosses' new 160-acre farm in the fertile Arkansas delta was a flooded 160-acre snake-infested swamp with hordes of mosquitoes.

"When they got there, the land wasn't even cleared; it was just a bunch of swamps and cypress trees. Papa didn't know nothin' about sawmillin' or loggin'. I think Momma (Othermother) was seventeen or maybe eighteen. Papa worked for the Sons in their loggin' business, and I don't think he hardly made enough money to pay rent and make land payments. They woulda' starved to death if Papa didn't get that job."

FISHIN' AND A TAXI SERVICE

Moon continued, "Daddy didn't tell me all this. Uncle Luther did when we were fishin' together in the early '60s on the Klamath River in Northern

23

California. I don't know when Daddy and Uncle Luther met, but I guess it was during the war. After the war, he worked for the Sons too.

"The Sons owned an ole' metal flat-deck boat they called The Kelly. Uncle Luther operated that. In the wintertime when the lakes were high, he'd hook to the cypress logs and pull 'em to the sawmill. They'd cold deck 'em and then sawmill 'em in the summertime. Daddy didn't want nothin' to do with loggin' before the war, and he didn't want nothin' to do with it when he got back, either!

"When he got out of the army, he bought a Winchester Model 12 pump shotgun. I regret I don't have that shotgun no more. Next, he bought a new car. After drivin' that ambulance in the army, Daddy was always fascinated 'bout cars. He always wanted a new car. He liked to drive people places, and so he started a taxi service. I guess that's how he made payments on the car. He was driving that new car when Momma and Daddy met. He started commercial fishin' again too. I think catfish was the big seller then, but he'd get lots of bass, too, so he made his livin' drivin' and fishin'."

COURTSHIP

As Moon shared the beginnings of my grandparents' courtship, I envisioned their first encounter.

The oldest Moss girls, Pearl and Willie, busied themselves setting the dinner table as Mamie finished up preparations for the evening meal.

"Pearl, did you ask Momma if I could go too?"

Willie was referring to the Friday-night hoedown in Marked Tree. The whole town turned out, the fiddler struck a chord, and the band joined in as young and old hit the dance floor. Standing shyly beside her sister in her light blue dress, Willie scanned the crowd. In the dim light on the other side of the room, she noticed two uniformed gentlemen deep in conversation.

Looking up, Mack's war-weary eyes instantly locked on the shy seventeen-year-old girl standing next to her sister across the room.

"Luther, see them girls over there? Let's figure out how we might strike up a conversation."

Walking home that evening, Pearl and Willie chatted nonstop, recalling every minute detail of their conversations with the two handsome soldiers.

HONEYMOON

"Momma and Daddy got married in Marked Tree or Lepanto, Arkansas, sometime in late 1919 or early 1920. They honeymooned at The Peabody Hotel in Memphis. They traveled down the St. Francis and up the Mississippi in a motorboat!"

I could see the newly married couple as they traveled. The boat bounced up and down in the slight chop; wispy green willow leaves shimmering in the midday sun. The twenty-horsepower Evinrude whisked the boat along nicely, Mack's new bride sitting close beside him on the seat. Willie's nervous excitement intensified when Mack announced, "We are about to enter the mighty Mississippi!"

Mack tied the boat to the Memphis dock, gathered the luggage, and walked over to pay the docking fee. Restless horses winnowed as the couple joined the small line forming near the end of the boardwalk, waiting their turn for the next coach.

"Watch your step. Destination, sir?"

"The Peabody Hotel."

Mack had seen Paris and wanted to share with his new bride as much of the world's grandeur as possible. Willie "oohed and aahed" over the beautiful flower arrangement in the large pewter vase on the table as Mack scanned the French architecture of the hotel's lobby.

"Willie, whatcha' think about startin' a family and settlin' down back in Mississippi?"

"I like that idea!" Willie exclaimed, already confident in the industriousness on display in her new husband. After a splendid time in Memphis, the newlyweds returned to Marked Tree, again by boat, and prepared for a move to Mississippi.

1920 — Startin' a Family in Mississippi

My imagination continued to provide the scenes as I imagined the beginning of my grandparents' life together. Well-wishers clamored about, saying their goodbyes and offering a small gift or a few bucks for the young couple's journey. Mack and Willie's aspirations focused on the cultivation of a new life of their own. Mack, restless to hit the road, carefully loaded his fishing gear and shotgun into the trunk of his shiny new car. Traveling southeast toward the Mississippi River, the high tips of pine needles along the roadside twinkled like Christmas lights in the afternoon sun. Crossing the Great Memphis Bridge, they journeyed south toward their new home. Luther and Pearl Spurgeon followed suit a few years later.

Reminiscing

Continuing our lazy car tour, Moon's stories shifted to his childhood memories of downtown Ackerman.

"Right here is where I grew up." He pointed out where the old white house used to stand. Jean adjusted the iPhone; I slowed the car to a crawl.

"Daddy owned quite a number of rental houses and land, all the way to where the railroad tracks cross West Main by the steel mill. Right there where the post office is, is where our garden was. He sold that land in the mid-forties so the city of Ackerman could build the new post office. Furr's grocery store would have been right there on the other side of the garden. Where it says, 'Timeless Treasures' would've been our back door. This street [Main Street] would've gone right through our back door if it didn't have a curve in it back then."

I recalled Aunt Ethelyn's description, "We first lived in Louisville, Mississippi, and Daddy worked as a salesman. During the Depression, he just did any kind of biddlin' job he could find. We still lived better than most because he had a war pension. When I was in the seventh grade, we moved to Biloxi. Daddy was going to raise chickens, but that didn't pan out, so we moved to Ackerman. We moved into the big house on Main Street with Uncle Will Bruce. When Uncle Will Bruce died, Daddy bought the house for a thousand dollars. Daddy was always a shrewd trader. I remember that house like it was yesterday. It was a big sprawling house with a big wraparound porch. We were all so happy. Daddy worked so hard to make sure we had anything we needed. He just knew how to make money. We always had plenty to eat and nice new clothes."

Contemplating Aunt Ethelyn's description and Moon's stories of the pain Mack experienced in Arkansas and France during his teenage years, I surmised, *Mack must have busied himself putting his natural entrepreneurial gifts to work, intent on creating a better reality for his new family.* He largely succeeded until his own death came knocking, and pain wrote another lengthy chapter, Moon's and mine.

Left to right: unknown, Willie Lee Sunn,
and Mack Sunn in a business suit.

27

CHAPTER 3

A BOY!

SUNN FAMILY

MACK AND WILLIE'S HAPPY UNION produced five children. Ethelyn, September 3, 1921; Jean, March 27, 1925; Barbara Ann (Bobbie), May 29, 1928; James William (Moon), May 19, 1936; and Patty Gail, October 24, 1941.

From the outset, Mack's first and only son, James William, was destined to be different—known by his family as "Jimmy" but to everyone else as simply "Moon," a nickname designated by his schoolmates. Mack was over-joyed to finally have a boy. There were important sensibilities a boy needed to know, especially related to hunting, fishing, and how to "turn a dime." Mothered by three older sisters, like Mack before him, Jimmy was afforded the absolute freedom of boyhood.

Left to right: Bobbie, Jean, Moon (around age 2),
Othermother, and Ethelyn (around age 18) in late winter of
'38 or spring of '39 (Patty was born in October of '41).

RESCUER

Moon continued, "I know it's hard to imagine, but we're prob'ly drivin'
right over where our pigpen used to be."

In the post-Depression, pre-WWII South, most families in rural towns
kept a few farm animals: mostly chickens, pigs, and a milk cow. Mack and
Willie were no exception.

"Patty tried to climb the fence around the pigpen because she wanted to
hold one of them cute baby pigs. She fell straight down right in front of the
trough. That big sow charged instantly and was gonna tear her to pieces,"
Moon recounted.

Hearing the commotion, eight-year-old Moon scaled the fence and, in
one huge leap, landed on top of the charging sow. Grabbing her two floppy
ears for reins, he rode the big sow rodeo-style around the pen. Othermother,
hearing Patty's sobs and Moon's yells, ran out, reached over the fence, and
pulled Patty to safety.

Aunt Patty recalls, "Momma told me when she got out there your Daddy was still riding the pig around and around the pen."

A predestined rescuer from birth, Moon would save many others from the jaws of death in years to come, but sometimes he arrived too late.

BARD

Moon continued to reminisce. "My sixth-grade teacher, Mrs. Ruth Mabus, instilled in me my love for poetry."

Crickets and tree frogs created a rhythmic cadence in the towering oaks as heels clinked against the boards of the long, echoey hallway in the old white house facing the railroad tracks. On opposite ends, Othermother and Jimmy slowly walked forward, exchanging places, their eyes glued to the text they held in their hands.

Aunt Patty recalls, "Momma would recite one line, your daddy the next—Longfellow, Keats, Poe. Your daddy had a gift. He could memorize entire long poems and never miss even a single word."

Moon can also remember every minute detail of every fishing article he's ever read—thousands over a lifetime. They are all sacred to him.

CHOCTAW LAKE

We exited Main Street in Ackerman and turned left on Highway 15, bound for Choctaw Lake.

The air was damp and cool; dense fog hovered over the water. The barely visible distant pines resembled tall gray ghosts presiding over past decades. It felt a bit eerie and surreal. Moon continued to recount his childhood, remembering his boyhood days with Mack at the lake. My memories of Choctaw Lake were mismatched: some fond, others nightmarish.

Moon continued, "This lake is beautiful today, but man you can't believe how beautiful it was back then before they tore down the dance pavilion and all the cabins. Daddy got the job out here because he knew more about boats, fishin', and I reckon business than anyone else around. I followed Daddy around the lake, and he taught me everything he knew. I guess while most kids were already workin' on the family farm, I was workin' for Daddy. I was like his apprentice, learnin' everything he knew. He instilled in me a kind of confidence about the outdoors I've never lost. I'll never forget those days."

Once again, Moon's recollections took me to a different place and time. I imagined Mack shifted nervously in the straight-backed chair, next in line to interview for operations director at Choctaw Lake.

Sam Moore's voice loudened, "Next!"

Two days later, the phone buzzed on the table in the hallway. "Hello, Willie Sunn speaking."

She covered the receiver, "Mack, Mack, it's Sam Moore!"

"Hello, this is Mack Sunn."

"Mack, the job is yours. I'm convinced you're the man for the job. Report to the lake at 7:00 a.m. Monday morning, and I'll show you the ropes."

Every morning, young Moon in tow, Mack drove the short distance from Ackerman to Choctaw Lake. Like Mack's experience in the sunken lands, Moon's life-shaping years were inextricably linked to water. Completely free to explore the wonder of his surroundings, entire days were spent paddling, swimming, catching crawdads, and fishing.

YELLOW CANOE

As we drove across the dam, I experienced flashbacks of being out in the water with Moon on a warm summer day fifty years before. I was being instructed in the finer points of canoeing.

I asked, "Remember, building the canoe together?"

"Yeah, I remember that and then bringing it out here and paddling around."

Building projects can cement the father-son relationship. Like Mack before him, Moon loves all sorts of boats, especially those you can paddle by hand and easily load on top of your car. Moon has rarely been spotted driving an automobile without some sort of watercraft tied on top. From Moon's perspective, "You never know when you might need it." Since boats are one of the important sensibilities of life, he ordered a wood-and-fiberglass canoe kit for us to construct.

"Shane, be over here on Saturday, and we'll start work on the canoe."

Momma dropped me at the street. It was mid-July, hot and humid. I hurried up the drive, under the canopy of tall pecans. An array of various and sundry long cardboard boxes lined the yard beside the sawhorses.

"Shane, help me open these boxes, and let's go through the packing list."

I don't remember much but a broken cedar rib, a few cuss words, handing him tools, messy hands, and the day he asked, "What color you wanna make it? We can make it any color you want by mixin' these tubes into the epoxy." I settled on yellow.

Finally, the canoe was finished. First order of business? Put it on top of whatever beater he had at the time and drive slowly through Ackerman to evoke stares and comments.

Next, off to Choctaw Lake, paddling the yellow canoe against the backdrop of emerald Southern pines and clear water. He taught me the J stroke and how to sit low in the center to navigate shallow water. He also demanded that I learn how to swamp the canoe in deep water and reenter it. This was accomplished by swimming underneath it at the center point, grabbing each side and pushing it upward, all the while treading water and then flipping it quickly right or left back upright.

He'd do it. I would try and fail. He'd do it again, and I would try and fail again. He would not let me give up until I succeeded, relatively speaking. Canoe upright again: good. But, of course, we were still in the water, so he had to teach me how to reenter the canoe without turning it over. This was done by swimming to the back and pressing down with your torso, and then sliding forward on your stomach to reenter the canoe.

He'd demonstrate. "Shane, swim to the back and press the weight of your chest against the back end."

I was eight, and my chest was as narrow as a two-by-four; I weighed about sixty pounds soaking wet. I tried, the canoe squirted forward, and I fell backward into the water.

"Watch me one more time. You've got to hold onto the sides when you press down with your weight and then squirm forward on your stomach."

With much effort, I finally managed to get into the canoe, but it wasn't a thing of grace or beauty.

"You're learnin'; let's go fishin.'"

While other boys were cutting the grass, watching TV, or doing their homework, I was a student in the outdoor education class of Moon Sunn. More importantly, there was something special about the yellow canoe. It wasn't only his; it was mine, and it was ours.

Easter Flood

Almost a decade later, in 1979, the Pearl River crested in Jackson, Mississippi, fifteen feet above flood stage. Many homes and businesses had water to the rooftops. Seventeen thousand residents were forced from their homes in Jackson and surrounding communities. Damages were estimated between $500 to $700 million. Today, that's $1.76 billion! Meteorologists describe "the Easter Flood of 1979" as a "two-hundred-year event."

Two days before in Ackerman, it rained fifteen to twenty inches in twenty-four hours. Exact records are sketchy. Othermother owned a rain gauge and kept official records for the state for over twenty-five years. After the historic flood, she told me, "This is the only time we got so much rain that it overflowed the gauge. It had to be over fifteen inches."

Boats were paddled down Main Street in Ackerman. The streams in and around Ackerman join to form the Yockanookany River, the chief tributary of the Pearl. Northeast of Jackson, the Pearl is dammed, forming the thirty-three-thousand-acre Ross Barnett Reservoir.

Moon decided to put our beloved yellow canoe in the road ditch in front of his house on Louisville Street and see how far he could get. His goal: Ross Barnett Reservoir, eighty-five miles as the crow flies! The water was turbulent and angry, Class 5 rapids in Ackerman, Mississippi. I think he'd watched too many Westerns where pioneers being chased by Indians encountered rapids and waterfalls. He was not to be deterred.

His first encounter with death occurred where the road ditch enters Town Creek near the present-day library. He had to make it underneath the bridge, which had maybe a foot of clearance in the rapidly rising water. Moon wedged the canoe under the bridge and then pushed down as hard as he could against the underside. He inched it forward until he made it out the other side.

Most men attempting this dangerous feat would have enjoyed their obituary in the *Choctaw Plaindealer* a couple days later. On second thought, it'd never occur to most men that this is what one would do when a flood hits Ackerman! Moon was so confident in his physical abilities, not in a proud sort of way, that the potential dangers never entered his mind. Moon was exhilarated, like a kid going on a ride at the county fair. Death encounter number two—heck, it was all a death encounter—occurred where the Yockanookany River flows under the old Gulf Mobile and Ohio train trestle just west of the old steel mill.

On this occasion, it resembled Niagara Falls as the speeding water funneled under the bridge, making three-foot waves, bilious spray, and huge whirlpools. Moon paddled faster, bobbing up and down in our yellow canoe on his way to Ross Barnett Reservoir. But the torrent was too much. The canoe's bow rose high to crest a wave, the stern dipped, and the wave behind flooded the back. The canoe flipped, tossing Moon headlong into the fuming turbulence. He tried to swim forward and grab the canoe, but the current sucked it under and carried it swiftly downstream. He angled for the bank, making it over and around the posts and pilings of the trestle and then through flooded bushes, limbs, and briars, finally making it to shore. He tried running downstream, but the river was so wide due to the flood that he couldn't spot the canoe again. He walked home, determined not to let the river claim our canoe.

And when I say determined, Moon redefines determination. The following days, as waters receded, he started searching the river, hiking through snake-infested thickets, picking up the next day where he'd left off the previous.

"It's got to be on that river somewhere."

Moon's philosophy for finding lost things? "If it's there, it can be found. If you can't find it, you simply haven't looked hard enough, long enough, or retraced your steps and movements accurately enough."

He found the yellow canoe four or five days later, thirty miles south near Kosciusko, Mississippi, wedged in a brush pile, badly damaged but reparable. He walked it to the nearest road atop his shoulders, went for the car, drove back, and loaded it up. It lay damaged in his backyard for almost a year, but one dog-day August afternoon when the fish weren't biting, he went to the hardware store, purchased the needed supplies, and repaired the canoe. Moon's only regret: "I didn't make it all the way to Ross Barnett Reservoir!"

From the back seat, Jean tapped me on the shoulder. I turned sideways and looked back. She smiled and gestured in a way that I knew meant, "This story explains a lot!"

Moon continued, "I don't think I'll ever do that again. I cracked it up and got to wantin' to get it fixed. I got it all fixed real good and then hung it up there in the garage, and I think it's been hangin' there thirty-five years. One day, I want to take it down and bring it out here and paddle it around on a Sunday afternoon. But I spent so much time gettin' it fixed and hung up there real good, I've never got around to takin' it down again. But I still believe I will one day. The other thing is that's just a lot of trouble when I'm just wantin' something to fish out of. So, I might never do it because most of these days like today would have been a good day to go fishin', and I guess I'd rather spend my time doin' that rather than takin' the time to fool around with the canoe."

I chuckled, hearing what I already knew: For Moon, other priorities line up somewhere behind fishing. But something felt right to me. The fact that our yellow canoe still hung in his garage symbolized something significant that happened a long time ago.

Yellow canoe hanging in Moon's garage.

DROWNING VICTIMS

Continuing our drive around Choctaw Lake, the sky darkened, and raindrops bounced and beaded on the lake's surface. The tree ghosts presiding, disturbing stories of the past hovered in the fog and pierced my brain.

As a kid, I remembered hearing accounts of Moon retrieving the body of a drowning victim near the dance pavilion at Choctaw Lake sometime in the late '50s. A young high school couple was canoeing together on the lake before a dance and somehow flipped their canoe. The boy couldn't swim, and he panicked and went down. Absolute pandemonium erupted among the large crowd gathered for the dance. Everyone was screaming and crying.

Someone yelled, "Go get Moon!"

Moon was already the "go-to" guy in any kind of local emergency. He arrived at the horrifying scene almost an hour later. A huge crowd had gathered on the pier. Moon's job: retrieve the body.

I remembered Moon's ghastly account of the event. "Sometimes it takes almost a day for a body to surface. I knew the lake was really deep off the end of the dance pavilion. So, I found an old, abandoned trotline with the hooks still attached and tied a brick on one end. The bottom is smooth there without any stumps or anything like that. So, I took the trotline and held it in one hand and swam back and forth, dragging the brick across the bottom. It wasn't too long before I hooked somethin', and I knew what it was as soon as I did."

I also recalled bits and pieces of the eerie description from Ty Cobb, Moon's lifelong friend and a high school classmate of the victim. "When Moon got him up, his body was doubled over in a knot, and his fingers were stiff and drawn. His eyes were still open and sorta gray with a faraway look."

Further haunting memories of Choctaw Lake continued to surface as if the tree ghosts owned the dark stories and possessed the power to suggest them to my brain. I recollected stories of numerous drowning victims that, as a kid, I'd encountered in more upfront, personal, and emotionally disturbing sorts of ways.

One afternoon, Moon and I were swimming on the wrong side of Choctaw Lake at the old, rotted 4-H pier. Moon wasn't about to pay the fee necessary to swim on the respectable side with a diving platform and sand rather than mud. He was instructing me on the finer points of swimming. I could swim, but in deep water, I was prone to succumb to fear.

"Relax, Shane, don't fight the water. Let's practice floating and treading."

An alarm blared from the respectable side.

Moon asked, "Are they blowin' that horn at us?"

Then he yelled, "No, Shane, get out of the water, there's an accident over there! Don't dry off. Run!"

Driving breakneck speed, sliding sideways, we turned right onto the levee road. Across the lake, I could see a crowd gathering at the end of one of the piers in the swimming area. Ramping all the speed bumps, we entered the parking lot. Moon ran down the hill; I followed. The gathered crowd pointed to an area of water off the end of one of the piers. Moon dove in and, within seconds, surfaced with a limp body on his right shoulder. He swam and pushed the victim toward the pier.

Someone in the crowd shouted, "Stand back!"

Moon pushed and a couple of bystanders pulled, managing to get the boy's lifeless body onto the pier. The Boy Scouts of America Lifesaving Merit Badge was on full display.

First, Moon checked for a pulse. I was unsure he detected one. Next, with his fingers, he pried open the youth's clenched jaw, checking his airway. Moon stuck his right hand into the boy's mouth and reversed his swallowed tongue. Then, he administered strong compressions to his back and chest with the insides of his palms, followed by mouth-to-mouth resuscitation, spitting water from his own mouth onto the pier. Another round of sharp blows to his upper back and more mouth-to-mouth. Suddenly, the boy puked up a gallon of water. Moon grabbed him, put him on his shoulder, and sprinted up the hill to the car. I ran behind.

"Shane, you're gonna have to sit on the front seat and hold him. He's still unconscious."

Adrenaline pumping, I did what I was told. I got in. Moon tilted the front bucket seat backward and laid the boy, who was older and larger than me, in my lap. I wrapped my arms around his chest.

"Grab his hair and try to hold his head up."

Speeding to the Choctaw County Hospital in Ackerman, the semi-conscious boy mumbled strange partial sentences, water and slobber running out his mouth and nose, dripping into my lap. Halfway to the hospital, we met an ambulance headed for the lake, its siren blasting. Pulling up to the main doors of the hospital, Moon ran to my side of the car, lifted the catatonic boy, and laid him on the hood. He resumed mouth-to-mouth.

"Run in there and tell them to bring a stretcher and some oxygen!"

I did. The boy lived. I had nightmares.

Boy Scouts of America Lifesaving Merit Badge.

LEE FURR

Other drowning memories surfaced when Moon arrived on the scene too late. Lee Furr was a salt-of-the-earth boy, beloved by the town, an important and proud member of the Ackerman Indians high school football team. One summer afternoon, Lee and a friend were fishing a local farm pond. Finishing up with a string of bass tied to his side, Lee waded toward shore. He stepped into a deep hole, went under, and then surfaced.

His friend asked, "Lee, are you all right?"

Lee smiled and said, "Yeah, the water's a little over my head."

He went under again but didn't resurface the second time. His friend ran for help.

That afternoon, Moon was out for a spin on his bike. In the distance, he heard panicked screams for help, so he peddled down the cutoff toward the pond. Halfway down the road, he met Lee's friend, who tried to explain what was happening. Moon sped to the pond, but it was too late to save Lee.

Like an ugly cancer, the hard-to-believe-and-accept news of Lee's drowning spread rapidly throughout Ackerman. Everyone was devastated. That day, Moon pulled his yellow Dodge up in front of our tract home and honked the horn. I hadn't heard the news. I ran out, thinking I was about to hear stories of his latest fishing exploits. Instantly, I could tell something was wrong; Moon was visibly shaken.

Looking at the floorboard, Moon said, "I've got some really bad news."

I listened to his broken sentences as he tried to explain what had happened. I couldn't listen. I felt stunned and nauseous. I burst into tears, slammed the car door, and ran inside. I tried to stuff it, but wept on and off for days, most of the time in private.

Lee's younger brother, John, regularly played with his friend Pete Long, who lived next door. I wondered, *What will I say to John the next time I see him? What can I say? Because Moon's my dad, will it remind John of Lee's death every time he sees me?*

I felt unduly connected and somehow responsible for the tragic event. *Why couldn't Daddy have arrived a little sooner?*

MICHAEL WILLIAMS

By now, it seemed as if the tree ghosts were laughing in some sort of mockery as another painful memory surfaced. Michael Williams lived in a black neighborhood across Louisville Street, a short distance north and east of the white subdivision where I lived. Although he was three years older, on summer days, we spent hours playing together beside the creek in the cow pasture that separated our neighborhoods.

Michael was black, bright, articulate, wore a big smile, and never met a stranger. By 1973, Michael had earned a starting position at cornerback on the Ackerman Indians football team, an important rite of passage in small-town Mississippi. At Choctaw Lake, boys challenged other boys to swim to the diving board platform. Michael, a poor swimmer, never backed down from a challenge. He started swimming for the platform, but about halfway there, panicked and went down. Moon was called to retrieve his body. I was, again, devastated. The entire Ackerman school system mourned Michael's death, a terrible blow to the whole community, especially the black community.

Rather than the structure of molecules, Michael's drowning was the topic of conversation in Gradie Ervin's Monday morning sixth-grade science class. Of course, Moon was central to the story. Proud of the fact Moon was able to help in some small way, I still felt the familiar guilt and shame. As a sea of emotions flooded the room, I retreated inside an internal shell, feeling like a bystander listening to a far-off conversation.

From there, I heard Gradie Ervin, my black science teacher, whom I respected, say, "If it had been a white kid, Moon would've saved him."

He glanced in my direction; I looked at the floor. *Why would he say that?*

I was confronted with the dark history of racism. I felt defensive, hurt, ashamed, and again somehow responsible. At the time, I didn't understand race or the pain black people had endured from centuries of mistreatment at the hands of white folks.

CAMP PALILA

The rain increased as we pulled the car beside the picnic pavilion at Choctaw Lake. Jean could tell I was distracted and flashed an annoyed glance that was a firm summons to reenter the land of the living. I tried but couldn't shake the painful memories. I wondered, *Was my childhood normal by any stretch of the imagination? How had growing up the only son of Moon Sunn really affected me?*

In the summer of 1973, when I was twelve, I took a week off from Little League baseball to attend Boy Scout summer camp at Camp Palila. The only merit badge I couldn't finish was swimming, which most of my friends completed with ease. I couldn't admit it, but I'd developed a real fear of the water. During our first day of swim sessions, the instructors pointed to a buoy in the middle of the lake we had to swim around to complete the mile swim. The mile swim was necessary to receive the merit badge at the end of the week.

All I could think about were dead bodies. *How could I be Moon Sunn's son and not swim a mile?*

I attempted to confront my fear, but it pressed inward with unrelenting fervency. On the following day, in the middle of the swim session, I slipped out of the water and walked away. Hating myself, I wandered into a day-old merit badge class on nature. The instructor seemed glad to see me. There were only two other boys in the entire class.

The instructor asked, "Where were you yesterday?"

"Oh, I was sick."

"Well, glad to have you. Sit down, you can catch up."

RESCUING RICHIE

The rain subsided; my memories brightened. Years later, because I was always fishing and always in and around water, I eventually conquered my fear. In 1977, my stepbrother Richie and I devised an ill-spent plan to go trotlining in a silver canoe on the Big Black River in Attala County. A week after surgery from a baseball injury, a metal pin protruded from Richie's right shoulder. The warmth of the sun and humid afternoon air surrounding us, we set our lines with goggle-eyed pond perch we'd seined that morning from a farm pond. That evening, we slept in the car under the bridge beside the river.

At daylight, stiff from a restless night, we awoke to flooding rain. We stood together under the bridge, hoping the rain would subside.

I prognosticated, "This rising river should be perfect for the catfish; how many you think we have on our lines?"

Richie responded, "This rain ain't gonna let up. Let's go find out!"

Richie couldn't swim a lick. Add mid-calf rubber boots and a shoulder injury, and it was more like he was a heavy cinder block waiting to sink to the bottom.

I instructed, "Go grab the lifejackets out of the trunk."

He retorted, "We're just going down there and right back."

"Okay."

Our mode of water transportation was Moon's silver aluminum canoe. We climbed in, with Richie in front and me in back. We paddled out into the raging current as the rain poured straight down in buckets.

In the middle of the river, we encountered a sunken tree lodged in the current, its skinny leafless limbs bobbing up and down, protruding upward in our direction. We miscommunicated. Richie tried to paddle right, I left. A sharp limb hit me in the chest. I leaned hard right, and so did Richie. The canoe flipped, dumping us both into the raging river. I detected panic in his eyes the moment we hit the water.

I screamed over the thunderous rain and current, "Grab the canoe. Grab the canoe!"

No use. Flailing to stay afloat, Richie was pushed downstream away from the canoe by the raging torrent. He disappeared below the muddy water. Holding the back, I tried to swim the canoe forward in the direction I last saw him. I couldn't push it fast enough. Full of dread, I abandoned the canoe and swam forward, turning and searching for signs of him. I glimpsed the back of his head surface, facedown, twenty yards in front of me. He disappeared again. I kicked hard in the direction I last saw him, fearing it might be the last.

Treading water in the angry river, I turned round and round, screaming, "Richie! Richie!"

Miraculously, the back of his brown coat floated upward underneath the water, only five yards in front of me! I dove and grabbed him around the waist. Richie locked his arms around my neck with such force I couldn't break free. We both went down. Somewhere in the bowels of the river below, I mustered my best left hook. The punch momentarily freed me from his death grip. Still fighting, I somehow managed to pull him to the surface. Energy spent, I knew the prospects of getting us both to shore were slim.

Something brushed my back: the swamped canoe, being pushed by the hand of God. I tried pulling Richie aboard, but the additional weight pushed the canoe under.

Above the rain and water's roar, I screamed, "Hold on!"

I slid backward down the length of the canoe, pressing the stern downward with my feet, attempting to lift the front end and Richie out of the water.

Semiconscious, in a state of absolute panic, he let go. I swam forward and grabbed his coat, pulling him on again. The harrowing process repeated itself several times, with me screaming, swimming, grabbing, and Richie determined to abandon the canoe.

Finally, slapping him hard across the face, I yelled, "Trust me, hold on, don't let go!"

I repeated the maneuver, this time managing to lift Richie's shoulders above the water. Beyond exhaustion, we floated downstream in the torrent at the mercy of the river. I spotted a sandbar at a sharp bend in the river ahead and realized, *This is our only chance.* Sliding my feet off the stern, I pressed downward with both arms, careful not to lower Richie too quickly into the water. Hoarse from all the screaming, I yelled again, "Hold on, hold on, don't let go!" So far, so good. Gripping the stern with both hands, I kicked hard for the bar. Ten yards out, my feet struck river bottom. I stood up and pushed the canoe onto the wet sand. Richie fell off and lay dazed in the sand, puking up buckets of muddy water mingled with pieces of hotdogs, the partially digested products of the previous evening. Totally exhausted, I collapsed.

Moon's voice awakened me from my extended memory trance. "Me and Daddy spent some wonderful years here at the lake."

The rain stopped, the sun penetrated the fog, streaks of narrow bright light reflected across the water, the tree ghosts vaporized, and I surmised, "Difficult, but worth being the only son of Moon Sunn."

CHAPTER 4

ENTREPRENEURIAL
FEVER

NOW BACK IN THE LAND of a current living and breathing conversation, I wondered why Mack and Moon's days at Choctaw Lake had ended, then I remembered Aunt Ethelyn's description. "Something was missing and too routine about that 'salaried job' for Daddy. The war pension always helped him do whatever he decided to do next. Daddy knew how 'to turn a dime.' He kept a big roll of cash in his front pocket. He made loans to anyone needing money right on the spot. He always took something for collateral, like a watch or a gun, anything he knew he could sell if the person wasn't good for the loan. He was never ruthless, but I do remember one of my schoolmates telling me, 'Mr. Mack charges such high interest.'"

With Aunt Evelyn's accounting, the long-ago past took form.

Mack reached over and turned off the bedside lamp, a palpable restlessness stirring inside.

"Willie, I like my job at the lake, but I think I can do better."

"You keep saying that, Mack, but there ain't too many good-paying jobs around here. What on earth would you do?"

The war pension provided just the cushion Mack needed, so he followed his gut and walked away from his job at the lake. He started slowly but soon excelled in his new entrepreneurial lifestyle. Mack became a freewheeling, self-employed entrepreneur, dabbling in various pursuits, including real estate.

Mack and Moon's fishing expeditions increased in direct proportion to an increase in his business. Young Moon watched and learned, not only the finer points of fishing, but also the freedom awarded those who have the self-confidence "to turn a dime."

EXPANDING FISHING HORIZONS

Moon continued, "When I was a boy, you had to drive all the way to the Mississippi Delta to get to really good fishin'. That Delta was like paradise, and I'll never forget goin' there all those times with Daddy. On trips to the Delta, Daddy usually caught more big catfish than you can imagine. He'd ice 'em down in #2 washtubs. Sometimes we'd stop off at a Delta farm and load the rest of the truck with watermelons. We were always sold out of fish and watermelons before the end of the next day.

"Most people don't realize that back in those days, fishin' didn't look nothin' like it does today. There were a few small farm ponds around that were usually hand-dug for livestock. Most good fishin' was on rivers, creeks, beaver dams, sloughs, and oxbows. Choctaw Lake is only a hundred acres, and it seemed like an ocean back then! The large flood-control lakes like Sardis and Arkabutla weren't finished until the early '40s. Grenada and Enid didn't even exist 'til the early '50s."

Franklin D. Roosevelt's New Deal, designed to put thousands back to work, drastically changed the fishing landscape in north Mississippi. The north Mississippi lakes constructed in the '40s and '50s not only created thousands of new acres of fertile fish habitat but also significantly decreased the drive time to excellent fishing for the citizens living near them. The Grenada Project encompassed 90,427 acres with thirty-five thousand acres at recreational pool level. Grenada Lake has approximately forty-eight miles of shoreline.

"At first, Daddy was a little slow to warm up to the idea of fishin' at Sardis because he liked to go to the Delta so much. In 1942, the federal government closed the dam and spillway at Sardis Lake. That lake had just opened, but they did that as a precaution to avoid any kinda potential sabotage during the war. They reopened it, I think in 1946. But man, when they did, you can't even imagine how many fish were in there. We couldn't get up there the first day, but we were there the next. We caught and sold enough catfish to buy a secondhand pickup truck. I think fishin' trips musta' got in my blood from an early age. For all of us livin' in Ackerman, goin' to Grenada was like goin' to the Gulf of Mexico. Daddy died before he ever got to fish Grenada."

I wanted to ask more about Mack's death but determined I should wait.

HAWAIIAN WIGGLERS

"I loved to go with Daddy on trips to the Delta. That's where I really learned how to fish. I knew I could catch a bass with a line and live minnow, but what I wanted to do more than anything else was catch a bass on an artificial lure. I fine'lee did that at Lake Washington."

I imagined Mack and Moon on their way to Lake Washington. The dense canopy of water oaks and cypresses drew long, dark shadows across the dirt road; pebbles clicked against the undercarriage. The pickup bounced and rattled, Moon riding shotgun, Mack attempting to dodge the numerous potholes, some deep enough to jar your teeth and rattle your brain. The two were bound for Lake Washington in the Mississippi Delta. The familiar terrain, venerated from youth, called to Mack like a siren. The important conversation on the front seat centered on the anticipated exploits of the next two days.

"I thought to catch bass, I needed to use a lure that resembled a small baitfish, so I tried lures like the Heddon River Runt and things like that.

One day I got frustrated, and Daddy said, 'Here, try this.' He handed me a Hawaiian Wiggler with a red-and-white skirt."

Still in use today, the Hawaiian Wiggler is one of the hundreds of lures designed to catch men, packaged with the picture of a thinly clad hula dancer on the box. But the Wiggler does a pretty good job with the fish too. Hawaiian Wigglers are made with a front spiral spinner. Two diagonal pieces of wire are suspended from the eye on opposite sides of the hook, making them weedless and good for casting in thick cover.

Hawaiian Wigglers postcard, circa 1950.

Moon tied on the Wiggler, disappeared to shallower water, and within a couple of casts, hooked and landed a nice three-pound bass. As they say, it is arguable whether he caught the bass or the bass caught him. One thing is for sure: from that day forward, he's never stopped casting spinner baits to bass.

"I remember takin' the bass up there and showin' Daddy. I think I was really sayin', 'Look, Daddy, I caught this one for you.'"

Moon's comment jarred me. I thought, *Wow, he's a lot more in touch with the true source of his motivations than most.*

I remembered Moon repeating the same advice to me when I was young. "Here, Shane, try this." And it was always a Hawaiian Wiggler. His instruction was likely because the Wiggler is weedless, and he was weary of constantly retrieving my lure from yet another snag.

But as we listened, I wondered: *Maybe it was because the deep waters of memory surfaced.* "Here, Jimmy, use this."

CHAPTER 5

STRAY DOGS AND STRAY FRIENDS

AFTER MEANDERING AROUND Choctaw Lake, we returned to Ackerman the back way. I couldn't remember the last time I'd traveled this road. Another childhood memory surfaced.

LIGE WEAVER

For more than a century, bootleggers and God's children combined at the polls to keep ole' Choctaw dry. The moonshine business thrived.

I was eight or nine when our fishing trip to Choctaw Lake was shortened by a substantial "gully washer." Lighting crackled in the distance, and the intermittent raindrops increased to a torrential downpour.

"Let's get out of here, Shane!"

We left the lake and headed for Ackerman the back way. Moon announced abruptly, "There's Lige!"

It sounded to me like he'd just spotted an important dignitary. We could barely see through the foggy windshield, the wiper blades slapping back and forth in the pouring rain. My head jerked sideways; Moon did an abrupt "one-eighty" in the middle of the road. Adjusting my eyes, I saw there in the middle of the deluge, walking up the side of the foggy road, Lige Weaver, wearing a long, dark, wet coat, a dripping brim hat cocked sideways on his head.

Moon rolled down the window. "Get in, Lige!"

I slid toward Moon as far as I could in the middle of the bench seat. Water poured off Lige, making big water spots on the cloth seat; I scooted closer to Moon. The strong smell of "likker" filled the humid air inside the truck.

"Where ya' headed, Lige?"

Lige shrugged his wet shoulders. "You ken let me out up har' at 'dat innarsect'n."

We stopped at the intersection.

"Lige, try to get somewhere out of this rain, if you can."

I felt relieved, repositioning myself on the seat, trying to avoid any wet spots. I was curious.

"Daddy, what's wrong with Lige?"

"Lige is kinda like an outcast. He's hard on the alcohol, and some say a little mentally deranged. Nobody in this town wants to have anything to do with him."

Driving the back way to Ackerman from Choctaw Lake, I remembered another childhood interaction with Lige.

"Get in, Shane, I'm gonna take Lige Weaver some of these fish."

We drove a short distance and stopped in front of an old ramshackle tenant house on the corner of Cherry and Louisville streets. Paint-peeled shutters dangled loosely from the windows behind the limbs of the overgrown trees. It seemed like we had just arrived at Boo Radley's house.

Moon exclaimed, "Man, they oughta' torn this thang down a long time ago!"

A gift of perfectly fileted bass in hand, Moon repeatedly knocked on the front door at the end of a long staircase ascending to the dirty unkempt rooms above. I watched from the front seat of the truck, wondering why it was so difficult to get Lige to the door. Moon tried again and again, with no response. Finally, he walked back toward the truck and scooped up a big handful of rocks from the graveled parking lot.

"Shane, hold these fish. I think Lige is in there."

I reached through the window and took the fish. Moon proceeded to toss one rock at a time against one of the shuttered windows above. Still no response. Every consecutive toss increased in velocity, the window and shutter responding with congruent volume.

Finally, the front door creaked open, and a scary-looking old man with dirty clothes and unkempt hair appeared in the entrance. Moon handed him the fish.

"Here you go, Lige. These oughta last ya' several days. I'll bring you some more in the next couple days."

Lige nodded his head in acknowledgment but didn't utter a word.

Moon would never ever admit that helping Lige was anything out of the ordinary. Sometimes a man is simply compassionate, not to impress anyone or feel good about himself—he just is. Moon taught by his actions. "You treat ever one the same."

Everyone, including Lige Weaver.

BARKER

Moon's kind soul extends to the canine crowd. He has always taken in stray dogs. Or, more accurately, according to him, stray dogs just kind of show up. They gravitate to him, or so he thinks. He'd never say it, but he has a soft place in his heart for the discards and rejects of the world. He'd never pay a dime to purchase a dog, but once they're his, Moon's all in.

He names them based on their most observable characteristics. Naming never required too much energy or imagination; the dog was simply called what it did. Scratcher, Growler, Jumper, and then there was Barker. One day, a half-starved feist mix, obviously mistreated by his previous owners, "just showed up" at Moon's house. In the grand scheme of life, it was foreordained, so Moon took him in and nursed him to health.

It wasn't long before Barker earned his name, and that's a gross understatement. Barker could bark loudly for hours without stopping to even catch his breath. He never responded to any commands, pulled on the leash like a Sherman tank, and was prone to bite. But Moon loved him anyway. I always wondered, *How?*

In the school of obedience training, Barker was already beyond the point of no return. This decreased most available options for pet care. If you let him inside, he ransacked the house. If you left him outside, he left. On these frequent occasions, Moon looked for him until he found him. Option three: attach Barker to a long lead in the front yard.

Moon never considered taking any long trip without Barker. Taking Barker anywhere was like bringing along an unrelenting terrible burden. One time, Moon finished packing, ready to leave for Alaska, but Barker had disappeared, having broken off his lead again—I'm sure to the relief and jubilant rejoicing of neighbors in a three-block radius. Most sensible people would've chalked up Barker's escape to the kind providence of God and simply left the unwanted nuisance and unimaginable trouble behind. Moon's take?

"Barker gets excited and nervous when he knows we are about to go somewhere."

Moon refused to leave without him, a luxury not even afforded homo sapiens. With extra time on his hands, he thought back through his supplies for the trip. "Maybe I need a little more food," he considered, which usually meant some extra bread, cheese, and sliced salami. So, he made a trip to Gilliland's Supermarket, and bounding up to him in the parking lot was Barker, doing what Barker does, ready for the trip.

CLUXEWE CAMPGROUND

One summer, years later, Moon and Barker joined my family for our biennial camping and fly-fishing trip to Vancouver Island, British Columbia. I was delighted to have Moon; Barker, not so much. Barker created chaos from the outset. He barked and barked and barked for no obvious reason other than to make sure everyone knew, "I'm Barker, and I bark."

Annoyed campers, there to enjoy the serene and peaceful setting of Cluxewe, shunned us like a new US leper colony had just landed. Moon kept Barker tied to his truck on the standard long lead, where he sat and barked all day. On Vancouver Island, this was akin to a sadistic form of animal cruelty. Most campers were from down island—places like Victoria and Parksville. Morning and evening, they walked their immaculately groomed dogs like contestants in the ring at the Westminster Kennel Club Dog Show. Barker barked, hissed, and growled at every contestant. I hid in the camper to avoid the disparaging glares.

Finally, the campground manager showed up; Barker snarled.

"You've got to do something about this dog. The whole campground is complaining."

"It's not my dog; it's my dad's."

"Well, your dad's registered at your site, and it's your responsibility to do something about it."

"Grrrrrr ..."

"Okay."

Later that afternoon when Moon returned from fishing, I said, "Daddy, we've got to do something about Barker. The campground host came down here around noon and said the whole campground is complaining."

"I know it; I'll try to figure somethin' out."

Next morning, Moon sipped a dark solution of cold water and Folgers coffee crystals, pulled on his waders, checked his flies, and, to my instant relief, untied Barker's lead from the truck. He imagined if he took Barker down the beach and tied him to a driftwood log while he fished, that would alleviate the problem. It only accentuated it. It wasn't long before I could hear Barker going at it, a half-mile down the beach.

Midday, all the tidy professional campers took strolls down the scenic beach.

"What sort of cruel villain would leave a poor, innocent, helpless, barking creature like this tied to a log on the beach?"

Thus began the daily dog rescues. The length and severity of "interventions" depended on how compassionate and brave the rescuer happened to be and Moon's particular mood that day. With milder interventions, Moon received a short lecture, said "thank you," and retied Barker on the beach. More determined rescuers showed up in the campground, with Barker in tow, verbalizing threats about fines and the Animal Rescue League.

On one occasion, I observed a would-be rescuer inquiring with nearby campers about the whereabouts of Barker's owner. The campers nodded and pointed down the road toward the leper colony. The wholly determined rescuer beelined for our camper. I hastily grabbed my fly rod, disappeared to the beach, and watched from a safe distance. The intervention grew to search-party proportions as the zealous rescuer collected a posse of other concerned campers. Barker in tow, the swelling posse blundered down the rocky beach, carefully inquiring of every fly- fisherman Moon's whereabouts, like there would be a lynching.

Focused more on the posse, I fake-cast in the shallow water near shore.

"Do you know where we might find a man named Moon?"

"No, I'm sorry, I don't, never heard of him."

Off again collecting new participants like a pilgrimage to Canterbury, the posse continued down the beach in Moon's direction. I followed the mob at a distance, slowly wading and half-fishing. Their determined search inevitably led to the discovery of the wanted perpetrator.

"Hey you out there! Are you Moon?"

Waist-deep, forty yards off the beach, Moon reluctantly waded toward the waiting kangaroo court. Tension building, I watched curiously from my observation post, wondering how this would end. Frustrated his fishing had been interrupted, Moon's very posture betrayed the fact this was not going to be pretty.

Telltale sign #1: Moon clenched his teeth as his whole body stiffened for the encounter. Sign #2: Like a cruise missile, Moon waded directly toward the blood-thirsty posse, his speed increasing with every step. I observed the mob's resolve visibly weaken. Eyes widened in fearful astonishment, some made half-turns while others stared at the water to avoid eye contact with the quickly approaching payload. Utilizing his directly pointed fly rod, Moon's scolding lecture ensued twenty yards from the crowd, his angry voice detectable above the breaking waves.

Like the Pharisees surrounding the woman caught in adultery, Moon's accusers gave up one by one and departed until only the self-righteous rescuer remained. Detecting weakness, with the zeal of a courtroom prosecutor, Moon went in for the kill.

"Give me my dog, now!"

Abandoned, alone, and frightened out of his mind, the bewildered man gave up and relinquished Barker to his owner. Moon took Barker, retied him to the same driftwood log, and resumed fishing. Barker seemed to enjoy the entire maddening affair. At least, it was one of the few times he stopped barking.

The posse gone, I waded closer.

"Shane, ya' catchin' any?"

"How'd that go!?"

"Them people don't understand what's none of their damn business."

"Whatcha usin'?"

"A shrimp pattern with a pink-and-chartreuse tail."

That summer at Cluxewe, most of the time unfazed, Moon patiently endured the daily attacks, still caring for Barker like the day he first took him in. Who else in the entire world would subject themselves to the endless trouble, much less the public humiliation of a dog named Barker?

When we packed to leave, I went to settle our account. I noticed a note scribbled at the bottom of the bill. It read, "Your father is welcome back, but not his dog!"

WD

WD, short for "white dog," was a very large, almost solid-white Alaskan Husky.

"WD *just showed up* one day while I was fishin' on the Kenai."

At the time, if Moon had known WD's characteristics, he should have named him "Follow."

"He'd lie on the rocks and just watch me fishin'. Evenings, he'd follow me to camp and sleep on the ground outside the tent. I guess I made the mistake of feedin' him. That year, a couple of days before I left, I fine'lee decided I didn't have room in the truck for such a big dog, so I drove him over to Kasilof and left him with a man I knew. Man, the next mornin', WD was already back, and that's twenty miles! I decided to load him up and take him with me back to Mississippi."

In Ackerman, WD followed Moon everywhere. It didn't matter if he was walking, riding his bike, or headed somewhere in his truck. Like the famous sled dog Togo, WD became famous for following Moon for miles simply to be with him.

"I don't know how that dog could do that, but he could. One mornin', I went deer huntin' out on the Game Area [the local term for the Tombigbee National Forest]. I had to take WD back to the house two times before I could ever get out of his sight. When I got home that afternoon, WD wasn't there. He didn't come back the next day either. Fine'lee, I went back out there where I was huntin'. I found WD dead on a hill not far from where I'd been sittin'. Some idiot had shot him. I think they thought they were killin' a white wolf or somethin'. I brought him home and buried him up there on the hill in the backyard."

Two summers ago, Barker escaped from his lead, and Moon searched for days. He never found him. No appropriate burial for Barker in the pet cemetery on the hill behind the house. Another stray "just showed up" to replace Barker. Moon departed from the usual and named her Judy.

How do you do, Judy?

Moon with a stray dog.

STRAY FRIENDS

Like the stray dogs, I thought about the numerous "stray friends" Moon has taken care of over the years, who, most of the time, just showed up. I realized Lige Weaver was only one example. I thought, *Moon's individualistic and relentless pursuit to reconcile his own pain inevitably made him sensitive to the pain of others and thrust him into the role of surrogate dad.* Usually, he offered "stray friends" his preferred therapy: fishing trips.

Aunt Patty recalls, "Your daddy always had all sorts of wily characters that followed him around, and he took good care of every one of them. He was like some kind of hero to all the young boys living in Ackerman."

I hesitate to refer to anyone as "stray"; maybe a better word is "different."

A couple of people come to mind, not only because they were Moon's good friends over many years but also because they are significant parts of this story, making multiple trips with Moon back and forth to Alaska. I also know I can never fully realize unseen and uncontrollable circumstances that contribute to the struggles and pain of others.

GEORGE EARL GRIFFIN

George Earl served time in the Mississippi State Penitentiary for killing his mother. Before that sad day, George Earl made five trips to Alaska with Moon.

"Most people couldn't get along with George Earl, but I could. He had all sorts of problems, mainly booze and drugs. You might say he was kinda lazy. He never kept any kinda job. On trips, he never fished very much but made himself the designated cook. George Earl liked to cook, and what I like to do is fish. I like to eat, but I ain't never liked to cook. I'll do it if I have to. George Earl could do anything when it came to cookin'. He knew how to get the fire just right, and he could cook in big cast-iron pots and skillets."

Then Moon, referring to Ty Cobb, his lifelong friend until Ty's death in 2015, said, "Ty had a real high IQ, but if you ever told Ty to go up there and cook the fish, Ty didn't know where to begin."

I chuckled, knowing Ty was good at lots of things, but apparently, cooking wasn't one of them!

JOHN PUGH

"John Pugh sprayed Agent Orange over there in Vietnam. I think he sprayed it from the back of a helicopter. He was never the same after he was in Nam. He got bone cancer from Agent Orange, and he had to get lots of treatments. He never walked too good after that. We went to Alaska together six or seven times. John's always been a really good friend. I think the first time he went was somewhere along about 1983."

Completing our car tour, as we ascended Moon's driveway, significant thoughts swirled around inside my head. I pondered not only how unique but also how rare Moon's treatment of others really was.

Moon and John Pugh with a Kenai River king.

CHAPTER 6

FISHIN' WITH MOON

DOUG LARSON was on to something when he said, "If people concentrated on the really important things in life, there would be a shortage of fishing poles."

After our car tour, we sat in Moon's den, looking at old photographs. Moon pulled out pictures of fish we'd caught together when I was a kid. I'd seen most of the pictures before, but contemplating my childhood now, the photos induced a discernable cathartic effect. I more fully realized the inestimable treasure Moon had imparted by teaching me how to fish. I also remembered the local fishing reputation I inherited and felt responsible to uphold.

I recalled numerous freely offered comments by various locals during those days.

"Moon Sunn can catch a string of fish out of that mud puddle out there."

"Ain't nobody can fish like Moon."

"He thinks like them fish think."

"Can you fish like yo' daddy?"

As king of the local fishing echelon, Moon, and his son, had an important reputation to maintain. Fishing wasn't something we did once in a while; it was something we did all the time. Life revolved around it. And fishin' wasn't something we did for a little rest and relaxation. If we rested, it was to fish, not the other way around.

Fishing with Moon was not only an adventure but, almost every time, a test of stamina and bravery. It didn't mean sitting beside each other at the lake, having a casual conversation, waiting for a fish to bite. It was more like an all-out fishing marathon. It didn't matter if it required wading for miles battling snakes, gators, thickets, brush, and gumbo mud.

I went fishing with Moon all over the place, but I learned my most valuable lessons at beloved Grenada. I still remember the smell of the methane gas bubbling to the surface as we disturbed Grenada's mud and decaying debris. Like different places, different lakes have different smells, and you remember.

Moon's lessons started before we shut the car door. Fishing gear was ready to go, fine-tuned the evening before the trip. Specific lures were selected depending on fishing conditions—H&Hs that Moon had reengineered and enhanced, the lure of choice. We always drove as close to the water's edge as possible—usually down some muddy road, hoping to get there and back again without getting stuck. Assembling our gear, which consisted of rod and reel, extra line, and lures that we carried on our shoulders in old army gas-mask pouches, we headed for the water's edge.

Lessons on "approach" ensued before we entered the water. Moon insisted first casts should always be made from shore. When Moon says, "Approach the water carefully," he means "stealthlike."

"Shane, never walk fast," or, God forbid, run to the water's edge.

"First, cast a few times from shore; sometimes the bass are in close, huggin' the bank. The first cast is always the most important. Most people spook fish you can catch because they make too much commotion. Don't tromp your feet, and try not to make too much noise."

Eyes focused, Moon crouched slightly, measuring every agile step as he approached the water. It was more akin to stalking a game animal.

I can't help it, but over the years, "fishing approach" has become a way I judge whether another fisherman knows what he's doing or not. To this day, when another fisherman approaches a lake or stream like a bull in a china shop, something recoils within me, and I have a hard time not correcting him or her.

Always making his first casts from shore, Moon entered the water as quiet as a field mouse. Waderless, often the water was so cold I could hardly stand it.

"Shane, your legs will fine'lee adjust and quit hurtin'."

Translated, he meant, "Turn blue and become so numb you can't feel them anymore."

"In the water, move caref'ly and try not to create any wake. Don't pick up your feet, but slowly slide 'em forward. Try to keep your lure from making big splashes on the water."

With Moon's casts, it was as if the water slightly parted its mouth to receive his lure. Mine looked and sounded more like they had originated from a grenade launcher. I watched as Moon cast with precision beside every dead tree, bush, or stickup.

"Shane, sometimes even a small stick floating on the water might be holdin' fish."

Pretty soon, I'd see him jerk sideways, setting the hook, always letting out an audible grunt, his rod bending and dancing as he played the fish. Once the fish was hooked, the job was to carefully land it in a manner that didn't disturb other fish.

"Shane, where there's one, there's always another 'un. I like to fight 'em, but I'd rather catch two."

Fighting the first, already anticipating the second, he kept his rod low in the water, the exact amount of tension on the line to avoid any unnecessary jumping and splashing. In this manner, he fought the fish until it tired, and then while lifting and pulling his rod backward with his left arm, he reached down with his right thumb and forefinger and grabbed the fish under the lower lip. He then looked it over, every fish a reflection of splendor and mystery. If I were there, he thrust it up above his head in my direction as if to say, "Look at this beauty!"

I always wondered if he did that when I wasn't around. He then released it or, if we were keeping the fish, he took a nylon string from the pocket of his cutoff jeans and tied the fish to his side.

Nylon string is an essential component of Moon's fishing arsenal; he keeps buckets of the stuff. Like a zealous member of an environmental beautification crew, he cuts down every abandoned trotline and collects discarded monofilament from the bushes of the lake.

"Abandoned line kills fish and water birds; I can't understand why people think it's okay just to leave it layin' around."

Off we went, wading farther into the lake, staying in eyesight of one another. Him fishing, me trying and learning. Moon has little proclivity for fancy bass boats and, more precisely, some of the people who occupy them.

"Some of them professional fishermen don't know what they're doin'. Look at them folks. They ain't catchin' a thing. All they are doin' is watchin' us. Shane, just *act* like you're fishin' until they move on."

I didn't know how to do that. How do you pretend you're fishing?

"If they see you catch one, they're gonna be right up here in the middle of us."

Pretty soon, the boat fishermen would yell across the water, "You boys catchin' any?"

Moon usually lied. "We caught a couple about a mile back up the lake."

If asked specifics, without speaking, he pointed in some direction. Pretty soon, they'd start their engine and head off in the direction Moon had pointed.

Moon also developed a theory that boats give big bass lockjaw. I'm not sure I agree, but he swears it's true. At least, you must give Moon's theories some consideration because they are all carefully formulated from endless hours in the school of fishing experience.

"Big bass have gotten used to the flash and movement of bass boats, especially the hum of them trollin' motors."

Moon swears that many times when the fish were biting, they'd stop when a boat approached. Once it moved on, they'd start biting again.

So, I followed, watched, and learned. On these memorable days, as the sun set on Grenada Lake, every ripple among the sticks reflected the brilliance of the world to come. Content, we loaded our gear and fish and spun back down the muddy road, headed for Ackerman.

"I think I'll take some of these fish and give them to Lige."

If Moon kept fish, it was always with others in mind. Maybe it was a way to maintain his position in the local fishing hierarchy, but I think it was because he knew others would appreciate them, especially the poor and elderly. After all, the fish weren't his fish. He was simply the conduit, distributing gifts of perfectly fileted bass far and wide.

BRIAR LEGS

We fished other places, many times until we could no longer see how to cast. I don't know why we never thought to bring flashlights along. I suppose that would've conceded the day's fishing was going to be so bad that we'd still be at it past dark-thirty.

On these occasions, I often found myself lost in some snake-infested thicket, surrounded by water, and somewhere at least two miles from the car. Trails formerly visible in daylight completely disappeared. For serious fishermen, the real problem is that you fish too long. You know fishing has impaired your decision-making ability when you tell yourself for the hundredth time, "This is my last cast."

"Shane, if you ever get lost, the moss always grows on the north side of the tree. On a starry night, you can always tell north by findin' the North Star; it's at the end of the Little Dipper. That star never moves. It always points north.

"If it's rainin', and you need to start a fire, find a holly tree. Holly has a kinda oil in it, and you can start a fire with it even when it's wet. The sticks that drop off below the tree are better than the green sticks.

"You always know west, unless it's really cloudy, because you can always see a little light in the west long after the sun goes down."

Fishing with Moon, getting lost was not the exception but the norm. One of the problems with being lost is you must first admit, "I'm not kind of lost, I'm totally lost." Once able to concede that, I always attempted to recall Moon's instructions. Problem was, most of his instructions were for worse-case scenarios, like if you had to camp out somewhere in the woods at night. On these inevitable recurring occasions, I could never remember exactly how a particular lake was oriented on the north-south axis.

"Is the levee, which most of the time I couldn't see anyway, facing east or south?"

The positions were almost always impossible to determine. *What now?* I would ask myself in those instances. *Make your best calculated guess and strike out in some direction that doesn't require swimming.* If I was off by one degree, it usually meant encountering briar patches only penetrable to rabbits, while slapping hordes of mosquitoes that were enjoying my sweet blood for dinner. Saw briars and short britches don't mix. The mosquitoes didn't even have to bite me; they could just feast on the warm blood already streaming down my legs from the cursed briars.

What appeared easy thirty minutes before now seemed impossible. I regularly found myself lost and entangled in an inescapable prison of briars, at which point, I tried to regather my senses and discern my whereabouts. In the darkness, trying to choose the least obfuscated path, most of the time, I recognized I was headed in the absolute wrong direction. Now, the immediate goal was to escape briar prison without any more flesh wounds.

That's when I yelled for Moon and listened, hoping to hear a reply or the faint honking of the car horn somewhere in the dark distance. After making recalculations, I was off again, wading through muck and mire in another hopeful direction. That's how I got "briar legs."

Most of the time, my legs looked like they had been subjected to a meat processer. They were often so bad, my mom, Farrah, had to take me to the doctor. Sitting in the waiting room in Dr. Pennington's office, I resembled the poor children in the UNICEF posters plastered on the walls.

The doctor visit and what followed usually went something like this:

"When did he have his last tetanus shot? Yeah, Farrah, he's got a bad case of impetigo. You'll need to fill this prescription and completely coat his legs twice a day with the antibiotic ointment. It's important to apply the ointment twice a day, once in the morning and once before bedtime. Are we ever going to get this boy raised?"

Next morning, Farrah ardently sought to follow Dr. Pennington's instructions to a T.

"I said, sit still, Shane," she impatiently instructed as she applied an overly generous amount of antibiotic "salve" to my briar legs.

Off to school I went, my britches sticking to my skinny legs like I had received a fresh application of Elmer's glue. In PE class, when I had to put on my gym shorts and display my skinny legs for the rest of the world to see, I wondered, *Why didn't I ask Dr. Pennington for a written excuse?*

Reluctantly, I pried my sticky, scabby legs from my jeans, attempting to hide my legs from other kids for as long as possible. Their legs looked completely normal. Mine? Abnormal—like they had encountered an angry wildcat.

Inevitably, I'd get the question, "What happened to your legs?" I knew any explanation proffered would be completely misunderstood. How do you answer—"I've been fishin' with Moon"?

FISHIN' IN THE DEEP SOUTH

In rural Mississippi in the '60s and '70s, hunting and fishing enabled folks to escape the indignity of low-paying jobs and the resulting poverty and to temporarily forget their problems. Both enabled you to put food on the table and feel a little bit better about yourself and your place in God's universe.

Social status wasn't measured by possessions; there were none to speak of. The real status barometer: one's hunting and fishing prowess. The number and size of bass and crappie on the stringer, the antler size of the white-tail buck, the beard and spur length of the tom turkey. Forged in the furnace of pain and indignity, hunting and fishing stories became currency, increasing your social status.

Acquiring more importance than weekly sermons, stories of catch and kill abounded. In Ackerman, fishing was more akin to religion, the patterns of weekly life bending and conforming to the next fishing trip, every part of it laced with meaning and transcendence. Mississippi might be near the bottom of every national list, but she's not last on the storytelling list, and we have the writers to prove it. Fishing tales were told and retold, each time better than before. Trophies of identity, the fish grew in size and number every single day.

Once a man told me, "I caught a catfish so big I cut its butthole out and made a hula hoop."

The biggest fish always "got back"—Southern for "escaped." Naturally, some of the characters in the drama became popular, famous, even legendary. As a particular character ascended the ladder of prestige, the demarcation between fact and fiction grew murky. I heard many stories about Moon that weren't true.

"Did Moon really … ?"

Most of the time, I learned to smile and say, "Yeah, I heard that too."

LOCAL FISHING REPORTS

Then there was the local fishing buzz told beside gas pumps at the local gas and grille establishments or in the aisle at the grocery store.

"Spurgeon Moss was in here a couple of days ago and told me Moon caught a nice string of bass up at Grenada somewhere off old #8. Spurgeon said Moon would kill him if he told anybody exactly where."

"Mike Melton said the water had risen almost a foot up 'ber since Monday."

"Yeah, I heard they shut down the spillway Sunday, and that water's gonna continue to rise."

"What's the weather forecast this week?"

"They're calling for more rain on Thursday."

"Folks are killin' the crappie at the old river run at Grenada."

"Donny Burton caught fifteen big slabs up 'ber Tuesday."

Facts had to be checked and rechecked for accuracy. Decisions about where to go on the next trip were determined based on careful analysis of the local news feed. You needed the cross-examination skills of a trial lawyer. It was a tricky affair, akin to a high-stakes poker game, the kitty awarded to those able to discern truth from hearsay. That's why Moon never revealed any secrets—ever!

"Shane, don't tell anybody where we caught these."

"Okay, I won't."

"Lyin's a sin, but sometimes bendin' the truth a little bit is necessary in the fishin' world."

Moon had learned from experience you didn't utter a word about the location of the latest catch, lest you wanted ten people from Ackerman there fishing your secret hole the next time you went. Opportunists abounded, and you learned to say absolutely nothing or tell white lies to avoid unwanted guests. So, we alternated between saying nothing and lying.

"Where'd you catch them bass?"

"Oh, we caught 'em late yesterday afternoon out at Choctaw Lake."

"I know that's not where you caught 'em. Where'd you really catch 'em?"

When asked, Moon's favorite answer: "I caught every one of 'em in the same place, right in the side of their mouth."

At school, I encountered boys whose dads had sent them on a "fishing-fact-finding-mission." They wanted to know the precise details of Moon's latest fishing exploits. They were so eager to know, it felt a lot like a deposition.

"I heard Moon caught a bunch of fish this weekend. Where'd he catch 'em?"

"He caught 'em all in the same place, right in the side of the mouth."

"Oh, come on, tell us."

"I told you, I ain't tellin'."

"Was it north, south, east, or west?"

"I told you, I'm not sayin' a word."

"I know where it was. It was Grenada, wasn't it?"

If I was too convincing it wasn't Grenada, they were more convinced it was. In these kinds of depositions, I learned that gestures worked better than words. Shrugs can't trap you like words can. So, most of the time, I responded by simply shrugging my shoulders. It got so bad, like private investigators, people carefully watched what highway Moon traveled when he left Ackerman on any given morning. The popularity was nice, the company not so much.

CHAPTER 7

MACK'S DEATH

Moon's 1949–50 school picture the year Mack died.

AFTER SCANNING OLD FISHING PHOTOGRAPHS, we sat in the dimly lit den in the fading light of the afternoon. I hesitantly asked Moon to tell us about Mack's death. Although it'd been seventy years, Moon's posture and short explanations revealed it was still difficult for him to talk about.

"It was a cold, overcast day in late November. Daddy hadn't felt well for a couple of days and didn't get out of bed that morning. Midmorning, Momma cracked the bedroom door to check on him, and he appeared unconscious.

She ran down the hall to call Doctor Williams. He arrived thirty minutes later and quickly determined Daddy had suffered a major heart attack. He called for a hot iron."

Before the days of defibrillators, apparently, hot irons were utilized in an attempt to jumpstart a dead heart.

"Daddy died on November 22, 1950; I was fourteen. You were born the day before his death, eleven years later."

I realized we were hearing *the* defining event in Moon's life. Weird, but the conversation seemed sacred. Of course, I wondered why he'd referenced my birth in this context.

I couldn't erase Moon's description of the hot iron. I thought, *As the searing iron was pressed repeatedly against Mack's chest, WWI etched another casualty atop her long list, thirty-two years after Armistice Day.*

Mack was buried on a rare snowy November day in Ackerman on a slight hill in Enon Cemetery. On a cold November afternoon forty years later, Othermother would join him.

The room was almost dark now as we sat in sacred silence. Moon handed me an old letter from Pearl, Othermother's beloved sister, that she'd written the week after Mack's death.

"Dearest Willie [Othermother] and Children: I still find myself unable to write you a letter. I still cannot realize Mack has left us on earth. To me he will always be alive and I shall speak of him as so. He will be with us for a long, long time; we shall not soon forget Mack. Of course, we will miss him but not forget him. He was a good brother to me. Luther [Uncle Luther] will surely miss him as we all will when we return. You will never know how I wished to be at your side, how I have missed you all, how close we all were while I was there. I hope the children aren't grieving too much. One always feels so for the children. ... I hope you have braced up and will be able to carry on. It is good that Mack left you so well fixed financially. That would be my biggest worry and

Luther doesn't seem too worried about how I would be provided for
if he should pass on. And he does have a bad heart. He liked to have
passed out when we first got the message about Mack. Said his heart all
but stopped, he broke down, took it very hard. Me, I couldn't believe it,
can't realize it yet, but though I've too done my share of weeping. You
are fortunate to have such fine older children. You can certainly rely on
them for any advice you need. These too with the rest of the family and
the friends and neighbors. This will be a saddened birthday for you.
Yet it can be one of the sweetest days you ever spent. I hope it will be
lovely. You and Pop [Will Moss] try to get together during the day, one
never knows. Two people like you and him can cheer each other up like
none of us could. I sent him a card, but you this letter. May God bless
you and make you happy. My deepest love to the children. Write when
you feel like it. Your Sis, Pearl — Monday night, November 27, 1950"

I read the letter and stared at the old AC window unit in the mottled light high on the wall above. It appeared antique, and I knew it hadn't been turned on for years. I visualized Othermother sitting in her easy chair across the room and remembered as a kid the palpable cloud of depression that descended on the Sunn family every year around Thanksgiving. I remembered asking her, "Othermother, why are you so quiet. You seem so sad. What's wrong?"

I remembered her painful reply, "This is about the time of year Mack died, and even after all these years, I've still not gotten over it."

Rick Bragg, in his book *Ava's Man*, describes the effect his grandfather's death had on his family. "After Daddy died, my momma told me, 'It was like there was nothin.'"[5]

Mack was the leader of the band, and everyone else tuned their instruments to the melody of his composition. Without him, the melody was

---

5   Rick Bragg, *Ava's Man* (New York: Alfred A. Knopf, 2001), 8.

gone, the family lost, left alone to figure out new notes. No two more than Othermother and young Moon.

Because Mack had been so successful in his quest to keep those around him happy and carefree, no one ever considered what life might be like without him. His death was an unexpected shock. The one thing Mack worked the hardest to prevent gained a new foothold and grew in the fertile soil of those he left behind who didn't have the slightest clue about what to do next.

Finishing the letter, staring at the air conditioner, Moon said, "It seemed so quiet around the house after Daddy died. Momma had never held any kinda job. Maybe she'd been a clerk down at the hotel by then, but she didn't even have a social security card! She didn't know anything about business or how Daddy provided for the family. She kept gettin' the war pension and made a livin' by sellin' the land and puttin' the money in the bank and drawing six or six and a half percent interest on it. She counted every penny and kept up with it. She also still rented the 'black people houses' down there by the lumber yard. When Daddy died, the first thing I remember thinkin' was, *I'll never get to go fishin' again*."

IT TAKES A VILLAGE AND THE BOY SCOUTS

I remembered Aunt Patty's words, "Ethelyn, Jean, and Bobbie were already out of the house. Momma was always good at raising us girls, but she didn't know quite what to do with your daddy."

So, I asked Moon, "What'd you do?"

"I don't know what I woulda' done if it hadn't been for Billy Moore and the Boy Scouts. Billy gave me a job at his drugstore on Main Street. I made $12.50 a week. I saved every penny to buy a 'glass' rod. Them fiberglass rods didn't come out 'til around 1947. I got my first one in 1951. *I've always regretted Daddy never got to use one*."

As they say, it takes a village. The good people of Ackerman became Moon's surrogate parents. School was a necessary evil, except for literature, history, geography, baseball, and football. Saturdays and every weekday after class or practice, Moon headed to his job at the drugstore. I could see him as a broken-hearted fourteen-year-old, taking his work seriously.

Dust specks flitted in the Saturday morning light streaming through the front windows of Billy Moore's drugstore. Working behind the counter, getting things ready for the day's customers, a palpable ache twisted inside Moon, searching for release. Disoriented, his financial source of boyhood independence gone, he was forced to determine a new way to live.

Looking over his round spectacles from behind the counter, Billy deadpanned, "Are they teaching you anything at that school, Moon?"

"Yes sir, a little."

After a vanilla milkshake with lots of malt and a few hours stocking, Moon helped clean and tidy things for the next day. The newspaper and magazine rack always needed attention.

"Hey, Moon, why don't you take those expired issues of *Field and Stream* and anything else you want? By the way, don't you need off early tomorrow for Boy Scouts?"

Moon read and reread every *F&S* article, especially the fishing articles.

"I liked the magazine articles describing where and how the writers caught fish and what kind of lures and flies they used. I read most of 'em from cover to cover. I still have some of 'em. I also loved the *Boy Scout Handbook*. I read it forwards and backwards. I liked the illustrations and lists describing what to do in any given situation or emergency."

Moon memorized the Scout Oath with the seriousness of a catechumen. "On my honor I will do my best to do my duty to God and my country and to obey the Scout Law; to help other people at all times; to keep myself physically strong, mentally awake, and morally straight."

In the upper echelon of important things, the Scout Law ranked just above the law of Moses. "A Scout *is trustworthy, loyal, helpful, friendly, courteous, kind, obedient, cheerful, thrifty, brave, clean, and reverent*, AND those who know Moon best would add "freaking tough!" Over the years, the various laws competed for ascendency. Some doubled and tripled in importance, while others dropped off the list. Moon would become an expert in the "thrifty" category. Mack could "turn a dime"; Moon can "stretch a dime."

EAGLE SCOUT

"I won the history award almost every year in school, and I'm proud to be an Eagle Scout of Troop 41, Pushmataha Council, Boy Scouts of America. I think in some way, the Boy Scouts helped me cope with Daddy's death.

"Niles Bashaw was older than me and already an Eagle Scout and member of the Order of the Arrow. He was the oldest son of the local Presbyterian preacher. He kinda took me under his wing and helped me realize I could be an Eagle Scout too. I don't know where I'd be today if not for Niles and his brother, Lewis. Their daddy got transferred to Florida. For years, they used to stop by and visit if they happened to be passin' through Ackerman.

"I loved the Order of the Arrow and worked hard to make sure my costume was authentic. I gathered feathers, fox and squirrel tails, beads, fur, and made leather from hides I tanned. I gathered different colors of clay to paint my face. I wanted to look like a real Choctaw warrior as much as possible."

Elected by their peers, the Order of the Arrow is a national honor society of the Boy Scouts, composed of scouts who best exemplify the Scout Oath and Law in their daily lives. OA uses imagery commonly associated with American Indian culture for its self-invented ceremonies to instill and recognize leadership qualities, camping skills, and other ideals.

Considering Moon's comment, "I wanted to look like a real Choctaw warrior," I thought, *I've never seen you do anything half-heartedly.* I imagined Moon in his costume, dancing with a group of his peers. Drums beat around the blazing fire as Order of the Arrow dancers hopped on one leg, then the other, orange sparks whirling around their head bonnets and painted faces. Louder, faster, drums and native chants joined the smoke and rose into the night sky. Moon morphed into the embodiment of a real Choctaw warrior. Forever a student of history, he knew that a bit more than a century before, on identical hallowed ground, the very same rituals had taken place.

Listening to Moon's descriptions, I realized the significance scouting played in helping him cope with Mack's death. I also thought, *That explains why, as a kid, locals told me, 'That Moon is part Indian' or asked, 'Shane, are you part Indian?'* It was their attempt to make sense of the otherwise inexplicable!

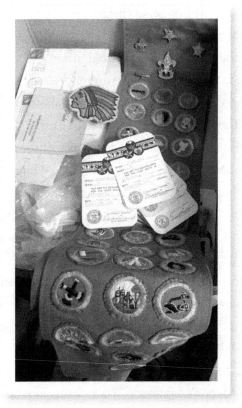

Moon's Boy Scouts of America sash and Eagle Scout pin.

GRENADA LAKE

You might think it odd that Moon seamlessly jumped from talking about his daddy's death to a long description of fishing Grenada Lake. But I already knew from this point forward, Moon literally sought connection with Mack by going fishing. This quest gave Moon his extraordinary drive to pursue the next fish, eventually propelling him back and forth to Alaska over forty times!

"I don't think they backed up Grenada until sometime in November of '53. In March of '54, only four months later, I was catchin' bass wadin' in them cotton fields. The first time I ever went up there, I went with Ed Sallis. He ran the hotel down here by the courthouse. His son, Edward Earl, was my age and a good friend, and we all went up there to Red Grass. I'd never seen Grenada Lake. It was a Saturday afternoon in the early part of March, a day kinda like today, really overcast. Ed had a wooden boat, and when we got up there, I looked at the boat and it was barely big enough for the both of them. So, I told 'em, 'Don't worry about me, I'll just wade.'

"They fished and fished and fine'lee came back and hadn't gotten a strike. I caught three bass in a flooded cotton field, about a pound or a pound and a half apiece. I took 'em home. Three or four days later, I managed to borrow a car and drive to Grenada by myself. I caught I don't know how many, but it was more than I'd ever caught in my life. I took 'em down to the *Plaindealer*, and they took a picture in front of the Western Auto Store of me holdin' them fish. All of a sudden, I became the best bass fisherman in Ackerman. The reason was, I was the first one to really learn about Grenada Lake. I always wondered what Daddy would've thought about that. I took Momma's new '53 Chevrolet up there a couple of times, and she didn't like that very much."

Listening, I remembered Moon's former comment, "Daddy died before he ever got to fish Grenada."

CHAPTER 8

MOON'S PHILOSOPHY
OF ECONOMICS — MPE

IN *A River Runs Through It*, Norman Maclean understood something unusual and significant about his brother, Paul. He says since Paul was too young to swing an ax or pull a saw all day, from an early age, he had two purposes: to fish and not to work, at least to not allow work to interfere with fishing. Moon and Paul aren't dissimilar.

As the unbearable pain of Mack's loss pressed inward, his memory and lessons pressed outward. This combination defined Moon from an early age and became the genesis of what I call Moon's philosophy of economics, MPE. When I was a kid, Moon's unabated determination to not allow anything to come between him and fishing was not only confounding, but it was also sometimes frustrating. So gradually, over the years, I defined Moon's behavior and gave it a name. Naming it, at least, helped me learn to cope with its extremes ... barely!

MPE isn't bad, simply different—very different. Put in its simplest form, Moon views money as a means to an end. Money equals time to fish or purchase whatever you might need in order to fish. The evil world exists to take your money in order to keep you from fishing. Therefore, both money and time are resources to be carefully managed so you can subdue the earth and fish as long as you please. You can either put money and time to work for you, or both, like the second law of thermodynamics work against you. In order to manage money and time, you must be willing to sacrifice for the prize: fish. This requires physical stamina and an iron will. Convenience stores and fast-food establishments are viewed with measured suspicion because they exist to waste your time and lift your money.

"All them kinda places try to do is get your money and waste your time."

Over the years, Moon has driven more miles to and from fishing destinations than any man alive. On these trips, he only stopped for the least amount of time and for absolute necessities, like fuel and, depending on which bodily function, sometimes the bathroom.

Once on a fishing trip, referring to a Coca-Cola with measured ire, Moon asked, "Shane, why do you drink those dang things? All they do is make you need to pee." As if the fish couldn't wait a couple more seconds for me to pee!

The value of any particular job was determined by how much time it bought you to fish. With the impulse of a stock trader, Moon soon realized jobs in and around Ackerman produced very little return on your time investment. Assembly lines and factory jobs in Flint and Chicago were better options because they offered heftier returns. Come hell or high water, Moon stuck to his philosophy with the fervor of a Marxist.

"The stuff you have to have becomes the stuff that weighs you down and, if you let it, will eventually steal all your freedom."

Freedom is interpreted as "fishing where you want as long as you want." So, he did whatever work was necessary for as long as necessary in order to fish more than necessary. The proportional relationships between jobs, money, and time were all means to one end: fishing.

Moon also believes in depravation. Like Elijah who was fed by the ravens, he thinks if you wait long enough, food will magically appear out of thin air. And most of the time, he is right.

1955 — Auto Assembly Line

"When I finished high school, I hitchhiked to Flint, Michigan, and got a job on an automobile assembly line. I left the day after my eighteenth birthday, which was May 19, 1954. I worked buildin' Chevrolet bodies they called the Fisher body #2. Fisher body number #1 was built for Buicks. I worked up there all summer and saved all my money and decided to come home that fall and enroll at Holmes Junior College. I majored in pre-med, but man, I wasn't passin' nothin'. I couldn't do that algebra, and I still can't. I decided I never wanted to be a doctor anyway. So, I quit college and went back to Flint. I got there on the first day of January 1955 and got the same job right back in the same place. Taze McIntyre, another boy from Ackerman, lived up there with me then. I was eighteen; Taze was nineteen."

Familiar with Moon's unrelenting commitment to stretch a dime in order to stretch his fishing time for as long as possible, I imagined the scene unfolding in Flint. The January snow piled up as Moon made his way back to the tenement house after another long week on the line. He opened the almost-empty refrigerator in the cold, unfurnished apartment, chugging milk from the jug while making a salami and cheese sandwich, his brain subconsciously calculating how much money he was saving. Any personal violations of MPE (Moon's philosophy of economics) were viewed as signs of weakness. You absolutely didn't spend your hard-earned fishing money on vices like beer or cigarettes or other needless items like good food. Why a ribeye when cheap salami works just fine? Steaks cost too much and keep you from saving every dime, which buys more time to fish. That evening, exhausted from work and his self-imposed malnutrition, Moon's time in Flint was about to end.

"When we got home from work that night, me and Taze were playin' on the unheated staircase at the apartment building. Taze was real strong, and he was always doin' all kinds of crazy stunts. Some of 'em looked like circus acts. He could put one hand on the wall and the other on the stair banister and flip up in the air and walk down the banister on his hands. Taze asked,

'Can you do that?' So, I looked at it real close and thought to myself, *If he can do it, I can do it.* I did pretty good 'til I got almost to the end of the staircase, and I lost my balance. When I saw I was gonna fall, I didn't want to hit my face, so I reached up to catch the wall, and my hand slid down and hit the glass in the front door. When I looked at that thing, I had a wide gash in my right wrist. No blood was coming out, and then all of a sudden, before I could put it down, blood hit me in the face in a big squirt."

The razor-sharp glass had severed ligaments, tendons, and the main artery.

"I knew I didn't have much time, but the problem at the boarding house was the parking lot was so narrow and icy, you'd have to push one car out to get another one out. There wasn't a car to get me to the hospital! Just then, Norman Hitt from Eupora came drivin' up in his new car. He saw what was happenin' and got me in there and drove as hard as he could toward the hospital.

The hospital was about ten miles away through terrible traffic. A cop thought Norman was a goin' too fast and pulled us over. Norman said, 'We gotta get to the hospital,' and he pointed over there at me, and the officer looked and asked, 'What's your blood type?' I said, 'A positive.' He said, 'Follow me,' ran back to his car and turned on his lights, and boy, he opened it up. Had it not been for him, I think I woulda' died. They say, I don't know if this is right or wrong, but they say you might live somethin' like a minute or two minutes after you bleed all your blood out. When we got to the hospital, I'd done quit bleedin'. Everything was blurry, and it seemed like I was lookin' through the wrong end of a telescope. They had A positive blood waitin' right there on the outside where the ambulances pull up. It wouldn't ten seconds before they had a needle in me with a transfusion goin'.

"I stayed in the hospital six or seven days, and the insurance was good. They told me I'd be lucky if I was ever able to use my hand again. I had several surgeries after that; I think the biggest one was a couple of days later. After the surgeries, I went back to the boardin' house, but I never went back to work on that assembly line anymore after that. I stayed at the boardin' house 'bout five more days. Then, I felt like goin' home, and so somebody took me down to the bus station, and I bought a bus ticket from Flint, Michigan, to Ackerman, Mississippi. I couldn't work at all, and it took me a long time to get well. I had to keep it in a cast or half-cast, for I don't know how long.

"Everybody always said, 'You bein' right-handed, how do you throw that bait castin' rod so good left-handed?' I guess I should have told the truth, but I said, 'That's the way you s'posed to do it cause the reel handles are on the right side.' But I wouldn't have thrown it that way if I hadn't gotten that injury. At first, I couldn't use my left arm to throw it, and I couldn't use my right hand enough to wind it, maybe just a little bit. It took me a long time to ever get over that injury. Once I got the cast off, I had to stretch my fingers out every day. I couldn't even feel 'em; they wouldn't move on their own."

Fly Rod Rehab

"Do you know how I got the use of this right hand again?"

"No, how?" Although I'd heard bits of the story before, I wanted the full account.

"It was by castin' a fly rod. At first, I couldn't even bend my fingers around the handle, so usin' my elbow as a brace, I lashed my hand to the cork handle. I'd cast it with my whole arm. I still cast a fly rod right-handed, but I cast a baitcaster left-handed. I'd stand out in the yard for hours and repeat two o'clock, ten o'clock. I did it every day; there wasn't nothin' else to do. Over the weeks, I started noticin' some small sensations returning to my hand. That gave me the determination I needed to keep goin'. Gradually I got to the point that I was able to grip the handle without havin' to tie my hand on there. From there, I made enough progress I thought I might actually be able to go fishin'.

"I went out to Choctaw Lake and fished with a popping bug. I remember the first time a bass made a swirl at that bug. I twitched the rod tip a little, and man, that bass took it. It made a big run, and I remember it hurt a little, but I was determined to not switch arms to fight the fish. Castin' that fly rod, and then I think actually catchin' fish, helped me forget about the pain enough to regain some fine-motor skills in my hand.

"You know every single muscle fiber is important when ya' fishin'."

"Yeah, I guess so."

Jean and I wondered if Moon was somehow suggesting that casting fly rods should replace physical therapy!

"Years later, I went back to Flint, Michigan. There was some pipeline work up there. I went by the same hospital. The doctor's name was Dr. Philip K. Stevens, and he was still there! He said he remembered me like it was yesterday. He wanted to show all the other doctors how good I could move my wrist. He said he was a real young doctor back then, and it was one of the first major operations like that he'd ever done. I told him, 'You did a good job.' He said, 'Well, thank you.'"

I glanced at the ugly scar on Moon's right wrist. It seemed natural because it'd been there my entire life. For me, the scar seemed like a family coat of arms that represents Moon's "never-quit attitude" whenever faced with seemingly insurmountable circumstances.

'38 PLYMOUTH

"Later that year, I got my first car and started goin' to Grenada a lot. I had a little money I'd saved workin' in Flint. I heard somebody say you could buy a 40 Model Ford with a V8 engine in Jackson for around a hundred or hundred fifty. So, I hitchhiked to Jackson to Jack and Ethelyn's. Jack, my brother-in-law, started helpin' me look.

"Every car I thought I was gonna buy, Jack said somethin' was wrong with it! I fine'lee gave up and decided to head back to Ackerman. Jack had a secondhand car he didn't use very much. It was an old 38-model Plymouth, and he just gave it to me. It had a three-speed in the floor. Jack said, 'Just go real slow in it. I never drive it over 45 miles per hour.' So I never did either.

But every once in a while, I'd let other boys drive it, and they'd drive it as hard as it'd go. I fine'lee learned not to let anybody else drive it. It got me to Grenada, and that was the main place I was wantin' to get."

I wondered if this was the inception of Moon's turtle-speed driving habit.

"Man, you can't believe how good the fishin' got at Grenada when that lake was about three or four years old. Once I was able to get a car, I realized I could go fishin' anywhere I wanted to, but mainly I drove to Grenada."

As we listened, I heard Moon's repetition: Grenada, Grenada, Grenada. Moon seemed obsessed with Grenada. Of course, I wondered why. Remembering his former comment again, "Daddy died before he ever got to fish Grenada," I knew there had to be a connection. I couldn't help but wonder: *As Moon drove alone to Grenada only three years after Mack's death, in his mind, was Mack sitting invisibly beside him in the passenger's seat? And at Grenada that day, as Moon landed fish after fish, I wondered if he whispered under his breath, "Look, Daddy, I caught this one for you; I caught all these for you."*

Moon's quest for the next fish redoubled.

FOREST RANGER SCHOOL

Moon continued, and as we listened, I discerned MPE lurking in the subtext of every single story.

"In the fall of '55, I moved down to Lake City, Florida, to attend the University of Florida's Forest Ranger School. I was tryin' to get a one-year forestry certificate. You could get one in one year! I wanted a job on the Game Area, but you had to have that certificate. Horace Long was the big boss back then. I knew him pretty good, and I figured if I could land one of them government jobs, I could do about whatever I wanted to."

THE TIMBER WOLF
1959

UNIVERSITY OF FLORIDA
FOREST RANGER SCHOOL

1959 forest ranger school yearbook.

BASEBALL

"I played baseball when I was down there in Florida for a semi-pro league."

Knowing Moon's undying love for baseball and having heard this story countless times, I envisioned the play at the plate.

A cloud of red dust fanned outward; Moon took the ball from his mitt and showed it to the umpire. "You're out!" He handed the ball to the ump and, like a proud rooster, strutted to the dugout, glorying in the fact he had just retired Pat Summerall.

"Pat Summerall was already famous by then. Before he played football, he was part of the St. Louis Cardinals farm club. In one game, I tagged him out in a close play at the plate. I don't think he liked that too much, but I knew how to block the plate real good. After the game, he walked over and congratulated me. He was a nice fella.

"After that, anytime I'd see him broadcasting a football game on TV, I'd always think about that play at the plate. I believe he died a couple of years ago. I've always loved baseball. I love everything about it. It boils down to a game of determination and confidence. I've played every position there is, but mainly what I liked to do was catch, and that's what I did most of the time. The catcher is the most important player on the field. We had a good team in Ackerman, and we beat every team around, most of the time. I had all the bats and catchin' equipment. I was kinda like the player-manager. I don't think we'd even had a team if I didn't round up all the boys.

"I got the certificate, but the Forest Service put a freeze on hirin'. I was out of money, so I moved back to Ackerman and did whatever odd-and-end job I could find. They were drillin' an oil well near Kosciusko, so I worked on that some. Before that played out, I had enough money to buy a red-and-white '57 Chevy Convertible. Mainly, I played baseball and fished Grenada."

There aren't many things that can distract Moon from his all-out obsession with fishing. Baseball is one.

1957 — US ARMY

Moon in his army uniform.

"I got drafted in 1957. I had to go to Fort Jackson, South Carolina. They could keep you in the army for two years. When I first got there, they put everybody through a bunch of tests. I scored the highest in my group in marksmanship and got designated "expert." They put all the experts in one group and got you to shoot every day. I became the expert of all the experts. I've always liked competition, and the harder it is, the better I like it. Back then, they did a lot of boxin' and wrestlin' on them bases. I didn't like boxin' too much, but I don't think I ever lost a wrestlin' match.

"I also scored the highest on the PT tests. They said they'd never had anyone score highest in both categories. That got the officers to start takin' a special interest in me. I wouldn't so sure I wanted any of that attention because my goal was to get out of there in two years. I qualified for paratrooper school, but you had to stay in for three years to finish paratrooper trainin'. I told 'em, 'I ain't interested in doin' that.'

"All the officers ever talked about was the Korean War. One officer, who was a Green Beret in Korea, kept pullin' me aside, tellin' me, 'A man like you could have a good future in the army.' He explained that in Korea, they needed expert marksmen to take out Chinese communists shootin' them big fifty-caliber machine guns. Somebody had to get 'em, and that was usually the best rifle shot in the company, and the smaller and more mobile you were, the better. I told him, 'I appreciate it, but I just don't think I can do it because I like to fish too much.'"

FORT GORDON, GEORGIA

"After basic training, I got a little time off, and when I went back, I was stationed at Fort Gordon, Georgia. On weekends, I drove to Santee Cooper and fished. I'd see people in boats, but I never saw nobody wadin'. I applied that 'Grenada technique' at Santee Cooper, throwin' that spinner bait beside every stick up, and man, you can't believe how many big bass I caught. I'd just sleep out there on the ground.

"Fort Gordon is only about a hundred miles from Fort Jackson. That officer would drive down there, still tryin' to get me to sign up for longer. I respected him and didn't want to disappoint him. I told him it was not because I didn't like the army or was afraid of combat, but it was really about the fishin'. He could never understand that. I fine'lee got him to go fishin' with me and taught him how to wade and cast. He couldn't wade too good, but he started catchin' bass, too, and we became good friends. I think that helped him understand what I'd been tryin' to tell him.

"Before Vietnam, pressure was put on Congress to cut the military because it was costin' the country a lot of money. They passed a bill to trim the military by about 30 percent, or somethin' like that. Because we had become friends, that officer helped speed things up for me. I don't know whatever happened to him; he was a very good man. I got my discharge papers, and I never saw him anymore after that."

Moon finished his army story, and I couldn't stop laughing. He wondered what was so funny. It was hard to explain, and I wasn't even sure I completely understood myself. Upon further reflection, I realize I was considering Moon's story from the officer's perspective. He learned what I already knew: nothing can deter Moon from fishing!

CHAPTER 9

LUTHER SPURGEON

Uncle Luther Spurgeon with a black bear.

ALL MOON'S STORIES ARE FISHING STORIES, but sometimes he "goes around his ass to get to his elbow." Like a good history professor, every detail—places, characters, and dates—is significant. Every feature employed joins the plot and converges at a common terminus: *fish*. Besides fish, the importance of place ranks high in Moon's view of the world. Why would anyone ever permanently leave Ackerman, especially your surrogate dad? I knew Uncle Luther held a place of high esteem in Moon's life, and Moon felt compelled to give the entire story of how Luther and Pearl ended up in San Francisco.

It was the summer of 1941, and residents checked the accuracy of their watches as the steam whistle blew at the E. Y. Pickle lumberyard in Ackerman, announcing the noon break. Lee Opel rushed home, the rusty spring on the screen door screeching and the door slapping loudly against the doorframe as he ran inside to share with Margaret what he'd just read in the *Plaindealer* want ads. "Margaret, welders are needed in San Francisco!"

"Uncle Lee Opel married Margaret, one of Papa and Mamie's [Will and Mamie Moss's] twin girls. Uncle Luther married Pearl, the oldest daughter. So, Lee Opel and Luther married sisters. They lived close to each other out there on the Choctaw Lake Road. Back then, there was hardly any work in Choctaw County. One day, Uncle Lee Opel read an ad in the paper, sayin' welders were needed at shipyards out in San Francisco. He went down to the telephone switchboard and asked Mrs. Powers to call the number for him. The man on the other end asked a few questions and if he could be in Memphis that evenin' for the six o'clock train. They worked out the details, and Uncle Lee Opel got the job. He hurried home and stopped and told Uncle Luther before he even told Margaret. Uncle Luther asked, 'How much money did you say they were gonna pay ya'?' Luther said, 'Man, it doesn't seem like there's that much money in the whole world.'

"So, Luther got the phone number and went down to the switchboard office and asked Mrs. Powers to call it for him. The man on the other end asked him how old he was. I think Uncle Luther was forty-one years old. The man asked him why he wasn't in the army, and Luther told him he'd fought in WWI but was still plenty healthy enough to work. That man hired him too!

"When they left Ackerman, I don't think they had anything but the clothes on their backs. In less than twenty-four hours, Uncle Luther was in

Memphis aboard a train bound for San Francisco. He went to bed one night out here in his house by the Game Area and didn't realize that'd be the last night he'd ever sleep in that house. They left their wives and all the kids here, and I think always thought they'd come back one day. But *they never came back*. The next summer, Uncle Luther hired a driver to bring Pearl and the kids to San Francisco. Pearl didn't even know how to drive. They took whatever belongings they could stuff into the trunk of the car. The house stood there for years just like it was the day they left it. It still had all the furniture and everything else in it.

"Daddy and Uncle Luther were always like brothers. I guess they had a kind of respect for each other because they shared that war experience. Nobody can really understand that unless they've been there. I know Daddy missed him. I missed him, too. I reckon he was kinda like a second Daddy to me."

As we listened, I already knew Luther's significance in Moon's life. After Mack's death in 1950, although already living in Northern California, Luther became Moon's surrogate dad for numerous reasons. There wasn't a man alive who knew Mack better than Luther. Mack and Luther experienced the hell of WWI, married sisters, resettled in Ackerman, and shared a common love of the outdoors. Pearl and Luther adored Mack and were thus able to sympathize with Moon's significant loss.

Luther knew stories of Mack's Arkansas days Moon had never heard that enabled him to connect with Mack, even though Mack had been dead ten years! Luther was also an example of someone who left Ackerman, risking everything he'd ever known, and reestablished himself in an entirely different place. For Moon, this produced an awareness that the entire world was at his doorstep—with one important difference. Luther was mobile chiefly for vocation. Moon is mobile chiefly for fishing.

"Do you know who is really responsible for Uncle Luther movin' to California?"

"No, no idea."

"One man—Adolf Hitler! If it hadn't been for Hitler wantin' to start that war, Uncle Luther would've never gone to California to weld in them shipyards."

"Hmm, I guess you're right."

I surmised, *I suppose if we can locate our pain and loss inside events beyond anyone's immediate control, it helps us arrive at better conclusions.*

SAN FRANCISCO SHIPYARDS AND SALMON FISHIN' THE KLAMATH

Sparks flew from a sea of welders, rushing to finish the next warship. Among them, Luther Spurgeon, glad to be contributing to the war effort and earning a decent wage.

"Uncle Luther made good money workin' in the shipyards. They'd never seen that kinda money around here. I don't know exactly when Uncle Luther started salmon fishin' the Klamath River, but I know it was while he still worked in the shipyards. He must've driven to Klamath on the weekends and when he had vacation time. Before he retired, he and Aunt Pearl built a house on the big bluffs overlookin' Klamath Bay and the Pacific Ocean. Aunt Pearl sent postcards to Momma when I was a kid. I read and reread every line, especially Uncle Luther's descriptions of the big salmon he caught. Sometimes he sent pictures of the salmon, and I couldn't believe how big they were."

1960 — GO WEST, YOUNG MAN

A semester of college under his belt, Moon set out for the West Coast to reacquaint himself with his second daddy and go salmon fishin'.

"I first went to California in early June of 1960. I decided not to take the '57 Chevy because it was pretty new, and lots of the interstate highways were just bein' built. They were always workin' on 'em, and you'd have to take lots of detours and sometimes just sit there in all that dust in a long line of cars. It's a long way from Mississippi to Northern California. It was even longer back then. So, I hitchhiked out there with a friend, Reggie McClure. They were cuttin' giant redwoods, and I got a job in the loggin' woods. Mainly, I went out there to salmon fish. When I got there, I started buggin' Uncle Luther to take me out salmon fishin'. He told me, 'Oh, they ain't no salmon in here yet; they don't ever show up 'til after the fourth of July.'

"I kept pesterin' him. I told him I just wanted to learn how it was done. I guess I worried him enough and so he fine'lee took me out. He told me not to expect to catch anything. I reassured him I didn't, that I just wanted to learn the ropes. He had 'bout a twenty-horse Evinrude on his boat. Dependin' on which way the tide and current were runnin', you'd motor up there and then drift with the current. Locals used about a pound weight, dependin' on how strong the current was. They trailed some kind of spinner or bait about three feet above the weight. Uncle Luther used anchovies. I ain't never liked usin' bait for nothin'. I prefer spinners. They used steel leaders that looked like a guitar string, and I could tell right off the leaders were robbin' the action of the lure. There was a nail in the gunnel beside each seat. You'd drop your line to the bottom and lay your rod tip against one of the nails to keep it from slidin' back or a big salmon jerkin' it overboard."

FIRST KING

"We got out there and hadn't been there ten minutes, and a big king hit and doubled the rod over. I grabbed it and fought it and fine'lee got it up to the edge of the boat. Uncle Luther tried to net it, but it came off. I said, 'Man, did you see how big that fish was?' Uncle Luther said, 'Yeah, they're bigger than that in Alaska.' I thought right then, *One day I'm gonna fish for king salmon in Alaska!*

"We started goin' back out there every day. I rerigged all Uncle Luther's leaders with strong monofilament, and man, we started catchin' the fish. Word got out, and a lot of other boats started showin' up, but none of 'em was catchin' 'em like we were. We didn't tell anybody about the monofilament. I don't believe steel leaders ever work a spinner as good as monofilament. The truth of the matter is I didn't ever want to catch 'em trollin' in the first place. I wanted to catch 'em with my feet on the ground, wadin'. I ain't never liked fishin' out of a boat. A boat gives you an unfair advantage. *You never feel the fish's full power* because once you hook 'em, you can just drift with 'em.

"Once I understood what the fish were doin', I figured out where I could wade and get close enough to catch 'em. I started catchin' 'em wadin', and those people couldn't believe I was catchin' 'em like that."

All Moon's descriptions sounded very familiar and true to form! I laughed again. Sometimes you laugh when you should cry, but that's the rest of the story.

Moon with salmon caught on Klamath River in 1960.

COAST GUARD RESCUE

Over the years, Moon's all-out pursuit of fish has brought him face to face with death. Most of the time, Moon's amazing physical fitness enabled him to escape confrontations with the Grim Reaper, but on this occasion, he needed help.

Moon continued, "Jack Bowman from Ackerman was out there workin' for the same company in 1960. Jack had polio when he was young and always had trouble with his legs. Jack told me he wanted to go fishin'. Because of his legs, I figured it was best to take him in a rowboat rather than wade. I'm not sure, but I don't think he could swim a lick. We couldn't ever get out there in the mornin' when the tide was right and the fishin' was best because we were workin'.

"We took off early one afternoon, and there wasn't another boat on the water! The tide was goin' out real fast, and the ocean was makin' giant waves, but the current caught us and started pushin' us toward the big rocks. Huge waves were crashin' against the giant rocks, causin' a huge spray. I rowed and rowed and fine'lee figured out all that was doin' was keepin' us stationary. We weren't goin' forward nor backward. When I stopped a second to catch my breath, the current pushed us closer and closer to the giant rocks. I fine'lee spent all my strength."

I thought, *For Moon, that's a lot!*

"I wondered if I could even get myself out. I knew I wasn't gonna be able to get Jack out. Just when I gave up and prepared for the worst, I heard this 'whop, whop, whop' of helicopter blades. I looked up and saw a big orange Coast Guard helicopter headin' right toward us. They hovered right above us and tossed down some ropes. I managed to grab one and tie it to the boat right before we hit the rocks. They pulled us until they got us out of the waves and current.

"One of the Coast Guard fellas told me later, 'Man, we debated about whether or not we were gonna make a final check that day. We didn't think there'd be anyone stupid enough to go out there in that. You better be glad we did!' I told 'em, 'I was glad.'"

As we listened, I thought, *No wonder when I was a kid, I worried myself sick every time Moon left for Alaska. I feared it might be the last time I saw him alive.* I remember carrying the ceaseless fear with me everywhere I went. Sometimes at night, I cried myself to sleep, asking God to watch over my daddy.

Moon concluded, "Uncle Luther died sometime in the summer of '68 during my first trip to Alaska."

CHAPTER 10

MARRIAGE AND
EARLY FAMILY LIFE

THE STORY NON-SUBTLY SHIFTED GEARS from Uncle Luther, now focusing on Moon and Farrah's marriage and my subsequent birth. I perked up; the tale was entering a realm of which I knew very little. I suppose divorced parents don't care to talk about memories of a failed marriage. That afternoon, Jean and I drove the short distance to my mom's house for an early dinner. Curious, my brain awash in Moon's stories, I asked about her recollections and corroborated them with details Moon had explained that afternoon.

Moon recalled, "In 1960, I stayed in Klamath until the work started slowin' down in early winter. I saved all my money and bought a bus ticket back to Ackerman. I married your momma on Friday, January 13, 1961."

Farrah in an Ackerman High School letter jacket.

Farrah, who's never at a loss for words, remembers, "I was a senior in high school. Me and your daddy decided to elope to Tuscaloosa, Alabama. Margaret Weaver and Dick Burney were our witnesses. I continued to live at home, and we kept it a secret until I graduated."

Moon remembered, "I knew when we got married, I had to have a job. I went to North Carolina and worked for a fella cruisin' timber. It didn't take me too long to figure out I didn't like that job too much, so I quit and hitchhiked back to Ackerman. My next choice was to drive back to Klamath, California, and take Farrah with me and work with the loggin' company. So that's what we did in the summer of '61."

Farrah remembered with disdain, "The '57 convertible didn't have any air conditioning, and when we drove across the deserts that summer, I felt like I was gonna suffocate. Your daddy would never buy anything to eat but Velveeta cheese, a loaf of bread, and that damned salami. The first time we were out there, I was 'pregnant sick' with you. I never hardly saw Moon. Ronny [my uncle and Farrah's youngest brother] was just a baby, and I badly missed him. I made Moon buy me a bus ticket home, and I stayed at Daddy and Momma's until you were born."

At this juncture, I remembered Moon's hesitant description that afternoon. "It seemed Farrah was likin' the trip as long as we were goin', but as soon as we got there and stopped, she became real dissatisfied. I'd come home from work every afternoon, and she'd be cryin'. I'd ask her what's wrong, and she'd say, 'I wanna see Ronny.'

"It was two weeks before I drew my first check. The day I got the check, I had to buy Farrah a bus ticket. She left the next mornin' and went back to Floyd and Kathryn's. After she left, I didn't have to rent as much of a room out there. For somebody that wanted to live like I wanted to live, they had a camp in the main part of the lumber mill. If you worked for the company, you could live there for nothin'. That's what I did and saved every dime. I worked to the end of September, then left for Ackerman."

It felt strange hearing Moon and Farrah describe the circumstances surrounding my entry into the world. I heard things I'd never considered. Like the fact Moon was in Northern California until six weeks before I was born! Like it or not, MPE and its extremes generate consequences—some unintended. Momma was pregnant with me, missing her family, and already growing weary of Moon's rambling ways.

Moon, me, a big bass, and a '57 Chevy convertible.

CHAPTER 11

THE WOOD FAMILY

FLOYD'S HOUSE

MOON'S RECOLLECTIONS now focused on the early days of marriage when he and Farrah lived with Floyd and Kathryn for several months, which again, somehow, I'd never heard about.

"I got back on Friday night and stayed at Floyd and Kathryn's. I was tired from the long drive, but Floyd said, 'You gotta get up in the mornin', tomorrow's the openin' day of squirrel season, we're goin' squirrel huntin.'' I really didn't wanna go, but when you stayed at Floyd's house, you had to do what Floyd said do.

"It was never the same for your grandpa after he fought in the Pacific. He had diabetes, and I don't think he ever felt very good. He still worked hard tryin' to put extra food on the table. He painted houses, hunted, fished, and grew a big garden. I think that's what helped keep 'em goin'. He kept a few pigs and had a smokehouse. He was really good at curin' hams."

As we listened, I remembered with fondness Floyd and Kathryn's home, which for me was a rare source of childhood stability. I also remembered Grandma [Kathyrn] telling me years before, "When Floyd returned home in late 1945, he only weighed 110 pounds. He was so weak and sick he couldn't even work. Farrah and I met him in Longview, Texas. Your momma was three years old, and she'd never even met her daddy!"

Putting the pieces together, I wondered how these circumstances affected Mom's childhood experience of family nurture. I recalled Moon and Othermother's stories of Mack's war experience and thought again, *The physical and psychological toll war has on soldiers and their families lasts for generations after the conflict. Furthermore, Hollywood's glorified version of war that I've loved over the years is deeply flawed. Who'd enlist if they knew they were potentially signing up for generations of family pain and devastation?"*

Illegal Doe

Living off the money Moon earned in California, two weeks before my birth, Moon and Farrah rented an apartment in Ackerman. Several days before my arrival, Floyd and Moon decided to celebrate the most important holiday in Mississippi: the opening day of deer season!

"I woulda' gone back to California the next summer, but I had to be in court. Floyd and I went deer huntin' on the Game Area. I shot through a buck and killed a doe. Back then, you couldn't use slugs on the Game Area, only buckshot. I've never liked using anything that causes the shots to spread, except if I'm a turkey huntin'. I was propped against a big oak, and a whole group of deer came down the hardwood hillside. I picked out the biggest buck; it was only about a six-point. I put the bead on him and squeezed the trigger. Floyd heard me shoot and came over. I was still leanin' against the same tree when he walked up; I'd never gone down there yet. We walked down the hill and found a blood trail and followed it a piece, and there lay a dead doe. Floyd said, 'You shot a doe!' I told him, 'No, I'm sure I shot a buck.' So, we went back and looked real careful and found a second blood trail. We followed it until it fine'lee played out. What happened was I shot through the buck and killed a doe behind it. We never found the buck. Floyd said, 'Let's go,' and I told him, 'I'm not gonna leave this doe laying here; somebody can benefit from it.' I ain't never believed in wastin' nothin.' I told Floyd, 'I'm takin' this doe to the game warden.'

"Back then, the wardens took deer to French Camp to help feed the kids at the boarding school. So, I skinned the doe and put the whole thing on my shoulder and walked all the way back to the car. We stopped at the game warden shack and told 'em what happened. Officer Carr wasn't there, but Officer Brooks was. He followed us back out there, and I showed him what I was shootin' and where I shot and the two blood trails. Mr. Brooks said, 'You did the right thing. I'll take the deer to French Camp.' Well, two days later, Wilbur Carr found me in Ackerman and wrote me a ticket. He didn't even ask me any questions or look at any evidence. He just wrote me a ticket for illegally shootin' a doe, which I did, but it was unintentional."

Listening, I recalled stories of Wilbur Carr I'd heard as a kid. Among the locals, Officer Carr had a reputation for strict enforcement of the letter of the law!

Moon continued, "I was determined from the minute I got the ticket to fight it in court. I killed it in Winston County, so I had to go to Louisville to the justice of the peace court. It was on the federal land, but for some reason, they prosecuted those cases then in local court. The court date was either in late '61 or early '62. I was my own attorney. They found me guilty! I didn't know many people in Louisville. I think if the trial had been in Ackerman, I woulda' won. I appealed it, but the next court date didn't take place until August. I was planning on leavin' in May and goin' back to California to do that loggin' work. But if I'd left, I woulda' been found guilty, so I had to stay 'til August for court."

Listening, it only confirmed what I already knew. Moon has a strong sense of justice, and his determination is unrelenting.

"We got in there that day and sat around for a while. Fine'lee before the court was even called into session, the judge called me and Wilbur Carr to the bench. He talked a little bit and then said, 'From what I understand, Mr.

Sunn, you are not guilty of illegally killin' a deer, and I'm dismissin' the case right now.' That got me out of there, but from that point on, Wilbur Carr was always lookin' for some kinda revenge. He was always tryin', any way he could, to bust me and your grandpa for the slightest violation until the day he retired. Not all of 'em, but some of them game wardens don't understand what they were put here to do. They assume everybody is guilty, and they think their job is to write you a ticket on some meaningless technicality. I've always believed in followin' ever bit of the law, *but sometimes the circumstances might necessitate doin' somethin' a little different.* Really, Wilbur was a pretty good fella, but I do know he'd been in the penitentiary for runnin' whiskey. Don't put that in the book! But I still think he was a pretty good fella, he just thought he had to do his job the way he saw it."

ILLEGAL PARKIN'

Years later, Wilbur Carr wrote Moon a ticket for illegally parkin' on the Game Area. The evening before, Moon had roosted a big gobbler. Rather than takin' the trouble to drive home, Moon decided to sleep in the woods.

Moon recalls, "The next mornin', when the turkey flew down, I made a couple of purrs on the call, and that big gobbler came right to me. Man, he had a long beard and big spurs. I'd been huntin' him a while, and I was sure glad to fine'lee get 'em."

When Moon walked out with the turkey, he noticed a yellow ticket stuck under his windshield wiper. The ticket was signed by Wilbur Carr.

"I didn't know it was illegal to sleep on the Game Area. I'd been doin' that ever since I was a kid."

His story seemed consistent with the Moon I knew. I wondered but didn't ask, *Was your truck parked by a "no overnight camping" sign?* In Moon's economy, certain things, like big turkey gobblers, take precedence over small technicalities of the law! I also wondered if there were a difference between "camping" versus "sleeping" on the Game Area.

Jasper Floyd Wood, Jr. (Uncle Sonny)

Finishing up dinner with Mom, Jean and I decided to go see Jasper Floyd Wood, Jr., my Uncle Sonny. Four years younger than Farrah, Uncle Sonny was a teenager during the years of Moon and Farrah's marriage. I knew he would be able to shed more light on this period.

"It's really hard to describe Moon's influence on me and my family. He was like a big brother to me. His strongest trait is pure determination. There ain't nobody as determined as Moon. There's no telling how many one-on-one basketball games we played, and he always won, twenty to nineteen. We'd play checkers, and me and your grandpa (Floyd, Sr.) were good checker players. Moon would play you until he beat you."

Uncle Sonny continued, "He fought the same way. One year before the annual Eupora Eagles versus Ackerman Indians football game, Moon shot a buzzard out on the Game Area and took it to the game and tied it up on the goal post. When all the fans poured through the gates, Moon stood under that buzzard and dared all the Eupora Eagle fans to try to take it down. He stood down there under the goalpost the entire game. I can't remember who won, I think Eupora, but I remember it being a real close game. When all the fans started leaving, a fight broke out. The police broke it up, but Moon announced it would continue at some place out in the country. Everybody got in their cars and drove out there. There seemed to be as many folks at the fight as there were at the game. When I got there, there was a big circle of people, and Moon was in the center fighting three or four big guys, and he was winning. When I got home that night, I told Daddy about the fight, and he said, 'Sonny, why didn't you help him?' I told him, 'It didn't look like he needed no help.'"

Greenheads on the Big Black

"One time me and your daddy went duck hunting on the Big Black River down below Kilmichael. It had turned bad cold. The sloughs were all frozen over. The river was running out of its banks because we'd had a lot of rain before the cold front. I was just walking around the sloughs, mainly trying to stay warm. Directly, I heard the old Winchester pump go off, boom, boom, boom. I hurried over to the river and saw the gun laying there and all Moon's clothes in a pile on the ground. There was one mallard drake laying up there on the side of the bank. Directly, I saw him way down in the middle of the river, swimming hard toward a duck. He grabbed that duck and put it in his mouth and swam toward the bank.

"When he got close to the bank, he pitched the duck up there and then turned in the current and started swimming hard back downstream. I couldn't see it at first, but there was another duck floatin' way down there, and he got it too! He got all three ducks, and when he got out of the water, he was completely blue and shaking all over, and his teeth were chattering. Your daddy has some sort of ability to warm himself up. He stomped around there and shook himself off like a wet dog. He put his clothes back on, and we built a fire. I think your daddy always wondered, *Am I as good as my daddy at duck hunting?*"

As we listened, I thought about Mack's old Winchester pump. I knew Moon regretted he no longer owned it. I also knew, come hell or high water, Moon believes in finishing what he starts, even if it means swimming naked to retrieve mallards in the frigid Big Black River!

GEORGE RHODES

Uncle Sonny continued, "Late one afternoon, the law came out to Daddy's house to get Moon to help them get George Rhodes in jail."

George Rhodes was an imposing man known for his sheer brute strength. Donning the physique of a Lithuania powerlifter, George could grab a car by the bumper and pick it off the ground and, if he wanted, flip it over. George's biceps and forearms were bigger than most men's legs, his chest and neck heaping with layers of bulging muscle, making him impervious to the normal effects of billy clubs and other devices used to immobilize problems. George was feared by the townspeople of Ackerman and all the citizens of Choctaw and surrounding counties. George occasionally went a little berserk, and like the demoniac in Luke's Gospel, no one could bind him.

One day, George imbibed more than usual in the local moonshine and went on a hell-raising vandalizing spree. The county sheriff and deputies knew something had to be done. Pulling up to his shotgun house, they found George's truck parked in the drive. Precipitous fear descended like a cloud.

The deputies conferred, "George won't give up without a fight, and I sure the hell ain't fightin' 'em. We can't shoot him; somebody's got to go in there and get him."

Another deputy retorted, "I've done lots of risky things, but by damned, I'll quit on the spot before I confront George Rhodes."

"What we gonna do?" asked the bewildered deputies.

The sheriff said, "I've got an idea. Let's go ask Moon Sunn if he'll do it."

Moon entered the house and found George passed out naked in the deep freezer, a jug of moonshine across his lap. George respected Moon because he knew everyone else was afraid of him. Moon talked to George for about thirty minutes, managed to get some clothes on him, and brought him out to the sheriff and deputies without incident.

BLUFF LAKE AND A CARP

Uncle Sonny continued, "I went all over the place fishing with your daddy. We'd go to Bluff Lake, wadin' and bass fishin'. There were so many sticks and button willows in there, I couldn't do it. But Moon could wade through anything. I've never ever seen anyone else like him.

"One time we were up there, and the bass weren't bitin', so Moon started fishin' for trash fish. He caught a gar in the Noxubee River that was as long as I was. He caught a big carp, and I asked, 'Why are you keeping *that*?' Moon just looked at me and smiled. He put the carp in a big bucket to keep it alive, and we took it home.

"Ronny was little then and kept a bank pole set out down there in the road ditch in front of the house. He'd go down there every mornin' and check his pole. When we got home that evening, Moon took the carp and put it on Ronny's line. The next mornin', Ronny came up to the house as proud as a peacock, holding the carp. The fish was almost bigger than he was! We never told him the truth about that until years later."

CORK BALL AND GRENADA LAKE

Uncle Sonny recalled, "Your daddy never slowed down; he was always up to something. He loved to play baseball about as much as he loved to fish. He'd always go to town and round up a bunch of boys and bring 'em out to the house to play cork ball. Before he left, he'd pour milk into a fruit jar, add two raw eggs and a tablespoon of sugar, and drink it down and then hurry out the door. He played cork ball like he did everything else.

"I remember goin' with Moon lots of times to fish Grenada. On one of them trips to Grenada, we had a flat on the way home. Moon didn't have a spare. He got out and looked at the tire and then got back in the car and 'turned up' the Grand Ole Opry on the radio as loud as it'd go, and we drove home on the rim! On some of them trips, he'd trade the bass we caught for gas."

I thought, *Uncle Sonny's descriptions are spot on!* As a kid, I'd watched Moon drink raw eggs before Rocky Balboa made it mainstream. I also knew Moon's determination is unrelenting—mind, body, cars, and tire rims are all subservient to the task at hand, which is, most always *fish*.

CHAPTER 12

DIVORCE

GROWING UP, I had vague memories of Moon and Farrah's horrible and intense shouting matches, but as an adult, I realized I only knew small bits and pieces of the circumstances surrounding their divorce. So, on the morning of day two, I hesitantly asked Moon about the divorce. My sister, Christia, was born in late '62, and in early '63, we moved from the apartment to an old white house in Ackerman with a large elm tree in the front yard beside the driveway.

OLD HOUSE

I remembered our swingset in the backyard, being stung by red wasps on the rickety back steps, and learning to ride a bicycle on the street in front of the house. I asked Moon about the house.

"I bought that house in 1963 and gave Dan King $4,000 for it. Your momma never liked that house too much."

Farrah remembers, "When we lived in that old house, your daddy had all his buddies over all the time: Charles Eudy, Billy Stricklin, Prep Taylor, Dick Burney, and Jimmy Vanlandingham. Billy Stricklin even roomed and boarded with us for a while. Your daddy liked bluegrass music and was trying to learn to pick the banjo. Cordell Langley would bring his whole family over and pick his guitar until the wee hours of the morning. His kids fell asleep all over the place, and they expected me to put them all to bed. The house was always like Grand Central Station.

"Moon would leave his hunting clothes lying on the floor, and I'd pick 'em up and try to wash 'em. The damn things smelled awful. He'd get mad and say, 'Hell, why'd you wash my huntin' clothes? I'd just got 'em smellin' just like I wanted 'em. He'd work three months and then try to stretch the money for the rest of the year so he could fish. We were always moving all over the place.

"In 1965, he landed a job at a timber company in Bay Minette, Alabama, scaling logs. We lived in a rented trailer. Moon worked and fished. One evening, he came home and announced, 'I quit.' Nothing would do but pack up everything that night and move back to Ackerman. I asked him why we couldn't wait until tomorrow. He had a bob trailer, but it wasn't covered. It rained all the way home, and everything we had got soakin' wet.

"We'd rented the old white house, so we decided to move into the old house in downtown, where all the Sunns used to live. Sometime way after midnight, we pulled the truck and trailer up in front of the house and found out Mrs. Sunn (Othermother) had rented it a couple of days before. I told him, right then and there, 'I'm not going anywhere else with you. I'm gonna stay put right here in Ackerman.'"

1966 — SUPERMAN

The marriage on shaky ground, in 1966 we all made a trip to California to see Uncle Luther and Aunt Pearl. We went in the red-and-white '57 Chevy convertible, with no air conditioning. We took in all the sights. We toured the Grand Canyon and the vineyards in California. Sitting in Moon's den, we reminisced about the trip.

Moon and me during the 1966 California trip.

Moon asked, "Shane, do you remember goin' to California when you were little and seein' them big redwoods? You were fascinated with them big carvins' of Paul Bunyan and Babe the Blue Ox at that Trees of Mystery park."

"Yeah, I remember parts of it."

Another vivid memory surfaced of Moon trying hard to pass the car in front of us. Moon wanted to be first in the long line so he could carry the red flag leading the other cars through the dusty, single-lane construction zone. I suppose experiences of terror lodge in a kid's brain, and you remember.

I also remembered Christia and me asking a thousand times, "When are we gonna get there?"

Moon occupied us by telling stories about Uncle Luther.

"Uncle Luther is just like Superman. He catches big salmon, and he has wings. He can jump off those tall mountains and fly all the way to the ocean."

Exhausted after a week of driving, we finally arrived at Luther and Pearl's late one night. I remember the yellow glow of the lamps in the dim light of the living room and the sound of wind chimes on the porch, tingling in the

Pacific breeze. Superman appeared much older than I'd imagined. Christia curiously eyed Luther up and down and, in the innocent way that only a child can ask, blurted out, "Uncle Luther, where are your wings?!" Luther chuckled, "I'm getting so old all my hair has fallen out and my wings have dropped off."

Moon remembers, "After our trip that summer, Uncle Luther only lived a couple more years, until the first year I made it to Alaska in '68. They'd already buried him by the time I heard about it. *I think he knew I was in Alaska, salmon fishin'.*"

Uncle Luther, Moon, Christia, me, and a Klamath River king in 1966.

NEW HOUSE

After describing our trip to California in '66, Moon continued his explanation in response to my former question about the divorce.

"I knew your momma didn't like that old house in town, so I bought seventeen acres from Mr. Rob McKnight. You know it was out there close to where Papa used to live. My plan was to build a new house on it. Mr.

McKnight didn't much wanna sell the land. But sometimes, I used to take some fish by there and give 'em to him, so I knew he liked me pretty good.

"One day I went out there and asked him, 'Would you ever be interested in sellin' me some of the land across the road?' He said, 'Let me think about it.' I went back a couple of days later, and he said, 'I'll sell you seventeen acres.' I asked, 'How much will you take for it?' He said, 'I'll take $2,000, if you don't think that's too much.' I tried not to act too surprised, so I told him, 'Can you give me a couple of days to see if I can round up the money?' I really had it right then, but I didn't wanna make it look too obvious."

Jean and I laughed out loud. Having learned the art from Mack, Moon, too, is a shrewd trader. He's especially apt at reading any situation and "holding his cards" to get the best deal possible.

"The next day, I gave him $2,000, and he gave me the title. Mr. McKnight told me, 'If you ever sell it, I want the first chance to buy it back.' I got Lamar Ray to start the foundation work. But I reckon Farrah had already made up her mind to follow through with the divorce. I took the title back and gave it to Mr. McKnight, and he handed me the $2,000."

Uncle Sonny recalled, "I remember telling Farrah to hang with the marriage. Moon was fixin' to build a new house on McKnight Road."

Moon and Farrah were babies of different world wars. Both had suffered consequential loss and therefore had different generational assumptions about what really mattered in life. Moon sought to deal with his pain by pursuing the next fish. Farrah needed a nice house and a husband with a steady job. The pain of loss seeps deep into the soul and trickles downhill into succeeding generations.

In 1972, John Fogerty of Creedence Clearwater Revival fame wrote "Someday Never Comes" about his own experience of generational divorce. When his father left, he told his five-year-old son John, "Someday you'll understand." Fogerty replies in the song he penned, "I'm here to tell you now, each and every mother's son, you better learn it fast, you better learn it young, someday never comes."

My life experience tells me Fogerty is right because I realize in some real way I've spent my entire life trying to get over Moon and Farrah's divorce. But someday *never* comes? That seems to me far too pessimistic. I believe that *someday*, on *that* day, at the dawning of the new heavens and earth, I will finally and completely understand.

WHAT NEXT?

I tried hard to remember what Moon did next, but details were foggy.

"What did you do after the divorce?"

"I was really upset, and I guess you could say disoriented. I really didn't know what I was gonna do. Vietnam started in '65, and in '66, the government was draftin' a lot of people. I thought, *Well I was pretty good in the army the first time*, so that's what I decided to do.

"I went to the same draft office that drafted me the first time and told them I wanted to volunteer. Ty went with me, but he didn't wanna get close to that draft office. He tried every way he could to keep from goin' to Vietnam for as long as he could. He figured out if he kept goin' to college, he'd get deferred. He'd finish one year and start the next. He fine'lee needed a few more graduate courses to have a doctorate, so he did that. Vietnam got Ty a PhD!"

We appreciated Moon's nonsubtle humor related to Ty. It reminded me of many other occasions when Ty and Moon bantered over one thing or another. I knew their ability to jest over each other's idiosyncrasies was a mark of enduring respect and lasting friendship.

"They told me they weren't takin' any older volunteers right then. I guess my life would've turned out different if they were."

I thought, *Yeah it would've, and mine too!*

"My first time in the army qualified me for the GI Bill, so I decided to enroll at Holmes Junior College again and major in history. I've always loved history since I was little. The GI Bill paid for a year of college for every year I was in the army. As a matter of fact, I was makin' money on the GI

Bill because it paid more money than the tuition cost at Holmes."

To me, Moon's description of loving history sounded almost like an understatement. The man is a walking, breathing American history book familiar with the subtleties of US history, as well as its dark pages. His description of making money on the GI Bill sounded completely true to form.

CHAPTER 13

NORTH TO ALASKA — 1968

MIDMORNING, we sat in Moon's den and heard tales of Alaska. As a kid, I thought going to Alaska was simply something Moon did. But with the backstory fresh in my mind, I realized deeper motivations were in play. Alaska beckoned, and something inside Moon told him he must oblige.

"In 1968, after the second semester at Holmes, I decided to go to Alaska. I first heard about Alaska from Uncle Luther. There were lots of local stories about people goin' up there and gettin' rich workin' on the pipelines. I really didn't know nothin' about Alaska or the Kenai River. I'd heard somethin' about the Kenai on a TV commercial.

"Every day, I'd see a TV commercial advertising car batt'ries. It showed a pickup piled up with snow and a man dressed real warm in a fur trapper hat, tryin' to start his truck, but the batt'ry was too weak. He replaced the batt'ry with I think they called it the 'Alaskan batt'ry.' His truck started right up, and then the man said, 'You gotta be tough to live on the Kenai!' That's the first time I ever heard about the Kenai, but I still didn't know too much about it."

As we listened, I recollected bits and pieces of Moon's visit with Christia and me a couple of days before he left. Christia was five and I was six, and we were busy playing in the front yard. Moon parked his old Chevy truck in the gravel driveway under the big elm beside the old white house. He walked over, and we sat together on the paint-peeled front steps. He told us he was leaving for Alaska and the North Pole where Santa Claus lived.

Christia said, "Tell Santa Claus to send us some presents."

Moon said, "Shane, be sure to play baseball this summer and be tough while I'm gone." At that point, I was trying to adjust to a new normal. The recent divorce did a number on me, creating a huge, gaping hole in the center of my heart, affecting, among other things, my confidence. I played T-ball that summer, and I was a lot of things, but tough wasn't one of them.

Bright sunshine streamed into the den from the east-facing windows and French doors of Moon's home, so we decided to move outside to the lawn chairs on the St. Augustine grass under the pecans and water oaks to continue our conversation. Sitting at the very origin of Moon's first and every subsequent trip to Alaska, I imagined what it must have been like.

Privet hedge in full blossom, heat and humidity already oppressive, pain from the recent divorce, Luther's words replaying in his head, "They're bigger than that in Alaska," Moon packed his gear, bound for the land of the midnight sun.

Billy Stricklin slowly ascended the driveway.

"Whatcha' doin', Moon?" Billy asked.

"I'm packin' up to go to Alaska."

"Alaska? Man, that's a long way, ain't it? Whatcha' gonna do up there?"

"I don't exactly know, but I plan on fishin' for big king salmon."

"Ya' think that truck of yours will make it all the way to Alaska?"

"I don't know, but I plan on tryin' it."

"Whatcha' gonna do if she breaks down?"

"That's a good question. I guess I'll hitchhike and then try to get a job."

"Good luck, Moon."

"Thank ya', Billy."

Moon changed the oil and filter of the '57 Chevy Apache, pouring Quaker

State 10W-40 to the precise dot on the stick, and he meticulously checked and rechecked his packing list—first and foremost, his fishing gear, careful not to leave one thing behind that might come in handy. Moon went over his list one last time: jack, bicycle pump, shovel, rods, reels, tackle, fishing line, salami, cheese, sleeping bag. Check, check, check.

Darkness descending, the western sky a faint orange, he started the Apache's engine and slowly pulled down the driveway on Louisville Street. Not fearing death or depravation, Moon was like young Jeremiah Johnson riding into the Rockies, ill-equipped and with a lot to learn, but wholly determined. Giddy exhilaration and palpable pain competing, he headed northwest on Highway 9, humming Johnny Horton's, "North to Alaska" about the rush for gold. Of course, Moon wasn't searching for real gold—his was a quest for the legendary king salmon gold.

THE ALCAN

He continued, "Back then, when you crossed the Canadian border, they always asked you where you were goin'. If you said Alaska, you had to be able to show them about $300 so they knew you wouldn't get stranded somewhere in Canada. I don't know how much money I had, but not a whole lot. I was thirty-one and turned thirty-two on that first trip.

"You can't imagine how tough the ALCAN Highway was in those days. There were big rocks on the road, and if you weren't payin' attention, they'd bust your oil pan.

"The rock dust was suffocating. Every time you stopped for gas, you had to blow out your air filter. That dust would get in everything it could—your clothes, your hair, and all your gear. I didn't have a camper on the truck the first time I went. What I couldn't fit up front, I had to keep in the back. That's why I had to keep my fishin' gear covered and tightly wrapped. I didn't want that damned rock dust gettin' all over everything. If there was one little crack, it'd somehow find a way to get in there. Every day, I'd see people stranded along the road with a sign, 'Alaska or bust.' Well, they were busted."

The history of the ALCAN is impressive. Work began on the Alaska Highway in April 1942. It was built to provide a supply line in the event of a Japanese invasion of Alaska. The highway is considered the engineering marvel of WWII and is described as "the largest and most difficult construction project since the Panama Canal."

On June 3, 1942, the Japanese bombed the military base at Dutch Harbor in the Aleutian Islands, causing more than a hundred American casualties. This event created a sense of urgency to complete the ALCAN as soon as possible. The Army Corps of Engineers encountered numerous obstacles, especially thick permafrost along and north of Kluane Lake, Yukon. The highway was not officially opened until November 20, 1942. Though its construction was a necessary and impressive feat, early reports said, "Driving the rock laden, snow-covered highway was nearly as difficult as the construction had been."

The highway was first opened to civilian use in 1948. "Much of it unimproved, rocks ate tires for lunch, and it was common to encounter folks stranded because they ran out of tires or had mechanical failures."

The total distance of the highway is 1,382 miles from Dawson Creek, British Columbia, to Delta Junction, Alaska. The distance from Ackerman, Mississippi, to Soldotna, Alaska, is 4,260 miles. That's if you take the most direct route, which Moon never does. He's completed over forty trips there and back again. That's 340,800 miles, based on the most conservative estimate. The distance to the moon is 238,900 miles. When I say Moon has driven more miles to and from fishing destinations than any man alive, I don't think I'm lying. The "Fishing Association of America," if there is such a thing, should present him with some sort of award.

Keep Drivin'

Moon is famous for the number of hours he can drive without sleep—a trait that should be reproduced only with extreme caution, if at all. He's also famous for making it to Alaska in mechanically suspect vehicles and on tires with little or no tread. Less impressive in the hierarchy of fame, he drives at turtle speed, and as previously mentioned, usually with some sort of boat tied on top of whatever junker he happens to be driving at the time.

"I fine'lee made it up there to Tok, Alaska. At Tok, you can decide to head north to Fairbanks or south to Anchorage. I'd been goin' north, so I didn't wanna go backwards, so I decided to head north to Fairbanks. Well, I 'pulled into Fairbanks,' like it says in that Johnny Horton song, and looked around. All the way up the ALCAN, I could never get the radio to work. I couldn't pick up any stations. I fine'lee got one in Fairbanks, and the first thing I heard was Bobby Kennedy had been assassinated the day before in Los Angeles. I think that was June the 6th."

Listening to Moon, I remembered the newsflash on the black-and-white TV in the darkened living room of the home where Farrah dropped me before school each day so she could make the 6:00 a.m. shift at the shirt factory.

"I stopped in a diner and bought a cup of coffee. I didn't even like coffee back then, but I thought it might warm me up, and I needed to find any information I could about work. I knew I had to get a job. I didn't have any more money for gas, much less food."

As we listened, I knew that when Moon says he's completely out of money, he always has at least a little bit left.

"I walked in there and struck up a conversation with a few people who were sittin' around. I asked 'em, 'Do you know anything about any work?' This one fella said, 'Man, there ain't no jobs here in Fairbanks; I've been out of work for three years!' So, I sipped on that coffee and picked up a newspaper layin' there on the table. The first thing that caught my eye was a picture of a man holdin' up a sixty-six-pound king salmon, and the caption below said, 'Kenai River, Soldotna, AK.' I thought, *Good gosh, that's what I came up here for.* So, I tore it out and stuck it in my pocket. I couldn't afford a room in a hotel, so I just slept every night on the front seat of the truck. I fine'lee realized they were tellin' the truth about no work in Fairbanks, besides, the salmon fishin' around there ain't much."

ANCHORAGE, RED LIGHT DISTRICT

"I decided to drive to Anchorage. Since Anchorage was the biggest city, I thought I might be able to get a job there. I parked my truck on Fourth Avenue, hopin' I might get a job cookin' or washin' dishes. That part of Anchorage ain't a good place to be if you don't want to get robbed or knifed. I guessed people wouldn't bother me because I didn't have anything. I slept on the truck seat and tried but couldn't get a job in Anchorage either."

WHITTIER, ALASKA

"I stayed in Anchorage about four or five days and fine'lee saw an ad in the paper; a few workers were needed at a sawmill down in Whittier. I'd never even heard of Whittier before, but I didn't have any prospects, so I left Anchorage and headed for Whittier. I wondered if I had enough gas money to get there.

"I'd always heard about them big money jobs in Alaska, but they didn't seem too easy to find. I drove down to Whittier, and I didn't know nothin' about that place. There was a military base there durin' WWII, and when the war was over in '45 and they got orders to leave, they just left everything sittin' there just like it was. You can catch big halibut in Whittier right off the dock. That was fifty years ago, and I've never been back to Whittier since that first time. I'd like to go down there again one day to see if that ole' sawmill is still there."

Moon drops bits of geography and history into most of his fishing stories. You will always hear a little about who used to live in a particular location, what they did, how they did it, and why it was important to them. You might also get an automobile health update, a detailed weather report, his current bank balance, and a briefing on whatever music he happened to be listening to that day. He is also prone to digression if he happens to forget some important, sometimes unimportant, detail. To him, all the details aren't diversions but important parts of the entire experience. Over the years, parishioners have wondered why my sermons have long discursive sections. At least I can say I get it honestly!

A JOB

"Back then the end of the road was in a place called Portage, Alaska. Now you can drive to Whittier, but you couldn't back then. You had to leave your car in Portage and then take a train through a long tunnel under the mountains. I didn't have no groceries. I parked my truck in the lot and paid fifty cents to ride the train; that was my last fifty cents. I left everything in the truck, except my fishin' rods. That truck was about twenty-five miles away from the mill.

"I got down there on the train and could see the sawmill out there on the bay. I walked out a long boardwalk and met the owners and told 'em I needed a job. They asked, 'Have you ever done sawmill work before?' I said, 'Man, I've been doin' it all my life.' I told 'em, 'I worked for a loggin' company in Northern California near the Klamath River, hookin' up chokers.' They told me they were from Oregon and knew all about that mill. They hired me on the spot! It was about noon, and they had me sign a form, and I was workin' by one o'clock. They put me on the green chain."

The green chain is the most constant and grueling work in the entire operation. Working on the green chain requires physical stamina and dogged determination. I knew Moon possessed both in abundant supply!

"They were cuttin' two by tens and crossties, and I had to pull 'em off the chain and stack 'em and then take the pilin's down to the burn pile. It was hard work, but I was just glad I had a job. Work ended the first day around 5:00 p.m., and man, I was hungry, but there wasn't no place to buy any food, and I didn't have any money or transportation anyway.

"I took my fishin' rod and went down to the edge of the ocean. I managed to catch two chum salmon. I ain't never caught many chums since; they don't come up the Kenai too much. You know they can get up to about sixty pounds! These were both five or six pounds apiece, and I took 'em back to the room and cooked 'em. Man, I was hungry, and they were sure good.

"The mill provided you a room with a little kitchen beside it that even had a refrigerator. I put the rest of the fish in there and ate it every meal. Until I got my first paycheck, those salmon gave me the strength I needed to do that hard work on the green chain."

DUNGENESS CRABS

"At quittin' time the next evenin', I noticed a rowboat tied on the end of the dock. I think it belonged to the company that towed the logs to the mill. I sat my fishing rods in there and rowed to an orange buoy I could see out in the ocean. I thought the buoy marked a channel or somethin'. I pulled the boat up beside it and cast a few times, but I could tell the water was pretty deep. I was curious about how deep, so I decided to reach over and start pullin' up the rope to find out. I thought the rope must be attached to a big anchor on the bottom. I pulled and pulled and pulled. Man, I couldn't believe the water was that deep! I was about to quit but felt whatever it was come off the bottom, so I kept pullin'. I got it to the top, and it was a big crab trap full of 'bout ten of them giant Dungeness crabs. I said, 'The Lord will provide!' I took the crabs and dumped 'em into the rowboat. I ate on them crabs for the rest of the week. Man, they were delicious. That ain't never hurt my conscience too much, but it sure did help my belly!"

Jean and I laughed. Moon abides by all the rules, including most of the Ten Commandments, unless dire circumstances warrant otherwise. The definition of "dire circumstances" might change depending on the severity of the situation you find yourself in. Grueling work and no money or food qualify as dire circumstances! I thought, *Most of life's greatest lessons are learned in times of deprivation.*

CHAPTER 14

A GOOD PAYIN' JOB

THE SECOND RUN

MOON CONTINUED, "At the sawmill, you worked six days, but you were off on Sunday. They paid me on Saturday, and that's when I realized I was only makin' two dollars an hour! I was makin' twice that much in Mississippi, but I was still thankful to just have a job.

"Now that I had a little money in my pocket, Sunday mornin' I paid fifty cents to ride the train into Whittier and buy some gros'ries. I went in the gros're store and bought a few things. Back then, handheld transistor radios had gotten popular, and they were cheap. I debated but fine'lee decided to buy one. I think I gave two dollars for it; it was about the size of a pack of cigarettes.

"While I was in town, I kept hearin' people say they were catchin' a lot of salmon on the second run. I thought they were referrin' to a second run of salmon, but then I realized they meant a *place* called the 'second run.'"

SALMON!

Most of Moon's stories are fishing stories, but you need a lot of listening patience to get to the actual fish-catching. Listening, we knew he was getting close when he narrowed his eyes, took an excited deep breath, and launched into the catching experience almost like it was yesterday. I wondered if this was a function of his incredible memory or simply his enduring love for fishing. I assumed both.

"The next Sunday mornin', I took the train back to Whittier. When the tide was low, you could walk down the edge of the ocean to where two streams came in. I got to the first stream and cast for a while, but I could tell there wasn't any fish in there. Now I know that's what they called the 'first run.'

"I kept goin' and got to the second stream, and man, you could see swarms of salmon in there swimmin' in formation! I used my spincaster and cast in there to 'em. I don't like usin' spincasters, but that's all I had. I think I was usin' a Mepps spinner. Almost as soon as the lure hit the water, I had one. I caught a whole *mess* of salmon!

"The tide was way out, and I looked down and saw something glistenin' in the sand. I reached down and picked it up. It was an old brass sword handle. The blade had rusted off, but I thought it mighta' been there since the days of Captain James Cook. I picked it up and put it in my pocket.

"I guess I fished a little too long! The tide came in real fast, and there was no beach left, so I had to climb over them giant rocks and through all them thick alder bushes to make it back. I was cold and soakin' wet when I got back into Whittier. I carried the fish and paid fifty cents to ride the train back to the mill."

As Moon recounted his tale, I knew his disdain for spincasters was because he's perfected the use of the baitcaster. I thought, *Mack could cast that thing like a magician; Moon, like a god.* I also surmised, *I suppose you could carry a 'mess of salmon' on the train back then.* But I did wonder about the smell and what other passengers might have thought.

"That's the first time I ever got into salmon like that, and I'll never forget that day. I guess the sword handle has always reminded me of it."

Today the brass sword handle occupies a prominent place on my bookshelf. Sometimes, I pick it up and ponder it. It reminds me of this amazing story. It reminds me of Moon.

Moon with "a mess" of Kenai salmon, 1968.

Brass sword handle found on the beach
near Whittier, Alaska, 1968.

THE KENAI RIVER

"At night, after work, I listened to the transistor radio, and you could pick up stations from all over the place. I kept hearin' an ad, 'Come on down to Mississippi BBQ in Kenai, Alaska.' I think that caught my attention for two reasons. It mentioned both Mississippi and Kenai. I still had the newspaper clippin' of the big king caught on the Kenai I'd tore out of the newspaper in Fairbanks.

"The next week, the boss told me they'd gotten into a dispute with the tow company, and there wasn't gonna be any more logs for at least the next couple of weeks. He told me, 'I'm gonna have to lay you off, but you're a good worker. Check back in two weeks.' I told him I would, but in the back of my mind, I kept hearin' that commercial, 'Come on down to Mississippi BBQ in Kenai, Alaska!'

"I rode the train back through the tunnel, got in my truck, and drove to Soldotna, Alaska. I drove right down there on the Kenai River where Centennial Campground is today. Back then, it was unimproved with only a few campsites and picnic tables. There wasn't another soul down there fishin'! That's where I caught my first big king salmon. I couldn't believe how hard it fought. I think it took me thirty minutes to land, and it only weighed about forty-five pounds. I couldn't believe how fat and beautiful it was. When I landed that fish, I thought about Daddy and Uncle Luther and wondered what they woulda' thought."

As they say, the salmon caught Moon. Or had the hook already been set years before? In coming years, Moon would become legendary among the bank fishermen on the Kenai River in Soldotna.

OIL RIG

"I still didn't have hardly any money. I fine'lee got a job on a drillin' rig between Soldotna and Kenai, but that didn't work out too good. I only had one or two changes of clothes, and you'd get real oily and grimy doin' that work. I had to wash my clothes every day, and so I needed a room at a place that had a laundry. I had to eat at a diner because there wasn't any place to cook in that tiny apartment. At the sawmill, at least I had a place to live and cook, and it didn't cost anything extra.

"I was only making $2.80 an hour, but I was spendin' that just to be able to do the job. I figured out—I was really workin' for nothin'. *I wouldn't gettin' to do much fishin' either*, so I worked about ten days and decided to try somethin' else."

UNION PIPELINE

"I fine'lee got one of them good payin' jobs. I realized I'd never get ahead workin' a job that paid $2.80 an hour when they had jobs in Alaska that paid $12 or $13 an hour. Someone told me about pipeline work not too far from Soldotna in Nikiski, Alaska.

"I drove down there to check it out. There were lots of people standin' around tryin' to get on, like there always is on them pipelines. I talked to some of the fellas standin' around, and they asked, 'Did you join the union in Anchorage? If your name ain't on the list, you can't get a job here.' I said, 'Well I think I did.' I tried to avoid answering that question too directly. I asked, 'How many people are on the list?' They said, 'Oh, about five hundred.' I said to myself, *I've got to get me some kinda plan if I want this job*. So, I made up a big lie. I reckon I shouldna' done that, but I did.

"The big boss on that job was a fella named Petey Hill. I finally got to talk to him and told him I was in Vietnam and got shot, but I was all right now. I rubbed a place on my side and said, 'Yeah, I was hit right here,' and kinda showed him but didn't lift up my shirt. I said, 'When I got back to Mississippi, my wife had done left me, and I went through a bad divorce. I drove to Alaska because I'd heard you can make a lot of money up here. I've looked and looked and can't find no work. I think I'll just go out here and take my gun and end it all.' He said, 'Man don't do that!' If he'd said, 'Go ahead, I don't care,' I would have known I didn't have no chance for that job. But when he said, 'Don't do that!' I knew I had a chance. I knew he was the one pullin' the strings, so I drove out there every day and talked to Petey Hill. I told him I'd done a lot of work on pipelines, and I'd describe what all you have to do.

"Petey said, 'Half these people out here don't know what you know. I can tell you've worked on the pipeline before. If I need a man, I have to call the union hall in Anchorage. You have to pay $300 to get on the list.' I didn't want to tell him, but I didn't have $300! As a matter of fact, I was so broke, I didn't think I could drive out there another day.

"He fine'lee said, 'The union hall ain't open on Sunday, so I can tell 'em I got in a bind and had to hire whoever was available. That way, I can hire you without gettin' in trouble with the union. Be out here Sunday mornin'. I'll tell them I needed an extra man.'

"I drove out there Sunday, and lots of people were standin' around watchin'. Petey talked to me a little bit and then walked up to the office like he was usin' the telephone. He walked back down there and told me to go up to the office and eat breakfast and fill out an application. Before I got through eatin', he said, 'Come on, just sign your name at the bottom; you can fill out the rest later.' He drove me out there, and there were about seventy-five workers in the whole group. There was only about ten in my group."

I pondered Moon's comment, "I reckon I shouldna' done that, but I did." I thought, *At least he's honest; he's not lying about lying.* But I also realized that fishing MPE and "dire circumstances" were pushing hard against an impenetrable standard. Lying about fighting in Vietnam is more serious than checking someone else's crab trap when you're starving. But I also thought about the occasions I've lied when the stakes weren't nearly so high. Most of the time, I am ashamed to admit, it was to maintain my paltry reputation when I had plenty to eat. I also knew for Moon it was about making enough money to buy more than enough time to fish.

KEEPIN' THAT JOB

"The main boss on my crew was George Bartell. His claim to fame was he could whip any man in Alaska. I worked as hard as I could tryin' to make an impression and make myself indispensable. I could do more stuff than any of the rest of 'em. After I proved I could do the work, I knew they weren't gonna lay me off or fire me. I was stackin' skids, and I'd done that before. In the South, skids are made of red oak, and they are as heavy as I don't know what. In Alaska, skids are made from spruce or fir, and they're a lot lighter than red oak. I'd been workin' on that green chain, so I was in real good shape.

"You'd lay the skids down and they'd place sections of pipe on top so they could be welded together. Then you'd back down the line and load the skids into the back of a truck and take 'em forward. A lot of people just stood around and watched, but they had the advantage of the union. I was so eager to *keep* my job I'd grab two skids, one under each arm, and load 'em or take 'em wherever they needed to go.

"I was a makin' $12.50 an hour and double time on Sundays. That was big money back then. They provided me a room and three meals a day. I'd take the check and put it in a pillowcase in that old beat-up leather suitcase."

WHIPPIN' THE TOUGHEST MAN IN ALASKA

"That summer there were a lot of pretty days with not much rain. Everybody kept talkin' about how George Bartell could whip any man in Alaska. We were all sittin' around eatin' the lunch they'd bring out there to you, and George Bartell said, 'Hey, Missip, do you think you can whip ole' Penn State over here?'

"He was talkin' 'bout a younger fella who worked with us who always wore a sweatshirt that said 'Penn State Wrestling Team.' I didn't wanna wrestle him, but I ain't never backed down from no challenge. Besides, I knew I already had job security. So, we got out there, and I pinned him pretty quick. He wanted to do it again, so I put him down again. Then Penn State asked, and

I'll never forget this, 'You know what the hardest thing to do in wrestlin' is?' I said, 'Naw, what's that?' He said, 'Wrestlin' somebody that don't know how to wrestle.' I said, 'Well, I wonder who it is who don't know how to wrestle?'

"Several days later, George Bartell said, 'Hey Missip, I bet you can't whip me.'

I was thirty-two then. George Bartell was a big ole' fella and stood about six foot five. I really didn't want to fight the boss, but he said, 'Come on, let's give it a go.'

"I knew I could do pretty good with big, tall fellas because I did a lot of wrestlin' in the army, and I always went up against a big, tall fella, and I always whipped him. So, we got out there, and I got ole' George Bartell down, the man whose claim to fame was he could whip anybody in Alaska. He said, 'Hell boy, get up off this fifty-five-year-old man.' I said, 'How old are ya', George?' and he said, 'Fifty-three.' I said, 'You musta' done all that whippin' when you were about thirty.'

"He was really tough, but I don't think he realized what a difference twenty years makes. Me and George became good friends. When it started gettin' cold and they started trimmin' the crew, George took up for me. Fine'lee when it was clean-up and put-up time, me and George were the only two people left out there. And I really wouldn't even in the union.

"George told me, 'When you go back through Anchorage, go by the union hall and pay $300, and you'll have a job for the rest of your life. We gonna be doin' this for a long time, as long as they keep hittin' wells and needin' to pipe oil to this refinery.' When I left the job, I had thirteen checks, and I hadn't ever cashed one of 'em. Each check was $1,400 or so apiece."

SILVER FISHIN' AND A BULL MOOSE

I know it might be hard to completely comprehend, but Moon redefines frugality. He can stretch money further than it is intended to be stretched and eat stuff that'd kill a normal person. He is not afraid of being hungry, and he never frets or panics in any situation. Neither is he ever concerned about where he might sleep on any given evening. Why? It's about the end goal, the prize—it's about the fish.

"After we shut down the pipeline work, it was late September, and the Silvers were in really good on the Kenai. *I hadn't been able to do any fishin'* while I was workin'. I went back to the campground, and I was catchin' silvers like they were goin' out of style.

"One day when I was fishin', a fella said they needed night work at the generator plant. They needed somebody to do a few things, but the job was mainly like a night watchman. Sometimes when luck or fate or whatever you wanna call it is workin' for you, you need to keep it rollin'. At first, I couldn't hardly get a job, and then I couldn't hardly not get one. I prob'ly shouldn't have accepted that job, but I told him I would. So, I fished in the day and sat out there at night in my truck and mainly slept.

"One thing I wanted to do in Alaska was kill a big bull moose with giant antlers. So, I quit fishin' during the day and started goin' huntin'. First, I hunted around local lakes, and all I was seein' was a few cows. One day, I was talkin' to a fella and he told me, 'Man you've got to hunt big bulls up high.' That'd never dawned on me, so I started drivin' to a place near Cooper Landin'. When I got to the big mountains, I'd pick one out, park the truck, and walk up it. I fine'lee got a big bull moose. You can't imagine how much work it took to get him. I was by myself, and it was a long way up the mountain. It took me almost three days to get it all. I took the backstraps, hindquarters, shoulders, and everything else, and then I had to get the antlers.

"I worked another week on the nightwatchman job and then counted my money. When I left Alaska, I had over $20,000 in hundred-dollar bills. That was a lot of money in 1968!"

Based on Moon's intonation and facial expression, I wondered, *How much money?* So I Googled it on my iPhone. I was shocked to discover that $20,000 in '68 is equivalent in purchasing power to $157,222 today. I thought, *Man, that was a good payin' job!*

Moon with a bull moose in 1968.

CHAPTER 15

SOUTH TO ACKERMAN

AS MOON CONTINUED TALKING about his return trip in '68, I considered Jean's question from the previous evening, "Where were you, and what were you doing when this or that happened?"

Since the divorce, always in the back of my young mind was the secret hope they'd somehow be able to work things out and get back together. Doesn't every kid hope for that more than anything? Although I'd never dare share my secret with anyone. Rather, I learned to stuff my painful emotions and attempt to live with them.

Finally in the fall, a letter arrived from Moon, announcing he'd be back in Ackerman in the next couple of weeks.

"Read it again."

Momma struggled to reread the chicken scratch on the postcard; I was glued to every word. Overjoyed, I didn't sleep very well during those two weeks.

HITCHHIKER

"The week I was lookin' for the best place to moose hunt, I saw a fella walkin' down the side of the road. I pulled over and asked where he was goin' and if he needed a ride, and he told me some of the saddest stories I've ever heard. He looked real depressed and told me he was stayin' at the welfare home, or somethin' like that, in Anchorage. He was from somewhere in Montana and heard his wife, or either ex-wife, was somewhere in Alaska, but he'd never been able to find her. He told me, 'I think she might be back in Montana somewhere.' I told him, 'I'm goin' back to Mississippi in two weeks and have to drive straight through Montana. I'll take you if you want to go, if I can find you in Anchorage.' He gave me a phone number, and I wrote it on a piece of paper. I can't remember his name anymore; I wish I could. I told 'em at the generator plant, 'I'm gonna work one more week, and then I'm goin' back to Mississippi.'"

NEW TIRES

"I worked another week and then looked the truck over, and it looked pretty good, except the tires. I saw a special in the paper for four new tires at Sears and Roebuck in Anchorage. I had to load all my stuff and give away most of the moose, so I didn't get to leave 'til 'bout dark. The next mornin' in Anchorage, I got the tires put on, and then I went by the union office. A sign on the door said, 'Closed due to death in the family.' I said to myself, *That gives me time to find the fella that needs a ride to Montana.* I called the number, and they told me how to find the place. I drove up, and the man runnin' that establishment was some kinda preacher or somethin'. The fella I was pickin' up didn't have a penny to his name. The preacher seemed concerned about that, and I told him, 'Don't worry about that, I have plenty of money.' The preacher said, 'Let me pray for you boys.' He put his hands on both our shoulders and said, 'God bless these boys and keep 'em safe' and stuff like that. I said, 'Thank you, I'll be very careful goin' back. I always try to drive real careful.'"

Listening, I thought, *Real careful and real slow!*

"I went by the union office again, and it still wasn't open, so I gave up on that. It was late October and not very cold yet; it was about thirty degrees or so in Anchorage. I just had one little coat over my short-sleeved shirt."

Moon still picks up hitchhikers. Somewhere along the way, he missed the bulletin it can be dangerous. He also has a soft place in his heart for anyone in need. I'd realized years before it was pointless for me to attempt to change his ways.

BLIZZARD

"We left around noon, and when we started gettin' east and over the high mountains, it seemed like the heater in the truck just quit workin'. When we got to Gunsight Mountain, way past Anchorage, but not to Glennallen yet, it was as cold as I've ever seen it in October. It was snowin' and the wind was blowin', and I could barely see the road. The other fella said, 'Let's get a cup of coffee up here at this station.' I didn't even drink coffee then, but I decided it might warm me up. It felt like the cold wind was blowin' straight through the truck. I had the heater wide open, and it felt like it wasn't doin' a thing. We pulled up to the café, the only one for miles and miles. A man ran out and said, 'Don't cut your engine off!'

"I didn't cut it off because I knew he was right. We ran into the café in the blinding snow and wind. It was warm inside, and I could see the thermometer outside—it read thirty below zero! I never thought I'd get into that kinda cold weather. I'd never experienced an Alaskan winter. Matter of fact, I ain't wantin' to see another one either.

"Before we left the café, I put some paper on the radiator to help the heater. That helped warm it up some. I was pretty tired and figured the other fella hadn't been doin' much, so I let him drive. I went to sleep. He went the wrong way in Glennallen, and we went 150 miles out of the way toward Fairbanks, and then we had to turn around and come 150 miles back. That was 300 miles, and we weren't a bit further than when we started. It was five or six hours later in the trip, and we'd burned a whole tank of gas! I lost my temper, and I fussed at him too hard, and he just hung his head down."

THE BLIZZARD "JUST FOLLOWED US"

"I had a set of chains but only for the back tires. I'd lay the chains on the ground, then get back in the truck and drive forward. Then I'd get out again and lay down in the snow to fasten 'em on. Man, the wind was blowin' the snow, and I couldn't see, and I felt like I was gonna freeze to death. I'd put 'em on and drive forty miles and hit a section with no snow, and I'd hear the chains hittin' rocks, 'plap, plap, plap.' So, I'd get out and take 'em off. I'd drive thirty miles and hit deep snow and get out, lay down, and put 'em on again. And it was like that all the way down the ALCAN. I think the blizzard just followed us.

"We didn't have any trouble crossin' the Canadian border. The fella ridin' with me had a birth certificate, and they let us go right through. It was dark and cold. The last time we looked, it was thirty below, and it didn't feel a bit warmer when we got into Canada."

JOHN HENRY MCCLAIN

"Near Whitecourt, Alberta, I saw a hitchhiker and thought, *Man he's gonna freeze to death if I don't pick him up.* When he got in, he was just shiverin', and you could feel the cold he was generatin' just sittin' in the truck a minute. I don't know how long he'd lasted if I hadn't picked him up. His name was John Henry McClain, and I'll never forget him; I still think about him a lot."

I wondered skeptically, *Does Moon really still think about a boy he picked up hitchhiking in Alberta fifty-two years ago on his first trip to Alaska?* Then

I remembered Moon has driven by the exact spot, on the same road to and from Alaska, over forty times in those fifty-two years. That's over eighty occasions to reminisce, so maybe he does still think about John Henry. Then I wondered, *What's motivated Moon to think about John Henry McClain for so long?* Obviously, a teenage boy hitchhiking in these conditions had more than a few problems in his life. Was Moon's memory simply nostalgia or was it more? Did Moon identify with John Henry because of his own pain and loss, recent and past? Might John Henry have reminded Moon of himself after Mack's death eighteen years prior? Or did John Henry remind Moon of his own children and his uncertain role in nurturing them moving forward? I didn't ask.

Moon continued, "That put three of us in the truck. We were about a hundred miles from the US border, and when I got down there, I had moose horns, cases of canned salmon, two passengers, and a bunch of other stuff in the back of the truck. John Henry was a minor, but I didn't know it was illegal to take a minor across the border. We got to the border just when it was gettin' a little light. So many things were illegal: John Henry was a minor, and the other fella only had one set of identification.

"It just so happened the first fella was born in the state of Mississippi: Biloxi, I think. It also turned out he'd spent ten years in the penitentiary! I had no idea about either of those things 'til we got down there to that inspection. Well, him bein' born in Mississippi, which his birth certificate showed, and me being from Mississippi, the officers couldn't believe we didn't know each other. When they find one thing wrong, they think everybody has done somethin' criminal. And that's good—they shouldn't let nobody that's dangerous get by, but a lot of 'em do anyway. But even the innocent ones they put ever kind of question to 'em you can imagine if they happen to get one little suspicion.

"They made us get out of the truck, and they went through everything. Well, they got on the fact of me and him both bein' from Mississippi. And when they found out he'd been in the penitentiary, they decided I must have been in the penitentiary with him. But he wasn't in the penitentiary in Mississippi; he was in the penitentiary in Montana!

"I never told 'em exactly how much money I had, cause they'd prob'ly thought I'd stolen it or somethin'. After they asked me the same questions for what seemed like fifty times, they fine'lee told us to just go on. I know they coulda' gotten me for taking a minor across the border. But they got so stuck on me and the other fella, they never even questioned me about John Henry McClain. I think they must have thought he belonged to me."

SHELBY, MONTANA

"We drove on down to Shelby, Montana. I decided to let the other fella drive again. I'd gotten tired, and I felt a little sorry for him since I'd fussed at him so bad the first time. I got in the passenger's seat and tried to get some sleep. I felt the truck crossing a railroad track, 'bump, bump, bump.' He'd gotten on the wrong road again, so he punched me and told me to wake up. He slowed the truck down and pointed and said, 'Eh, does that sign say Montana?' I looked out there, and it said, 'Post Office.' He didn't even know how to read! That was the reason he'd gotten mixed up the first time, but I didn't know that. Because I'd fussed at him so bad, he didn't want to make another mistake. I let him keep drivin', but I knew my sleepin' was over because I was gonna have to be the navigator.

"We were lookin' for his wife, or ex-wife, or any other relatives. Then I found out he'd never found her since he'd gotten out of the penitentiary. We drove thirty miles out in the country to a place he thought he lived one time. There'd be one little road and the next road would get even littler. We were drivin' through cattle country and sometimes woods. We fine'lee came to a house that looked like it hadn't had nobody livin' in it for twenty-five years. Bushes and trees were growin' up around the place; you could barely even see the house! He said, 'I believe this is where I used to live, but I'm not completely sure.' I knew nobody lived there, but he got out of the truck and started walking around the yard. I'd gotten a little concerned after learning he'd been in the penitentiary, and so I figured that was my chance to get back in the driver's seat. We never found the man's wife, but we fine'lee found somebody in the next town that knew him. So, I just left him there. I don't know how I got into that situation, but that fella really needed help."

I thought about all the inconveniences Moon has endured over the years taking care of numerous wily characters. Listening, I felt nothing but admiration and respect.

MEXICO OR MISSISSIPPI?

"That left me and John Henry in the truck. John Henry first told me he wanted to go to Mexico, but when he found out I was goin' to Mississippi, he wanted to go to Mississippi too. That mornin', we drove down to Great Falls, Montana, and then headed east.

"A little way out of Great Falls, I heard the old Apache start makin' a 'plump, plump, plump' sound. The road sign said 110 miles to Lewistown. I saw a Chevrolet dealership and pulled in. It was about closin' time on a Friday afternoon. I told 'em, 'This truck is hardly runnin', and I don't know what's wrong with it. I'm coming back from Alaska and want to get it fixed as quick as I can.'

"I could tell they didn't want to deal with it. The other thing, I looked pretty rough. I knew what they were thinkin': *This man ain't got enough money to fix his truck.* I started to show 'em my money but decided I'm still not sure about John Henry McClain, so I didn't show 'em no money."

I thought, *Moon may be tenderhearted, but at least he ain't stupid!*

Moon continued, "The way I do that is keep one roll of hundred-dollar bills in my left pocket and just get one out at a time and keep the change from that hundred in my right pocket. I never touch my left pocket 'til I spend every penny of change. That was before the days of credit cards, and I never thought I'd ever own a credit card, but a credit card is a lot easier. They stood around lookin' at my truck, and I asked, 'How much is that little Ford sittin' over there?' They said, 'That ain't for sale.' I felt in my right pocket and took out eighty-seven dollars. I told 'em, 'I'll give you eighty-five dollars for it.' They said, 'Naw' and walked off. I said, 'See 'bout gettin' my truck fixed then. I'd like to leave sometime tomorrow. I'm goin' over here and get me a room in this motel.'

"That meant I had to get a room for John Henry, too, or turn him loose. It looked like John Henry would rather be with me. I'd bought him a good supper a time or two, and he'd taken to me.

"They got to lookin' at the truck and listenin' to it a little bit. I could tell they still didn't want to bother with it. They walked back over, and one man kicked the dirt a few times. He asked, 'How much did you say you'd give us for that Ford?' and I said, 'Eighty-five dollars.' He said, 'I believe I'll take it.' I handed him eighty-five dollars, and he signed the title and had me sign it at the bottom. It was a black 1949 two-door businessman's coupe. It was shiny black and didn't have a scratch on it!

"They didn't offer me anything for my truck, so I rented a tow bar. First, I found a flat place and changed the oil in the Ford coup. I'd never towed nothin' like that before and didn't know how to hook it up. I bolted the tow bar on the Ford and backed up to the Apache. Somehow, I managed to get it all hooked up. But I couldn't figure out how to hook up the lights, so I pulled the light switch in the Apache only halfway out so I'd have lights in the back without running down the battery in the Apache. The Apache's parking lights shined in front and the taillights in back. I didn't know how to hook up the brake lights and blinkers, and I sure didn't want to take a day to see if I could figure out how to do that. I left the Chevy dealership in the '49 Ford Coupe pullin' the Apache. I drove all night. John Henry seemed excited."

I wondered, *With all the money in his pocket, why did he bother to tow the Apache?* But then I remembered his undeterred frugality and all the junkers he'd owned over the years. Plus, I realized he needed a way to haul all his gear and the various and sundry things he'd purchased in Alaska. I surmised, *Oh, the Apache must have served as a trailer!*

PULLED OVER IN MINNESOTA

Although Moon generally takes the most direct route to and from Alaska, while trying to avoid as many big cities and interstate highways as possible, sometimes he takes a scenic detour for no apparent reason, but only when returning *from* fishing.

"I'd never been through Minnesota and wanted to see that, so instead of cuttin' down through Missouri, I kept going east to Minnesota."

Listening, I wondered about the sanity of his choice, especially since he was towing a large pickup behind a '49 Ford Coupe!

"I got to a small town with a square, kinda like in Oxford [Oxford, Mississippi]. About halfway around it, two cops pulled me over. One walked up beside my driver's window and said, 'Mister, your tow lights ain't workin'.' He didn't say anything to John Henry. I guess he thought he musta' belonged to me. He walked to the back and said, 'Make your brake lights work. Mash ya' brakes.' I slid out of the Ford Coupe and opened the Apache *door and pulled* the lightswitch all the way on. I reached down and pressed the brake pedal with my hand. Then he said, 'Try ya' right blinker,' and I pushed the stem up, and it blinked. 'Try ya' left blinker.' I pulled the stem down, and it blinked too! The officer said, 'Good.'

"They didn't even know I was in the truck! It had nothin' to do with what I had hooked up. As a matter of fact, they had never even made blinkers for the '49 Ford yet. So, it didn't even have no blinkers! I got out of the Apache and leaned against the coupe. They walked up and asked, 'Where ya' been?' I told 'em I'd been in Alaska, and they got to lookin' at the moose horns. They both said they really wanted to go moose huntin'. I told 'em about fishin' in Alaska, and they got interested in that too. I told 'em I didn't have much of a camera, only a Polaroid, and I showed 'em a few pictures of the last silvers I caught. They kept talkin' and wanted to know where in Alaska. One of 'em said, 'Boy, I'd like to go fishin' in Alaska someday!' They got so enthralled, they forgot all about the lights! They fine'lee said, 'Go on,' and so, I went on."

MEMPHIS, TENNESSEE

"I kept drivin' and never got stopped again. By Sunday mornin', we were gettin' close to Memphis. I couldn't believe how hot it was. Six days before it was thirty below, and it felt like a hundred in Memphis.

"John Henry kept telling me he wanted to go to Mississippi. I felt sorry for him, but I wouldn't bringin' John Henry with me to Ackerman because Momma still owned and lived in this house then. So, when we got to Memphis, I asked him, 'Have you ever worked in a hotel?' He said, 'Naw.' I said, 'Well you gotta have a place to stay.' We talked a little bit, and I said, 'You can cook, can't ya'?' He said, 'Yeah.' I said, 'I'm gonna take you to one of these big hotels.' It might have been the Peabody, but it was a big downtown Memphis hotel. I drove round and round the parking lot, towin' the truck, and fine'lee figured out how to get around to the back. I looked real careful, trying to figure out where the kitchen was. I got out and walked over to make sure.

"I came back and told John Henry, 'Go through that door right there. Tell 'em you're a good worker and want a job washin' dishes, and you can cook, and you can clean rooms. Tell 'em you've got to have a job.' I handed him forty dollars. And I never thought I'd see him again, which I ain't. I think he got a job because I watched and saw him talkin' with a fella. I got out and looked real close, and the man was pointin', and John Henry was shakin' his head in a positive way, and so I reckon he was tellin' him what to do. I pulled out and got mixed up in all those Memphis interchanges, and I like to never got out of there. I fine'lee pulled on into Ackerman. I never go back through Whitecourt, Alberta, and not think about John Henry McClain. After all these years, I wonder whatever happened to him."

Moon's repetition of his fond memory and concern for John Henry McClain made me think my former musings at least had some merit.

HOME AGAIN

On a bright autumn afternoon, Moon pulled up in front of our new tract home in the black '49 Ford Coupe towing the Apache pickup. Momma had sold the old white house, presumably without Moon's permission. The bed of Moon's truck looked like Santa's sleigh arriving from the North Pole, loaded with gifts. On second thought, maybe more like the Grinch's sleigh leaving Whoville. Giant moose horns protruded from the back, a red-and-white, three-speed English Racer leaned against the side, a Radio Flyer snow sled, part of the cornucopia.

Moon said, "Up there in Alaska, people pawn all their stuff for the price of a plane ticket home, and you can buy it for nothin'."

Mainly, I remember the tight embrace. I didn't want to let go. I carefully watched Momma's nonverbal clues. She seemed genuinely happy to see him.

ARGUMENT

That evening after dinner, I heard their voices escalating from the den.

"Why did you sell the house without telling me?"

"How was I gonna tell you when you were somewhere in Alaska in the middle of nowhere?"

The fight intensified to familiar terrain. They were yelling and screaming, and I could hear every word from my bedroom. Like a racquetball being whacked against one wall then the other, maze-like emotions whirled inside my head. I covered my ears with my pillow, attempting to silence the rising pain. Warm tears streamed down my face and dripped off my chin. My heart wanted one thing; my head told me this was headed somewhere entirely different. My hopeful dream fading, the reality of a permanent divorce confronted me like a mocking jester. I wanted to go down the hall and intervene, but what kid is that brave?

From somewhere deep within the well of my anguished soul, an inhibited sound escaped. I screamed out loud.

"Shane, is that you?" Silence.

"Christia, is that you? Come here." Silence.

My secret longing was buried underneath a heavy pile of crumbling bricks, and I had only one choice: learn to live with it. But that's much easier said than done. *The Wild Rose,* a song by Caroline Herring based on a poem by Wendell Berry, comes to mind, "Great roots of night they grow, the things that hide come out again."

HOLMES JUNIOR COLLEGE — 1969

Moon continued, "I've always regretted not going back to Alaska in '69. I would've gone back, but Ty convinced me to go to Holmes Junior. I'd already quit Holmes twice!

"Really, I wasn't too interested in college, but what attracted me was I wanted to play baseball. When I played in the Ackerman league, we played Weir and Louisville and other teams like that. W. A. Miles always caught for the Weir team. By then, he was a professor at Holmes. One day I ran into him in Ackerman, and he said, 'Moon, if you come down to Holmes, I know you can make the baseball team.'

"The baseball season had already begun when I started playin'. I got to catch some. I didn't have the best arm to second, but I never let any balls get past me. I could always figure out how to block 'em up.

"The last game I played, I got to pinch hit. I batted twice and got two hits, so I ended my baseball career batting a 1.000. After the game, the coach told me I'd be startin' the rest of the season. But the next day at practice, he walked up and told me that I had used all my college eligibility because I'd gone to forestry school in Florida. My baseball playin' days ended right there.

"Because I was goin' to college, I didn't go back to Alaska until five years later. I don't know why I let Ty talk me into goin' back to college. That was the biggest mistake I ever made. I finished college and everything, but what I should've done was what George Bartell told me to do and gone back to Alaska the next summer. But like I said, it was baseball that got my attention. I've run into George Bartell in Alaska several times over the years, and he told me, 'Man, you should've come back; all of us that retired from the pipeline have got it made.'

"If I'd retired with the pipeline union, I'd a never had to worry about anything else. I don't know whatever happened to ole' George, but he was a really good fella."

As Moon described his regret for not returning to Alaska in '69, I had an entirely different take. Had he, I'd never been afforded the formative years I spent with him while he completed a history degree at Holmes Junior College and Mississippi State.

CHAPTER 16

GROWING UP MOON
SUNN'S SON

AFTER MOON'S RETURN from Alaska in late '68, life resumed, not as before, but at least we went fishing together.

WALNUT, MISSISSIPPI

On fishing trips with Moon, Ty Cobb was often riding shotgun, me sitting between them or in the back seat. Ty was almost a foot taller than Moon, well shaven, usually sporting a nice mustache, and with eyes that were gentle and kind yet inquisitive. Moon and Ty argued about everything—history, politics, and public education policy. The escalating ire of unresolved disagreements often bled over into the day's fishing plans. Annoyed with Moon's recalcitrant fishing ways, Ty challenged. Moon stuck to his convictions, not changing one thing to accommodate Ty or anyone else. I believe this was why we seldom went fishing in anyone else's vehicle.

Sometimes arguments escalated to epic proportions, but usually nothing a day of fishing couldn't resolve. However, there were exceptions. On occasion a big blowup erupted, and they'd avoid each other for a couple of weeks. But they always reconciled. Real friendships can withstand terrible disagreements and come out the other side unscathed, even stronger.

"Your daddy is just plain stubborn, but he ain't gonna change his ways. I guess that's what makes him who he is."

It was consoling to know someone else understood and sympathized with the trials and triumphs of Moon's kamikaze version of fishing.

I recalled a time when I was eight and we rose well before dawn for a day of fishing at a new watershed lake near Walnut, Mississippi. Riding in the back seat, I listened as Moon and Ty bantered about the latest politics. Ty, a moderate Democrat and philosopher of sorts, despised the oppressive ways of the past, still endorsed by powerful Dixiecrats. Moon didn't care much for the rising young Republicans who had no clue what it was like to be poor and not a landowner. I couldn't understand much of their conversation, but I knew whatever it was they were arguing about was very important to them. They were getting passionate and raising their voices. Ty quoted statistics to strengthen his argument. Moon countered with knowledge and familiarity of the local people, always defending the marginalized.

As they philosophized about what needed to be done, I dozed in the back seat. I awoke from my slumber when the conversation changed to fishing. They wagered on who would land the most fish that day.

"Whoever catches the most fish wins a steak dinner, and whoever catches the least has to whistle Dixie all the way home. The only exception is if you happen to catch the biggest fish—that works like a 'get out of jail free card.'"

"Shane, you in?"

"Yeah."

Armed with a push-button green Johnson Century, I didn't stand a chance. The lake was new and boasted a healthy population of bass in the one-to-two-pound range. Ty had received a personal invitation from a friend at Mississippi State. I was relieved to know we weren't sneaking into some lake Moon assumed he owned.

We fished the entire day in the hot sun without even a break for lunch. I was sleep-deprived, and by early afternoon, my legs felt like I'd tied cement blocks to both feet. Harsh reality set in as I watched Ty and Moon catch fish after fish. I'd only managed to hook and land two fish the entire day, hours apart.

I muttered to myself, "I'm gonna have to whistle Dixie all the way home."

The sun sinking on the western horizon, Moon announced, "We'll need to be headin' out of here in a couple more minutes."

Moon's DNA coursing in my veins, I tried to muster energy for one last cast. A bush in the water, taller than all the rest, caught my eye. Faithless, I drug my lead- cladded feet forward, so exhausted I could barely lift my arms to cast. I pressed the button of the green Century and managed a high-arching "moon-cast" ten yards beyond the bush. I cranked the reel handle, pulling the chartreuse spinnerbait toward the bush. Suddenly, everything stopped.

I announced, "I'm hung."

"No, you're not, look at your line!"

My rod doubled over, and I reeled like there was no tomorrow. I felt a new surge of energy as I fought the big fish.

"Hold him, Shane! Back up."

I did. Moon grabbed the big bass as it slashed about in the shallow water.

He held it up. "Man, that's a big bass! It'll easily go over four pounds. I didn't think there were any bass in here this big."

I could tell Moon and Ty were genuinely impressed.

My whole body smiled. "I won the 'get out of jail free card'!"

"You stayed at it, Shane, you really learned how to fish today."

Something felt right inside, heck, even right in the entire cosmos. I'd ascended the pinnacle of the world's pantheon by catching the biggest bass. Some part of my wounded heart was instantly wrapped in a new veneer. I mattered; I could catch big bass. I don't remember who won the steak dinner, but I got one too!

Me with a big bass.

PUSHUPS, COD-LIVER OIL, AND MPPF

The Apostle Paul said, "Physical *training is of some value*, but godliness has *value* for all things, holding promise for both the present life and the life to come."[6]

Moon's philosophy of physical fitness focused on "the present life" part. Fishing, at least the kind we did, was an extreme sport accessible only to the physically fit. Long before Richard Simmons and the exercise obsession caught fire in the US, Moon was already a phys-ed freak. Had there been a fishing Olympics, Moon would've been a regular on the podium. The more fit, the more fish-catching potential you possessed. If you happened to be tournament fishing, which Moon despises, physical fitness put you atop the leaderboard before your hook hit the water because it enabled you to wade

---

6   1 Timothy 4:8, NIV.

for miles through impenetrable thickets and gumbo mud and endure the entire day without eating a morsel.

So, during my youth, fishing birthed a second child, MPPF, Moon's philosophy of physical fitness. Isometrics, pushups, chin-ups, toe raises, anything that might give you an edge and increase your fish-catching potential.

Scattered in random places in Moon's house, one encountered chin-up bars, spring-loaded stretch contraptions, barbells, dumbbells, weight benches, and ab wheels.

An isometric ninja, he advised, "Shane, you don't necessarily need any of this stuff to get really strong. Your joints work like hinges. Your muscles are attached to your joints by ligaments and tendons. When you push or pull somethin', one muscle does the work while the other muscle offers resistance. Here, let me show you. Put both hands on top of mine. Pull down on my arm as hard as you can."

I pulled as hard as I could, and he might let me gain an inch or two.

"That's resistance. Now, with both hands, try to hold my arm straight," at which point, he lifted me off the ground.

"That's called the lever; it's the muscle workin' when you push or pull somethin'. You need to learn how to work both kinds of muscles. That's why you gotta be careful when you're weightliftin'. It can make you muscle bound; that's a fake kinda strong. If you lift weights, you need to concentrate as much on the downward motion of the bar as you do when you're pushin' it up. On the downward motion, you need to give it as much resistance as you can. Then you're makin' sure you're workin' both kinds of muscles."

A bit annoyed by the way-too-long and detailed exercise and physiology class, I replied, "Yeah, okay."

Mistake! A better response would've been to ask a question about fishing to hopefully divert his attention from the impending "run-through." Lesson, practice, further explanation, further practice—that's how you learned.

"Shane, see how many one-handed pushups you can do." It didn't take a soothsayer to figure that out. "None, zero, zilch." Moon could do more one-handed pushups than most men could manage with two.

He'd demonstrate. "One-handed pushups are good for you because you have to offer more resistance. Start with one arm and then try the other one. Most people have a dominant arm, so when you get where you can do a couple, concentrate more on your weaker arm."

"Okay," feigning my growing impatience, secretly hoping class would soon end.

Then he'd pull out the ab-wheel!

"Shane, grip both handles, start from your toes, keep your back straight, and see how far you can roll the wheel forward. Go out as far as you can."

"Plop!" I hit the floor.

"Find the position where you can't go any further and just concentrate there. Roll the wheel to that point and see how many times you can go back and forth. When you think you've done all you can, try hard to do one or two more. The human body is amazin'; it can go a lot farther than you think it can, even when you feel like you've already reached the point of exhaustion."

By now, I had "maxed out" in more ways than one!

HEALTH FOOD

But then I was likely to receive a follow-up lecture on the importance of healthy food. All food was looked upon with certain suspicion—it might make us fat or sluggish and keep us from fishing. MPE and MPPF were always in mortal combat when it came to food selection, all food evaluated accordingly. If food must be healthy but inexpensive, our options were limited. There was never any kind of junk food lying around Moon's house. Matter of fact, there was never much food of any kind lying around. Only the bare necessities, and most of the time, it was "just lying around."

On visits, a quick scan of available cuisine made me feel like I'd either encountered a desert hermit on a religious fast or a fur trapper in Alberta. Moon believes the healthiest foods come right out of the woods or water.

During one exercise session, I remember a smoked deer shoulder just "laying out" on his kitchen table. You couldn't miss it! A sole hunting knife lay beside it. No need for any kind of fancy utensils. We had to take time to wash those and put them back in some drawer.

Moon walked over, trimmed off a piece, plopped it into his mouth, and started grinding away. Then he handed me the knife, which was the signal I was to do accordingly. That's when we knowingly nodded at each other. It was a communal caveman form of dining. I guess that's why I identify with the scene in *Dances with Wolves* when Kevin Costner shares a big bite of bloody buffalo heart with a Lakota warrior. Nod. Nod. Nod again. "Te-tonka!"

When I first saw the movie, I said to myself, "I know that! I've done that before!" Nod. Nod—skinning knife, smoked deer shoulder!

Moon pontificated, "Protein is the most important of all them food groups. Carbohydrates burn up quickly; protein feeds your muscles and gives you that long-term energy."

Anything else just "lying around"—and there were lots of other things—contributed to Moon's overall fishing fitness regimen. Chief in his arsenal: cod-liver oil and wheat germ oil. There were other bottles and jars of awful-smelling, homemade concoctions that you dared not ask about the contents, lest it remind him to get you to try a little.

Moon never made me do much of anything. But before the divorce, when I was still under his everyday tutelage, he did make me swallow a big spoonful of cod-liver oil. Only once a day if I was lucky!

"That'll make you grow big and strong." I didn't want to grow big and strong if it meant having to take a gulp of that awful-tasting stuff. I had a certain propensity for Hostess Honey Buns and Twinkies.

"Don't eat that stuff, it'll kill ya'. Read what they put in them things."

Of course, on fishing trips, I learned to just hide a Honey Bun and then scarf it down in three or four bites behind some tree and stuff the evidential wrapper in my pocket. But I could never do this without feeling a bit guilty and fearing I was one step closer to the graveyard. But man, they sure tasted good. I secretly wondered if Moon ever violated his own health-food code, and although I tried, I never found any incriminating evidence.

ARCHIE WHO?

How does a single individual take on Messiah-status in a young kid's imagination? That's what Archie Manning did in mine. In the late '60s, in poor, racist Mississippi, people needed hope—no one more than me. After the divorce, I remember crying privately in my room for what seemed like hours. I was lonely and an emotional wreck. So, I listened to Stan Torgerson, the voice of the Ole Miss Rebels, describe every play with David-and-Goliath-like detail.

"Here come the Rebels!"

"The Rebels are knockin' on the door of the promised land."

"Archie rolls right, he avoids one tackler, he hits Floyd Franks, thirty, twenty, ten, five, he scooooores! Wooh, hooh, mercy!"

"Manning, the six-three redhead, brings 'em to the line ... there's Mitchell from Columbus, Coker from Clarksdale ... Manning sprints right, he avoids a tackler ... Floyd Franks ... he hits Floyd Franks, thirty, twenty, ten, he scooooores! Touchdown! Touchdown, Ole Miss!"

"Number eighteen brings them to the line. The Rebels are knockin' on the door of the promised land. Lyman, did you get that number?"

It felt like I was sitting in the stadium, maybe even on the sidelines. On sunny days, I took the radio to the yard and lay in the grass, not daring to risk interruption by the chaos in the house. If Momma yelled, looking for me, I hid. On rainy days, I locked myself in my room. Early the next week, I anticipated the ensuing coach's show and highlights like the Second Coming.

Moon bought me a copy of *Rebel Coach: My Football Family*, John Vaught's autobiography, and like a Bible storybook, I mainly looked at the pictures. I loved the one of Coach Vaught sitting in a delta swamp, shotgun in hand, blowing a duck call, greenheads lying beside him on a log.

Mainly, I liked the three pictures of Archie. My favorite: the 1969 Tennessee game, Archie's arm cocked and ready to fire, Jack "Hacksaw" Reynolds in hot pursuit. My least favorite: the Houston game, because that's when Archie suffered a broken arm. The picture of the burned-out cars beside the Lyceum, the army truck, a gas-masked soldier, scattered debris, fallen road marker, and smoke—I didn't understand. That picture seemed out of place.

Moon was working on a history degree at Mississippi State. I turned nine on Monday in late November 1970.

"Shane, open your birthday present." I hastily ripped into the envelope. I was elated—two tickets to the annual clash for the golden egg!

It was a cold overcast day, and we sat bundled on the visitor side, adjacent to the Mississippi State student section. I unpinned my "Archie Who?" button from my shirt and put it on my coat so all the State fans could see it. Pregame, beside myself with excitement, I spotted my favorite Ole Miss players: Jim Poole, Bob Knight, Floyd Franks, Wyck Neely, Wimpy Winther, Elmer Allen, Skip Jernigan, and Vernon Studdard.

"Do you see Archie down there, Shane? That's him near the thirty-yard-line in the long white coat."

"Yeah, I see him!"

Three weeks before in the Houston game, Archie had suffered a broken left arm. Interim head coach Bruiser Kinard led the Rebels onto the field; Charley Shira, the Dogs. Beloved legendary Rebel coach John Vaught had suffered a heart attack in mid-October. Future NFL quarterback Joe Reed led the maroon and white; Chug Chumbler, the navy and crimson. The Ole Miss offense sputtered most of the day. Late in the fourth quarter, Ole Miss trailed, 19–14.

Smelling blood, chants loudened from the State student section beside us. "Go to hell, Ole Miss, go to hell." I tried to hold back tears. State's drive stalled; they had to punt. There was still hope.

Moon leaned over. "Shane, don't worry, Vernon Studdard is gonna run this one back for a touchdown."

I watched the punt rise high in the air, exceeding eye level, fishtailing toward the east endzone. Vernon momentarily hesitated and then ran forward to field the punt. He fumbled; State recovered. Pandemonium erupted in the State student section, louder, deafening. "Go to hell, Ole Miss, go to hell!" Tears streamed down my face; I couldn't hold them back.

"Let's go, Shane, and see if we can beat some of this traffic."

State fans streamed toward the exits of Vaught Hemingway, funneling into the narrow corridor, still bellowing their evil chant. A State fan noticed my tears and zeroed in, "Archie, who? Archie, nobody, that's who!" then rejoined the sickening chorus.

I surmised, "State fans must be wicked; they don't like Archie, and they don't mind saying 'hell' and telling other people to go there."

The Manning Passing Academy

In 2013, I had the privilege of a conversation with Archie. My son, Moss, was attending the Manning Passing Academy at Nicholls State University in Thibodaux, Louisiana. Hungry, I decided to take a break from watching quarterback drills and stargazing. Below the stadium, waiting in line for a hotdog, I detected a familiar Mississippi drawl.

I was curious, so I introduced myself. "I'm Shane, from Denver; my son's here attending the camp. I used to live in Mississippi."

"I'm from Mississippi too."

As I dressed my dog, we casually conversed about all the people we knew in Mississippi—it's just what real Mississippians do.

"What do you do?"

"I'm a Presbyterian minister; my parish is in downtown Denver."

"Well, that's terrific."

"What do you do?"

"Oh, I'm Archie's personal assistant; I'm in charge of his scheduling. How'd you like to meet him? That's him sitting over there on the golf cart."

"Sure, I'd love to."

"Archie, this is Shane Sunn. He's a Presbyterian preacher in Denver."

I was donning a Denver Broncos football T-shirt.

"Peyton and Ashley sure do like it out there in Denver."

"Yeah, Denver's a great place to live. Think we can win the Super Bowl this year?"

"I don't know; that's hard to do."

I told Archie I listened to Stan Torgerson call every game he played at Ole Miss. I wanted to tell him what he'd meant to me over the years, but I knew he'd endured a thousand such tales. I wanted to tell him when I was a kid, I had an "Archie's a Saint" bumper sticker on the blue pegboard in my room and that I'd watched every Saints game.

How does a grown man convey to an icon sitting in front of him on a golf cart the full significance he'd played in his life? Words seemed inadequate. I tried anyway.

I launched into the story about the day long ago when I attended the 1970 Ole Miss–State football game with Moon, not omitting many details. Archie patiently listened. I finished, feeling like a complete idiot.

Archie looked up and said, "That was a long time ago!"

I replied, "Yeah ... yeah it was."

The truth is, on that day in the humid air of south Louisiana, this story was incubating in the deep waters below.

Archie Manning and me at Manning Passing Academy.

CHAPTER 17

DESEGREGATION

WHEN I WAS A KID, the turbulent currents of systemic racism were whirling all around me. Real forces that affected everyone, myself not excluded, but I simply failed to recognize them on any significant level. Like an oarless raft in a big ocean, I was at the mercy of the currents. The Choctaw County public school system was desegregated in 1970, the year I entered fourth grade. I don't remember a lot about it other than some of my former classmates left our public school for Winston Academy, a white private school. I also remember white adults making a big fuss, asking every question imaginable, such as, "What's it like going to school with *blacks*? Although they used another term.

I was already racially confused. In 1967, my first-grade teacher, Mrs. Black, was white. Mrs. White, my reading teacher, who worked with the Title One Program, was black. She was motherly, an exceptional reading teacher, and always took a special interest in me. In 1970, integrating was the least of my concerns. It was interesting, erased the doldrums, and afforded a bunch of new friends. My more immediate distress was that in the late-sixties Christ-haunted South, divorce was a social stigma. Divorcees, who didn't measure up to the mores of Mayberry, were viewed with measured contempt. Having divorced parents landed you in a social class reserved for poor folks or heathens. Or maybe that was just my perception because I wanted nothing more than to be normal, like all the other kids, but I wasn't.

Other kids asked me sensitive questions like, "Do you live with your daddy or your momma?"

What that really meant was, "You're not like us." I felt the shame and wore it like a scarlet letter.

We no longer went to church on Sundays. I suppose neither Moon nor Farrah wanted to be reminded of their recent fall from grace. When my friends talked about their families and what they were doing at church, I disappeared and found other groups of kids to talk with who weren't card-carrying members of the local Mayberry mob.

Like a silent cloud, pain, shame, and loneliness followed me, suggesting, "You are worthless." I tried to dislodge it, but it was always there, all the time.

One day, my homeroom teacher was absent, so we inherited the privilege of a substitute. Her attire and fake smile betrayed the fact she was a proud emissary of Mayberry.

She asked, "Class, how many of you are Baptists?" Three-fourths of the kids raised their hands. I squirmed.

"How many of you are Methodists?" Most of the rest of the class raised their hands. I slumped in my desk.

"How many of you are Presbyterians?"

I'd never even heard the word before. Pam Irving raised her hand. I slipped my hand up a little late because I knew there wasn't going to be a fourth question, and I didn't want to be counted among the heathens. I guess that's how I became a Presbyterian.

I wondered, *Why had most of my black classmates not responded?*

IZOLA DOTSON JACKSON

Mrs. Izola Dotson Jackson was my homeroom and geography teacher. She curled her hair and wore horn-rimmed glasses, bright flowered dresses, and numerous beaded necklaces. I was a bit ADD and had a hard time sitting still for extended periods.

"Shane, come on out here. I'm gonna have to get Dr. John a holt ya." Dr. John was her paddle.

She took me into the hallway, and before she let Dr. John do his work, she put her hand under my chin and lifted my head. She demanded we make eye contact.

She paused, looked deeply into my eyes, and said, "Shane Sunn, God bless your little sweet cherry pie soul. Turn around and put your hands on your knees."

Then she tapped me on the rump a couple of times, so lightly I could barely feel it.

"Don't tell anybody it didn't hurt."

"Okay, Mrs. Jackson, I won't."

My shame cloud momentarily vaporized; I didn't know what a Christian was, but whatever it was, I knew Mrs. Jackson had to be one.

Izola Dotson Jackson.

THE MISSISSIPPI SOVEREIGNTY COMMISSION

Remembering my own experience of race and having observed Moon's impartial treatment of others over the years, Jean and I were curious. "Tell us about your views on race."

"When I was young, I wasn't old enough yet to understand the race situation. At first, I was just a goin' by what all the people I listened to said. They were all older than me, so I guess I was just takin' a kid's impression of it and how the people in this town felt about it. In the 1950s, Choctaw County was tougher on the race issue than anywhere else in Mississippi. So, I guess I was pretty much for the whites to start with. But I quickly realized that wouldn't right. Black people deserved what they were strivin' for, and the only way they could do that was to bring it into the light. So, I switched around and got for them. That had to be a gradual thing."

Moon's comment that "in the 1950s, Choctaw County was *tougher* on the race issue than anywhere else in Mississippi" jarred me. Then I thought, *Of course, it had to be. After all, Choctaw is only one county removed from Neshoba, the site of the horrific murders of James Chaney, Andrew Goodman, and Michael Schwerner in 1964, and only two counties removed from Leflore, the site of the brutal lynching of Emmett Till in 1955.*

So, that evening, I consulted Google concerning race relations in Choctaw County in the '50s and '60s. I read this from the May 5, 1969, *Congressional Record*: "A few Southern systems have sought to meet Federal guidelines to avoid cutoffs, but the overwhelming majority of white authorities say financial pressure won't persuade them to change their methods. 'Darn it, it's just not right to penalize the children because we aren't in compliance,' says W. M. Perrigin, superintendent of schools in Choctaw County, Miss. 'If we aren't in compliance, let the courts deal with us.'"

I thought, *I remember Mr. Perrigin like it was yesterday. He hired Ty Cobb to work in the superintendent's office.* I kept Googling and read the following from the files of The Mississippi State Sovereignty Commission, a state agency created in 1956 to monitor "race agitators." The files weren't officially opened until 1998, and then, only partially until years later.

"The Mississippi State Sovereignty Commission monitored the events in Choctaw County beginning in 1959 and kept records of race relations and civil rights demonstrations in the area. In 1959, a number of city and county officials reported no active National Association for the Advancement of Colored People (NAACP) chapter, no racial tension, and no 'agitators stirring up trouble or trying to integrate the races.'

"In 1961, Superintendent of Education W. M. Perrigin confirmed the difficult place that teachers and school officials occupied. He stated that teachers 'would not do anything to endanger losing their positions by indulging in any kind of agitative activities or belonging to the NAACP.' In 1960, however, many officials noted that African Americans, especially younger ones, were more demanding, but only twelve African Americans were registered to vote by 1961.

"In July of 1961, the MSSC placed six Rust College students from Ackerman on file for participating in boycotts in Holly Springs: Jessie M. Robinson, John H. Davis, Maudean Brown, Frederick H. Brown, Catherine Blackman, and Gradie F. Ervin."

Gradie Ervin was my sixth-grade science teacher and PE instructor! I knew and interacted with many of the others mentioned in the files, or their children, on a regular basis, but I had never considered they were being monitored. I thought, *I wonder how that must have felt; that explains a lot.* I paused and let it sink in. I felt deep shame and an almost overwhelming sadness. I continued, now focusing more on events surrounding public school desegregation. I read the following from *Mississippi History Now*:

"In 1968, the U. S. Supreme Court ruled, in *Green vs. County School Board*, that freedom of choice had proved ineffective and was no longer an acceptable method of school desegregation. A year later, the Supreme Court in a landmark decision, *Alexander vs. Holmes*, which spoke directly to thirty school districts in Mississippi but ultimately to the entire South, ordered the immediate termination of dual school systems and the establishment of unitary systems. Mississippi public schools underwent a dramatic change in *1970*. After sixteen years of delays and token desegregation, the U. S. Supreme Court ordered the dismantling of the state's dual school system. Federal intervention toppled Mississippi's *ninety-five-year-old 'separate but equal' educational system* in which white school children went to one school system and black school children went to another one."

I thought, *Wow, ninety-five years! That's almost a century! My fourth-grade year was more significant than I've realized.* In 1970, the "N-word" was part of common everyday vocabulary, even in private conversations among white kids at school. The deplorable word was often preceded by words like "them" or "those." I remembered Moon never ever used the word. Neither did he mind telling people who used the word in his presence to *never* do that again. He instructed me to do accordingly. He referred to African Americans as "blacks," "black people" and most of the time, just "people."

Moon told me, "Whatever makes you think you're better than anybody else, ain't nothin' but a lie. Most people don't really know who they are. Some people think your skin color means somethin', but it don't."

CHARLES THOMAS

Now well past midnight, I continued my trip down 1970 memory lane and thought about my black principal, Charles Thomas.

In 1970, Mr. Thomas was appointed assistant principal of the newly desegregated Choctaw County school system. Mr. Thomas was highly educated but black. Like keeping someone on a sports team that you never intend to put in the game, Mr. Thomas served a puppet role for the Mayberry mob. My interactions with Mr. Thomas increased during junior high.

"How ya' doin', Moon junior?"

He asked his question on a regular basis. I was familiar with bullshit, but there was something different about the way Mr. Thomas asked his question. It wasn't a casual question to evoke a meaningless conversation; he genuinely wanted to know. I slowly risked sharing tiny bits and pieces of my struggles at home. He listened and responded with a knowing, sympathetic smile and always gave me a warm pat on the back. I knew he understood; I knew he cared. Thinking back, I should've asked him how he was doing as principal of a desegregated segregated school system. In the summer of '73, with Moon in Alaska, Mr. Thomas gave me a job cutting grass at the school. *Why was he so caring and generous to a white kid?* Considering the existing racial landscape, he certainly didn't have to be that way.

My curiosity peaked, and I continued my obsessive Google search. I discovered that in 1983, after years of discriminatory promotional denials, Mr. Thomas was demoted and put in charge of the school transportation system. Like George Bailey in Bedford Falls, Charles Thomas responded the way he always did. Undoubtedly disappointed and hurt, he made the very best use of his new position. He cared for the bus drivers and the safety of every child. He made a careful study of all the unsafe bridges in the county and worked diligently to procure the funds necessary to replace or repair them.

I remembered 1983. Already a student at Ole Miss that summer, I coached the local Dizzy Dean 12–13-age baseball team in Ackerman. After a hard day's work on the green chain at the lumberyard, I collected the boys who needed a ride to practice. The problem was I couldn't fit them all into my car. I recalled a conversation with Mr. Thomas. "Shane, I'm not using this truck for anything. Just keep it until the season is over. Here's some extra money for gas."

Mr. Thomas loaned me his purple truck. I drove all over the dusty county roads, picking up players like Robert Coleman, Corey Burton, Donald Sibley, and Eric and Shaston Coleman, fitting as many as possible on the front seat, the rest in the back.

My eyes burning and seeing double sentences, it was time to come back to the present. I powered down my laptop and crawled into bed beside Jean.

MR. JIMMY SUNN
   Social Studies
MR. CHARLES THOMAS
   Jr. High Math
MISS ERIN MOSS
   English - Speech - Bible

Moon and Charles Thomas, *Smoke Signals*, yearbook, 1974.

CHAPTER 18

FIGHTIN', GAMBLIN',
AND TOUGH

NEXT MORNING, after my second cup of coffee, I sat at the dining table in our Airbnb, pondering Moon's stories from the previous day and my interactions with him as a kid. I jotted down notes, attempting to connect dots.

FIGHTIN'

When I was a kid, while other boys talked about their dads in normal sorts of ways, I periodically received reports that Moon had been in some brawl up at the crossroads and had beaten the hell out of three guys at once. Exact details were always hard to discern, with multiple and varied versions of what actually happened when the fists flew. But the stories must have been at least partially true because Moon's face divulged the visible battle scars that proved it. Because I wanted my dad to be like their dads, I didn't care for hearing about Moon's fights or talking about them.

Other boys shared things like, "My dad's construction crew is helping build a new apartment complex in Columbus." How should I respond? "My dad is in Columbus too—street fighting. They should try to get together sometime"?

I recalled Moon telling me, "Shane, them big guys tire easily, and if you can take their initial licks, pretty soon you can beat the hell out of 'em."

I wondered why he told me these sorts of things; maybe he thought I needed some personal self-defense instruction because I was skinny as a rail. I certainly didn't have any immediate plans to fight anyone, much less a big guy!

Sitting in the Airbnb, I searched for a plausible explanation for why Moon fought. Something didn't square; he was usually friendly and nice to everyone. Having read the holy writ of fishermen, *A River Runs Through It*, numerous times, I remembered Norman Maclean's description of his and Paul's toughness. Norman said, "Paul and I held in common the knowledge we were tough. This knowledge increased into our twenties. But I was tough by being the product of tough establishments—the US Forest Service and logging camps. Paul was tough by thinking he was *tougher* than any establishment."[7]

Norman's description made sense to me. Like Montana, in the rural agrarian South of the '60s, most jobs—farming, construction, and logging—required "real-man strength" and daily initiative to constantly battle the awful heat and humidity. Blue-collar men had to be "tough" to survive, so sometimes they fought to prove to themselves and others they were "tough" enough for the daily grind. But in the rarefied humid Southern air, sweat and blood comingled and sometimes bred a fighter tougher than all the rest. Like Paul Maclean, forged on the anvil of the pure determination he applied to fishing, Moon believed he was not only "tougher than any establishment," but he also believed he was *tougher* than most anyone around, and so he fought to prove it.

---

7   Norman Maclean, *A River Runs Through It* (Chicago: University of Chicago Press, 2017), 10.

For Moon, fighting was embedded in a discernable feedback loop between MPPF and fishing. Knowing you can wrestle nature's worst offerings and come out on top creates a kind of expanding confidence that extends into other arenas, like fighting and gambling. Moon holds the conviction that every synapse and muscle fiber can be harnessed for overall body strength. "How many one-handed pushups can I do? Chin-ups? What are my limits?"

Of course, you really don't know unless you are willing to test them. So, test the boundaries to see if there might happen to be any. Of course, the goal is to *win* the fight at all costs. If you lost, it meant either you weren't determined enough, or you were unconscious.

Fighting, like fishing, was simply a test of the will. Moon may not be bigger or stronger; he is simply more determined than anyone else. The bigger the challenge, the more determined Moon became, and that's what made him "tough"—and that's why he fought.

GAMBLIN'

I remembered a day when, as curious kids are prone to do, I rummaged around in the console of Moon's yellow Dodge. "What's this?" I considered out loud, discovering a folded piece of paper. It was a summons to appear in court for illegally gambling within the Ackerman city limits, not exactly a paradigm of moral virtue. I refolded the paper and carefully returned it to the exact spot I found it. I didn't want him to know that I knew.

Several days later, a local man, let's say, not exactly known for an upstanding reputation, told me, "Moon's the best poker player around; he wins lots of money. He's good at poker because he's the best bluffer I've ever seen."

My moral fastidiousness in overdrive, I nodded but didn't say a word. I silently wondered how much money Moon had taken from the man. Like fighting's relationship to MPPF, gamblin' enjoyed a proportional interrelationship between MPPF and MPE.

I know about Moon what Norman knew about his brother, Paul. Norman said, "Paul liked to bet himself on anyone that would fish with him. It was sometimes funny and other times not so funny to see a boy wanting to bet himself who was almost sure to win."[8]

What is it about individuals who live in order to fish that makes them susceptible to vices like fighting and gambling? By gambling, Moon could double, triple, and quadruple his money, which doubled, tripled, and quadrupled his fishing time, negating the necessity to focus on other things, like work. Although he liked the challenge, gambling wasn't so much about the gambling; it was about the money, and the money was about the fishing. It was a calculated and shrewd form of MPE. Unless, of course, you got caught and fined for gambling in the Ackerman city limits! Both fightin' and gamblin' were conceived and birthed in the imitable air of MPE and MPPF, each formed by the unquenchable desire to catch the next fish.

Maybe my explanation is some form of wish fulfillment, and Moon simply liked to gamble and fight. But having observed him for eight decades, I think it's pretty accurate. The real genesis of Moon's unwily ways was, and is, "Look, Daddy, I caught this one for you."

ETV TOWER

Continuing to consider Moon's local *tough guy* reputation, the scenes of more memories presented themselves.

In the gas station restaurant, locals sipped their weak coffee, munched on their homemade sausage and cheese biscuits, and pontificated about the ETV tower being constructed on Dido Road. Curious and with nothing better to do, like they were the builders themselves and like a trip to the county fair, they regularly drove down Dido Road to get an up-close look at progress on the tower. Armed with the latest knowledge, they gave the authoritative

---

8   Ibid., 8.

report next morning at the gas station.

"You know that tower is how ya' gonna see *Sesame Street* and *Mr. Rogers Neighborhood* on TV."

"I don't know, I think it's some kinda nuclear defense system they ain't tellin' us about!"

Like the Tower of Babel pressing into the heavens, the tower was a local marvel in Choctaw in '73. Counting site elevation, the tower rises 1,759 feet above sea level.

I remembered as a kid asking Moon, "How'd you get all that orange and white paint all over you?"

"Oh, I climbed the ETV tower out there on the Dido-Mt. Salem Road and painted the top and put the big light bulbs up there for them."

"How'd you get that job?"

"I guess they were lookin' for somebody brave enough to do it, that they didn't have to pay too much."

Curious and secretly annoyed Moon had engaged in yet another death-defying feat, I ventured, "How'd you do that?"

"Well, I rode the elevator up there about a thousand feet, and then I had to get out and climb the rest of the way up, about a hundred more feet, and put them big light bulbs on the top. They gave me some tools and a backpack with the lights and bolts in it. They told me they would pay me extra if I painted the top section. That's easy money. So, after I got the lights put on, I climbed back down and got on the elevator and got the paint buckets and stuff and went back up there and painted the upper section."

"Were you tied in or anything?"

"Well, I was when I was painting, but I didn't need anything when I was puttin' the lights on."

"Why not?"

"That harness just got in my way."

At that point, I realized Moon had free-climbed the last ninety feet of an 1,100-foot tower. My toes tingled as Moon nonchalantly described all the details.

"I couldn't believe how windy and cool it was up there. I could see all the way to 'Starts-ville' and Louisville."

I wanted to tell him not to volunteer for anything like that anymore, but I knew that'd have been like telling a monkey not to eat bananas.

SNAKEBITE

One day, Moon rode up on his three-speed English Racer, wearing cutoff blue jeans and an Ole Miss T-shirt. I guess cutoff jeans were the style in the early '70s, if not for everybody, at least for Moon. Most of Moon's cutoffs were so threadbare he could sit on a dime and tell you whether it was heads or tails. I instantly noticed an enormous red-and-blue bump on the front of his right shin. Like Sherlock Holmes, my young mind analyzed the situation. *Those aren't just fishin' legs. Maybe he was bitten by a dog while riding his bicycle?*

Introductory question of my cross-examination: "What happened to your leg!?"

"Oh," Moon said, casually glancing down at his swollen leg. "I got bit by a water moccasin while I was fishin' the other day."

Of course, that was an entirely insufficient explanation. What kid says to that answer, "Oh, okay," and moves on to conversations about Little League or the weather?

I asked, "How'd that happen? You've always told me snakes won't bother you when you're wading."

"I guess I did say that, but I've been wadin' since I was a kid, and this is the first time I've ever been bitten."

The huge, ugly purple hematoma on full display, his answer wasn't the least bit comforting. In fact, it was downright disturbing, so I continued my query.

"Okay, so, how'd it happen!?"

Feigning an air of complete aloofness, Moon deadpanned, "Oh, me and Ty went fishin' at that watershed lake down there near Carrollton on Saturday.

Ty waded down one side, and I went down the other. I was more than a mile from the car on the east side of the lake, and I noticed a water moccasin out there in front of me with its head stickin' up out of the water."

Incidentally, water moccasins are an everyday sighting in the South's numerous lakes, ponds, and rivers. But most people observe them from land, piers, or boats. Most wade-fishermen at least have on a pair of waders, offering some protection from underwater brush and snakes. Even then, if they happen to spot a snake, they are likely to rapidly exit the water, loudly articulating their favorite cuss words. That's when some self-righteous know-it-all, who'd never get in the water with the snakes in the first place, pontificates the common folk myth, "You know water moccasins can't bite underwater." The fact is, they can!

I suppose Southerners try to comfort one another with such nonsense; otherwise, the magnanimous snake infestation would empty all the swim beaches. Stories abound of snakes dropping from limbs into fishing boats, the wary fisherman sinking his boat trying to shoot the terrifying reptile. Moon, on the other hand, always clad in his standard cutoff jeans and old tennis shoes, completely ignores the snakes.

He's told me a thousand times, "Shane, them snakes won't bother you, and all them waders do is slow you down."

My take, *Yeah, and keep your legs from looking like they've been put through a sausage grinder.*

"That snake went under, and I didn't think a thing about it. Then I felt this weight on my right leg, and I thought I'd gotten tangled in an underwater vine or somethin'. I pulled my leg forward like you do when you're wadin' and get tangled up."

He demonstrated by pushing his leg forward, still sitting atop the bike.

"I did that, but whatever it was just stayed wrapped around my leg. Then it felt like somethin' was stingin' me. I lifted my leg, and that big ole' moccasin was coiled up around my leg with his mouth wide open and them fangs stickin' in there. He had me right here just below the knee, where you see the marks."

Leaning on the bike, he thrust his leg up for my examination. I saw two bright red marks about an inch apart, sunken and enclosed by swollen flesh, slight cuts extending from each mark. Moon's hypothesis that all waders do is slow you down was growing weaker by the moment.

"What in the heck did you do?"

"I grabbed the moccasin behind the head and unwrapped him and threw him off."

Most men's lives would've ended right there from shock or cardiac arrest. Moon followed the *Boy Scout Handbook* he knew from beginning to end better than theologians know the Bible. The only difference is most people read the book assuming they will be administering aid to others, not themselves!

"I waded to shore, and I know you ain't supposed to do this, but I couldn't suck the poison out because I couldn't get my head down to where the bite was."

He leaned forward again to demonstrate the obvious. "I cut my leg at them fang marks and squeezed it to make it bleed. That's the way you get the poison out of there when you can't suck it."

I now realized I was receiving in-depth instructions on what to do if I was ever bitten by a snake at some location on my body where I couldn't suck the poison out. He had my undivided attention!

"I started feelin' a little nauseous, so I started walkin' back toward the car."

I would've been puking my guts out, but Moon's stomach is impervious to most things because of the horrendous things he's learned to eat while living off the land.

"When I got to the car, I drank a lot of water. That helps the poison not be so concentrated in your bloodstream."

Moon keeps a supply of rinsed-out milk jugs filled with water in his truck, always at least one on the front seat. Even today, he'd never consider a Nalgene bottle or Hydro Flask when rinsed-out milk jugs work just fine. Hot water is just as good as cold.

"I got up there and honked the horn for about ten minutes, tryin' to get Ty to come back. But he never came back. After a while, I started feelin' better, so I went back fishin'."

I would have called a search-and-rescue helicopter, but that was long before cell phones.

"Haven't you gone to the doctor? You know snake bites can cause terrible infections."

"All them doctors do is take your money to tell you what you already know."

Such statements always made me want to argue with him, but I knew it was pointless.

"I've been icin' it and rubbin' a little of that triple antibiotic salve on it twice a day."

"Well, that's good."

Remembering these stories, I thought, *Not only was Moon next-level tough and daring, but he also didn't seem to be afraid of anything—tall towers or cottonmouth moccasins!*

CHAPTER 19

ALASKA — 1973

NEXT, I REMEMBERED Moon's description the previous day of his second trip to Alaska in '73. That summer, Moon embarked on a pattern that continues to this day—Ackerman to Alaska and back again. The pattern has slowed the past decade, but it hasn't stopped! I was eleven and turned twelve that November. I had to adjust to the pattern.

"I graduated from Mississippi State that spring, but I had to wait 'til school got out around mid-May before leaving for Alaska. I was plannin' on goin' in my old car, but then I learned Ty was wantin' to go. I knew my car wouldn't fit all the gear we needed to bring. Ty had just bought his brother John Magyar's truck, but he hadn't paid for it yet. Ty thought he could take his pickup to Alaska and sell it for two or three thousand dollars more than he owed on it. I'd already been up there before, and I knew that wouldn't gonna happen. Then I learned George Earl wanted to go too. Ty didn't want George Earl to go, but George Earl had more money than Ty did. Ty had a PhD, but back then he didn't have a dime to his name. I didn't have much money either. I'd climbed the ETV tower, and that helped pay off some of my school bills, but I think I only had about three hundred left, and you can't get to Alaska without no money. There was a lot of conflict right there at the beginnin'.'

"So, I elected for George Earl to go, and that made us have to use Ty's truck because there was no way to get there otherwise. I also knew that truck would do a lot better on the big rocks up on the ALCAN. When we were gettin' everything ready, Mr. W. M. Perrigin stopped by and hired Ty to work in the superintendents of education office. Ty told him, 'I was just fixin' to go to Alaska.' Mr. Perrigin said, 'Go, but be back by July the 5th.'

"One problem was figurin' out sleepin' arrangements. I knew about a truck shell camper Harold Stephenson owned. Harold bought it in Alaska while he was in the Air Force. It sat in his garage untouched for five or six years, and he wanted to get rid of it because it was takin' up too much room. Me, George Earl, and Ty went over there and looked at it. I paid him twenty-five dollars for it.

"Then, I had to figure out how to get it on the truck. I had to make lots of measurements and adjustments. I built a frame for a three-quarter bed in the back. I realized two men weren't gonna sleep back there together, so I got an army cot and made a tent sort of thing out of canvas to put over it, to keep whoever decided to sleep on it out of the rain. George Earl didn't help do any of the work, but he claimed the camper bed right off the bat. Ty said he really had a lot of back trouble, and he needed the bed, but he finally agreed to sleep on the cot. I told 'em I was the smallest, so I'd just sleep up there on the truck seat.

"We fine'lee got the truck all ready, and we decided to leave the next night. I told 'em, 'Bring ever thing ya' takin' and let's go through it.' I didn't want 'em bringin' a bunch of extra stuff. Ty was bad about bringin' stuff he didn't need. That always makes things a lot harder. Sometimes I carry more than I need, too."

I thought, *I've never seen Moon carry too much stuff. Rather, usually the bare necessities, if even that.* Moon was a minimalist before minimalism was cool.

"We fine'lee got all that settled, and I told 'em, 'We really need a good camera. You'll see lots of things and catch a bunch of big fish, and you're gonna want to get pictures of all it.' Ty said, 'I got the camera covered.' I said,

'Okay, I can mark that off the list,' but I guess I shoulda' looked at that camera. We counted all the money, and I told 'em, 'Give it all to me. I'll take care of the money.' I knew our money was tight, and I knew what they'd do with it. They'd spend it on a bunch of junk food and other stuff we didn't need."

Factoring in MPE and MPPF, Moon's account sounded true to form!

WHOLESALE GROCERY

"We left Ackerman the next night and drove to Columbia, Missouri, and got there about nine or ten o'clock in the mornin'. I knew about a wholesale grocery store where you could get things real cheap. We went in there and bought like fifty pounds of potatoes, twenty pounds of rice, ten pounds of beans, ten pounds of cornmeal, and some salt meat because I knew that'd keep. Oh yeah, we also got five gallons of corn oil and some onions.

"When we were payin' for all that stuff, I asked the fella, 'Y'all wouldn't happen to have any film for this camera would ya'?' He said, 'Naw, but there's a camera shop right across the street, and they have everything.' We went over there, and I showed 'em the camera and told 'em we needed some film for it. I thought, *Man, this is an old camera.* It was a Kodak 620. That fella took one look at it and said, 'They ain't made film for this camera for about thirty years, since the end of WWII. I don't know where you could get any, but it's gonna be hard to find. Here, let me sell you this camera.' I told him, 'We don't have any extra money, but thank you just the same.' We tried one or two more places, and they said the same thing, so I said to myself, *I reckon we'll just have to do without one.*"

WE ARE MOUNTAIN MEN!

"We drove and drove and stopped and slept most nights. George Earl in the camper, Ty on the cot, and me on the front seat of the truck. I did most of the drivin'.

During the day, we all rode on the front seat. George Earl and Ty were pretty big fellas, and it was pretty crowded. We fine'lee got up there somewhere in the Yukon territory. Ty and George Earl had never seen big snow-covered mountains before, and they kept sayin' they wanted to climb one of 'em. So, we pulled over beside a big 'un.

"The movie *Jeremiah Johnson* had come out sometime the year before. We all piled out of the truck and started up the mountain. We didn't get very far up it 'til we hit pretty deep snow. We went about a hundred more yards, and the snow was gettin' deeper and deeper. They fine'lee said they were ready to turn around. Heading back down the mountain, I yelled as loud as I could, '*By God, I are a mountain man!*' You could hear it echoing down the sides of the mountains. Ty and George Earl joined in, and all the way back down the mountain, we yelled, 'By God, we are mountain men!'"

I remembered the movie, a personal favorite, but I also recalled numerous men around Ackerman telling me, "I wish *I* could live like your daddy!" I detected a twinge of envy in their voices. In the early '70s, the spirit of the beat generation was very much alive, and I think they meant, *Oh, to be free from the everyday constraints of work and family.* Their comments invoked a sort of epiphany for me. I had no idea anyone wanted to be like Moon. It felt reassuring that some of my friends' dads wanted to be like mine.

Ty and Moon—Yukon mountain men!

LAKE TROUT ON THE RANCHERIA RIVER

"We got to the 'Ranchero River [Rancheria River], pulled over, and decided to camp for the night. I took a spincaster down to the river, and I think I was throwin' a #4 Mepps spinner. I cast a couple of times and hooked and landed a big lake trout. It was well over ten pounds.

"George Earl took it back to camp, and me and Ty kept fishin'. George Earl couldn't do many things well, but man, he was a good cook! When we got back, George Earl had built a fire, fried the lake trout, and made some french fries and hushpuppies in a cast-iron skillet. I told him, 'Man, this might be the best meal I've ever eaten.' If you bragged on George Earl a little bit, he'd do it even better the next time."

GRIZZLY HUNTIN'

"Next mornin', we loaded up and drove somewhere a little southwest of Tok. We decided to pull over and camp again, figurin' that'd put us into

Soldotna at a good time the next day. We stopped along another river; I don't remember which one. George Earl announced he wanted to go huntin'. That time of year, the sun stays up a long time. I told him to go ahead; I figured he'd be back in a little bit. He took my Winchester 30-30 and walked down to the river. He was back in ten minutes and said, 'Man, there's the biggest bear down there I've ever seen!' I don't think he'd ever seen too many bears before. I was already tryin' to lie down on the front seat, but George Earl insisted me and Ty come have a look at the bear. I fine'lee got up, and we all went down there.

"'Do you see 'em?' 'Yeah.' At first, I really didn't. I just wanted to get back in the truck and go to sleep. When I fine'lee saw him, I couldn't believe how big he was! He was a giant grizzly with a big hump on his back. He was on an island in the river, diggin' up willow shoots and eatin' 'em. George Earl asked, 'Do you want me to shoot him?' I said, 'Man, naw, give me that rifle!'

"We watched him for a while and then decided to head back and get some sleep. We got to the truck, and Ty announced he had decided to let me have the cot for the night. I told him, 'We've come this far like this, and it ain't gonna change now.' He said, 'What am I supposed to do?' I told him, 'That bear ain't gonna bother you.' I don't think he was too convinced. He took the 30-30 and walked around for a few minutes, lookin' down toward the river, and fine'lee got in his cot.

"Before I crawled back in the truck, I scooped up a big handful of rocks. When things got quiet, I'd roll down the window and toss one down the hill. You'd hear it bouncin' around, and then you'd hear Ty's sleepin' bag unzip. I'd raise my head up a little bit and see him walkin' around the cot with the 30-30. I kept him at it most of the night. You know it never gets too dark up there in Alaska that time of year."

CENTENNIAL CAMPGROUND

"We fine'lee got to Centennial Campground on the Kenai late the next afternoon. I walked down to the river to almost the exact spot I fished in '68. It wasn't no time until I had a big king on. I landed it and decided to keep it because we really needed the food. I took it to camp and cleaned it and cut it up. I walked over to throw somethin' away in the trash barrel and noticed a yellow paper bag. I picked it up, and there was not one but two boxes of unopened Kodak 620 film in the bag! That's how we took all the pictures."

Listening, we weren't only amused; I thought of other times during Moon's epic adventures when trash cans provided exactly what he needed. And sometimes it wasn't film but food!

CHARLES CALLOWAY

Over the years, Moon's proselytized many and converted some with his version of the Kenai salmon fishing gospel. His friend Charles Calloway was one.

"Charles Calloway moved to Alaska a summer or two after my first trip. I told him all about the trip in '68. Charles's wife, Alice, already had a sister livin' in Anchorage. I think they must've moved sometime in 1970. So, they'd been there almost three years when we got there that summer. Charles mainly worked and fished on the weekends. He'd caught some salmon, but he'd never gotten into the big kings yet. There was hardly anybody fishin' on the Kenai back then.

"George Earl didn't fish much, but me and Ty got to catchin' those huge kings, so I went into town and called Charles on the telephone. I told him where I was and said, 'I caught one over fifty pounds this mornin'!' Charles said, 'We went over to some place way east this weekend and caught two reds, but they didn't even weigh but about five or six pounds apiece.' He asked, 'Did you really catch one that big?' I said, 'Yeah, I really did. I might catch another one.' Charles said, 'I believe I'll take the rest of the day off!'

"He was livin' in Anchorage, and he'd never been down to the Kenai very much; he'd always gone the other way down toward Valdez. He borrowed his sister-in-law's black Cadillac and came drivin' down there in that. I met him at the Kenai River Bridge, and he followed me on down to the campground. We had one big king on ice, and he looked at it, and I could tell he was impressed. He said, 'Man, that's a big fish!'

"Charles hooked one that afternoon, but it managed to get off. I think it broke his line. I caught another one and gave it to him. He took the fish back to Anchorage in his sister-in-law's black Cadillac! Charles already owned a pickup and camper. So, he, Alice, and Greg came back the next weekend and stayed the rest of the summer. Alice insisted on cookin' for everybody. That kinda put George Earl out of a job. But man, could she cook! Greg, who lives up there today, was only about this high, and we all fished from the bank.

"There were lots of big buildin' projects in Soldotna back then. Charles checked around and found he could get a lot of work. He laid carpet and floorin'. He ended up startin' his own floorin' business, and then decided to build a house on the Kenai downriver from the campground. He built most of it himself. They moved into the house in '76. Charles could do anything he put his mind to, and I think what was on his mind then was fishin' the Kenai anytime he wanted."

Moon helping young Greg Calloway land a Kenai king.

Kenai River bank fishermen. *Center:* Moon, Charles, and Alice and Greg Calloway. *Right:* Edgar Griffin.

TIDE BATHS

Impervious to frigid water, Moon fished the Kenai River in his standard Mississippi fishing apparel: cutoff blue jeans and old tennis shoes.

Curious bystanders asked, "How's that man do that?"

Those who knew him usually responded, "Moon's got a built-in thermostat; he can turn it on or off whenever he wants to!"

A more accurate explanation is that when Moon gets after fish of any variety, he can tune out everything else and channel all his senses to the task at hand.

Paul the Apostle said, "Do you not know that in a race all the runners run, but only one gets the prize?"[9] Moon's prize on the Kenai? Monstrous king salmon. He harnessed every muscle fiber accordingly. It wasn't so much negation but a fine-tuning of the senses—mind over matter to win the prize. Not just aware, but hyperaware; not less intensity, but more.

"All them waders do is slow you down and get in ya' way."

And keep you warm, unless you're Moon!

In the early years on the Kenai, Moon became legendary not only for his scant, funky fishing apparel but also for his preferred method of personal hygiene. He took Tide baths. As in Tide, the laundry detergent.

"There weren't any bathhouses in the campground then, and to take a shower, you had to drive all the way to town and pay for it. I wouldn't gonna do that, so I just started bathin' in the river."

Moon's philosophy of bathing was another extreme version of MPE. It wasn't only that he refused to pay money for a shower; he didn't want to waste time to drive to town when he could be fishin'. So, he used Tide and bathed in the frigid river.

---

9   1 Corinthians 9:24, NIV.

INNOVATION

Ron Judd, former outdoor writer for *The Seattle Times,* said, "Humans engaged in this for millennia have learned that success necessitates thinking like a fish."[10]

On the Kenai, Moon was an innovator of the "bank-fishing technique" from the day he arrived. The good folks in Ackerman got it right: "Moon thinks like them fish think."

BAITCASTERS

"When I first started fishing in Alaska, most everyone used spincasting reels. I never did that; I always used a baitcaster. Baitcasters enabled me to throw two casts to their one. The important thing when ya' salmon fishin' is to keep your lure in the strike zone for the maximum amount of time. I learned the best way to do that was by usin' a baitcaster, just like the kind you use when ya' bass fishin'.

"The problem with baitcasters then was the drag. Big kings could burn up the drags on their first big run. That would cause your reel to jam, and then they'd break your line. So, I started takin' the drags out of every one. I'd thumb 'em. That way, I could let 'em run and even reel the handles backwards to give 'em line if I needed to. That way, when they made a powerful run, I wouldn't dependin' on the drag to do all the work."

LURES

Moon was also an innovator in the lure category.

"Most big kings are goin' a long way up the river, so they are usually real deep. A lot of people are pullin' their lures right over the top of 'em. I realized

---

10   Ron Judd, "In the Business of Tackle Some Big Ones Get Away," *Seattle Times,* July 5, 2012, wenatcheeworld.com.

that pretty quickly. Back then, no one was makin' lures heavy enough to get down there where you needed to be with enough action to coax a strike. So, I started to doublin' Pixies [a salmon spoon]. That way, I was gettin' three strikes to everybody else's one.

"The best lure was the Little Jewel made by Luhr Jensen. I bought a whole bunch of 'em when they were makin' the one-and-three-eighths-ounce one. But when the company was bought out, they quit makin' that size. When I realized that, I didn't wanna share 'em too much with anybody else 'cause I realized you couldn't get 'em no more. If I happened to see that size anywhere, I started buyin' ever one I could find."

Moon is usually charitable with his fishing lures; however, his generosity has limits. He might share a good one but never his best one. To do so would be a violation of his modus operandi. He's always searching for the slightest advantage. On the Kenai, Little Jewels became more valuable than gold. And the bank fishermen hoarded them accordingly.

"Fine'lee, I had only a few left. Around the same time, some fellas from New Zealand started comin' up there. One of 'em asked me what I was catchin' all my fish on. I didn't much want to tell him. But fine'lee I showed him one. He said, 'I've got a big metal die cast machine back in New Zealand.' So, I gave him one, and he copied it and started makin' 'em. Every year, they'd bring a whole bunch of replicas. Bobby Dale Martin [another Kenai convert from Weir, Mississippi] had a few of the originals and became friends with the New Zealand fellas, and so we all started usin' the ones they made. They're the best lures for big kings, fishin' the way I liked to fish back then."

SALMON RODS

"In the early days, most store-bought rods strong enough to handle big kings were made for spincasting reels. I needed a rod strong enough for baitcasters, so I figured out how to make my own. What I did was take the best baitcaster rod I could find and then reinforce the whole thing. The biggest pressure kings put on the rod is right above the handle. If it ain't strong enough, they can break it in half. So, I got some strong thread and epoxy and reinforced the whole thing. I've still got some of the rods I made back then. Fine'lee some manufacturers started makin' rods that'd work with baitcasters, so I started usin' them."

Hippie Moon with a Kenai king.

Moon's early salmon rods donned every color of the rainbow. Bob Marley and reggae salmon anglers would've felt right at home!

EXCEL FISHIN' LINE

"I don't remember if it was that year or the next, but a fella on the bank yelled down, 'Hey, what kinda line ya' usin'?' I looked up and said, 'I'm usin' twenty-five-pound Stren doubled four feet at the end for a leader.' He asked, 'Have you ever tried Excel line?' I said, 'I ain't never heard of it.' He told me he had a bunch in his truck, and he'd give me some. I said, 'That'd be fine.'

"Turns out the man was a representative for Excel fishing line at the beginnin' of Bass Pro Shops. He headed back to his truck, and while he was gone, I hooked into a big king. It was in the sixty-pound category. He came down and watched me fight the fish, and when I fine'lee landed it, he asked, 'Do you mind if I snap a quick picture or two?'

"I held the fish up, and he took several pictures. I put the fish back, and we talked a minute. What I was really wantin' to do was get back to fishin'. He fine'lee said, 'Here's my card. Why don't you stop by Bass Pro in Springfield, Missouri, on your way back to Mississippi?'

"I didn't think I would, but by the time I headed back that year, I started hearin' about all the good deals at Bass Pro. I had to drive pretty close to Springfield, so I stopped in there. I had the fella's card, so I asked one of the workers if they knew him, and they did. I met him, and we talked a little bit about how the rest of the salmon fishin' had been, and he invited me up to this big office kinda overlookin' the whole thing. He pulled out the pictures and showed 'em to me. I have to admit they were some pretty good pictures! We sat there a minute, and he asked, 'Do you mind signin' this piece of paper giving us the rights to use these photographs?' I said, 'I'll be glad to do that; you've already given me a bunch of line, and it worked pretty good.'

"Anyway, the truth was I didn't catch that fish on Excel line; I caught it on Stren! I don't know if that qualifies as false advertised or not, but Bass Pro sure sold a lot of fishin' line as a result of them pictures. A fish caught on Stren became the first big marketin' push for Excel mono line."

Bass Pro should have offered to outfit Moon for the rest of his life, but he'd have said, "No."

"All that would've done would've been to keep me from fishin' the way I like to."

Bass Pro ad featuring Moon in the upper right.

TY AIN'T NO GOOD TRADER

"That year, I set my green army tent back in the woods a little bit. The campground fee wasn't much back then, but the campsites weren't any better than the woods, and I wouldn't gonna pay no fee."

MPE! Not to mention Moon's never seen a tent he doesn't like. He loves the smell of canvas and feels as much at home in a tent as he does his own house, maybe more!

"Ty had to be back by July 5th, so he started tryin' to sell the truck. But Ty ain't no good trader. His first mistake was to tell people he had to sell it before the first week of July. He oughta' held them cards in the hole and not let anybody see 'em. The locals knew all they had to do was wait, and they'd get a good deal. The only fella really interested in it worked for Charles, and he just waited Ty out. The price dropped every day the closer it got to July. Ty thought he was gonna make money on that truck, but he ended up losin' a lot of money. I think he lost about three thousand, and the fella that bought it got the camper too.

"Hilton Jones, Charles's brother-in-law, had to buy Ty a plane ticket home. Matter of fact, he had to buy me one too! I stayed to the very last day before I had to be back to teach. I got into the silvers [Cohoe salmon] some before I left. Charles drove me to the airport in Anchorage, and I paid Hilton back as soon as I got back to Ackerman.

"It's hard to describe the kinda energy, excitement, and camaraderie of that summer. I miss Charles and think about him driving his sister-in-law's black Cadillac down there every time I cross the Kenai River Bridge in Soldotna."

I could tell by the cadence of Moon's description and the excited look in his eyes that the memory was still exhilarating. What is it about shared experience in pursuit of a common goal that galvanizes friendships? I know one thing: fishing with friends does that. I suppose even more so if you belonged to the small clan of bank fishermen on the pristine Kenai in '73.

For Moon, the '73 trip reaffirmed what he experienced in '68, and this many years later, one might say, charted a destiny. Beginning in '73, Moon returned to Alaska every summer for twenty consecutive years. And then, the streak only ended because he was turned back at the Canadian border!

Moon wearing standard Kenai fishing apparel.

CHAPTER 20

HISTORY TEACHIN' AND LAISSEZ-FAIRE PARENTING

IN THE FALL OF '73, I turned twelve and entered seventh grade, which meant I moved to Ackerman High School where Moon taught. What do you say when you haven't seen your dad since the previous spring, and one day you meet him in the hallway at school? Maybe it was my age, but somehow, I'd adjusted to a new normal, which wasn't normal at all. More was in play than simply our atypical father-son relationship. Moon's philosophy of parenting is *laissez-faire,* hands-off, don't interfere, let boys be boys—that's the way they learn.

"When you go to college to be a schoolteacher, your last semester they put you on what they call the teachin' block. I don't know why they called it that, but all it amounts to is practice teachin'. I think you were in the seventh grade when I did that."

FIGHT

I asked, "Do you remember when I got in a fight with Ed Reid one morning before class?"

"Yeah, I remember. You had him down on the floor of the classroom, and there were a bunch of other kids standin' around."

I don't remember exactly why Ed and I got into a fight. I wasn't prone to fighting, and Ed's a nice guy. I suppose seventh-grade boys will be seventh-grade boys. What I remember was the gathered crowd suddenly became gravely quiet and directed their collective concerned attention toward the classroom door. I looked up, and there stood Moon, the high school history teacher. Everyone expected an intervention and subsequent disciplinary action. Moon didn't say a word; he just walked away.

"Why didn't you say anything?"

"I prob'ly didn't want to. I was just glad you were winnin'."

HISTORY CLASS

Older kids told me with regularity, "We love your daddy's history class." Curious, I asked, "Why?"

"All he ever does is tell good stories. If you don't know the answers on the test, you can go up to his desk, and he'll tell you. You can do pushups for extra credit. If you can do a one-handed pushup, you get an A!"

Moon is, by nature, a history teacher. However, let's just say his teaching methods are outside the realm of the ordinary. His philosophy of education centers on personal motion and storytelling. Moon's classrooms really didn't need desks. In his way of thinking, history and pushups combine in a seamless web to produce real learning.

An outside observer might think he or she was witnessing a new, innovative high school history learning program with a few fishing stories thrown in for good measure. I think Moon's teaching method was a holistic philosophy of life he developed early on from following Mack around Choctaw Lake.

Life itself is living history. If you read it in a book while sitting at a desk, you won't retain it. Learning history must be intertwined with motion and stories. I'm not completely sure his students learned a lot of history, but they heard good stories and always got good grades!

CHARLES PEAY

"Do you remember the time we had to go to court because my buddies and I were caught turning out the traffic lights on Main Street?"

"Yeah, I remember that; it almost kept us from getting to go fishin."

During my junior high and high school days, Charles Peay was a police officer in Ackerman. He was beyond strict and had a reputation for enforcing the letter of the law.

Former chief of police Malcolm McMinn recalls, "Officer Peay had been to Vietnam, and I couldn't ever get him to understand being a police officer in a small town was different than being in an army at war. It didn't matter who you were; one time he gave Mayor Glasgow a ticket for failing to use his turn signal."

One Friday night, I was staying with Moon. We'd planned a big fishing trip for Saturday morning. That evening, with nothing better to do, a group of my friends and I devised a mischievous plot to engage Officer Peay. We knew how to turn off the traffic lights on Main Street. On the utility poles adjacent to the lights (there aren't many!) were switchboxes about eight feet off the ground. The poles were equipped with metal spike steps, making the switchboxes easily accessible.

We turned off the first traffic light, hid in the nearby shrubs, and waited. Pretty soon, Officer Peay's patrol car appeared, driving slowly down Main Street. From our hideout, we watched with bated breath. He stopped under the darkened signal, backed up, and pulled over. He slowly got out of his car and, with hands on his hips, walked back and forth, carefully analyzing the situation.

High drama, we covered our mouths to mute our uncontrollable laughter. After a thorough walking inspection, Officer Peay climbed the utility pole and restored the power. We instantly felt emboldened, and our plans enlarged. We waited until his car disappeared down the street, ran out, and turned the light off again. This time, we split up. While some waited in the bushes beside the first light, the rest used the back alley to position ourselves under the traffic light on the next block. Officer Peay climbed the first pole again. While his back was turned, we ran out and shut off the second light. For a while, Officer Peay must have imagined some strange electrical phenomena was underway.

We subdivided, extending our nefarious adventure to the third traffic light. Officer Peay drove in circles, climbing poles and restoring power. We all met in the central alley, laughed a couple of minutes, and repeated the process. The riskier it became, the funnier it was, and the better we liked it. Boys don't know when enough is enough, and we were bound to be caught.

Officer Peay finally realized something sinister was in play and drove his patrol car slowly down the alley. We sprinted for cover, hiding under whatever we could find. The search light's intense beams reflected around and underneath every object. We held our collective breaths. Somehow, we managed to escape his initial search. We watched from our various positions as his patrol car exited the alley.

"The coast is clear!"

Exhilarated by our narrow escape, we reassembled in the alley and told war stories, each trying to outdo the other about exactly how close the beams had come and how close we had come to apprehension.

We never considered Officer Peay might radio for backup. Standing red-handed in the alley, another patrol car appeared out of nowhere. It was too late to run. Pee Rooster emerged from his car with a big grin.

"Now ya' boys knows you shouldn't be a doin' this. It might cause an acceedent. Y'all go on home, it's gettin' late out har."

At just that moment, Officer Peay screeched in, lights flashing, like he was busting a hardened drug ring.

"Hands up, get against the car!"

He frisked us like we were packing assault weapons. Terror reflected in the eyes of my friends.

"Now Officer Peay, dese boys don't mean no harm, they jest tryin' to have a little fun, you ain't gonna arrest 'dem, is ya'? You donts have enough cuffs to go round, no way."

Like we were escapees on a most-wanted list, Officer Peay read us our rights and instructed us one by one to get into the patrol car behind the cage.

"My daddy's gonna kill me!"

"I'm gonna be grounded for two whole years!"

I knew Moon wouldn't care one bit. Officer Peay drove us to the county courthouse, which served as the police booking station and temporary jail.

"You can't put 'dem boys in jail, dat right 'dar is Doug Gilliland's son. You know Mr. Gilliland, donts ya'?"

Malcolm McMinn recalls, "I remember getting a phone call from Officer Peay late that evening, and it took me ten minutes to get him to back down. He took it on himself to be the adjudicator of the law. He thought his job was to arrest, prosecute, and sentence. I finally convinced him to drive all you boys home in his patrol car and have a conversation with your parents."

This time, rather than being packed in the back like sardines in a can, I got to sit in the front seat, which I didn't know at the time meant I'd be delivered last. I watched from the patrol car's front seat as Officer Peay drove from house to house, describing to parent after parent details of the horrendous crime we'd committed. I observed the lowered heads of my friends and the stern faces of their parents.

Finally, it was my turn.

"Where do you live?"

"I'm stayin' with my dad this weekend; we're going fishing tomorrow. He lives at 199 South Louisville Street."

Getting out, I noticed Moon had everything loaded for our fishing trip.

I stood beside Officer Peay in the garage as he repeatedly knocked loudly on the door.

"He must be asleep or in the shower; I'll get him."

Moon was in the shower.

"Daddy, there's someone out here who needs to talk to you."

"Who needs to talk to me at this time of night!?"

"Well, it's Officer Peay."

"Well, all right, tell him to hold on just a minute."

"Okay."

I invited Officer Peay inside. He slowly scanned the eccentric room filled with stacks of fishing magazines, rods, reels, hunting knives, and fishing lures, and didn't utter a word. Moments later, Moon appeared in cutoff jeans, towel in hand, still drying his thick dark hair.

"Mr. Sunn, right?"

"Yeah, what's wrong?"

Officer Peay launched into a detailed description of events, including how I had "intentionally abated a police officer." I could tell Moon was getting bored and a bit angry with the long detailed description.

"You mean to tell me that's what all this uproar is about!? *They were just bein' boys.*"

"Well, tomorrow's court day, and Chief McMinn has instructed me you will need to appear with your son in court, and Mayor Glasgow has agreed to address the boys on the importance of safety and obeying the law."

"We're goin' fishin' tomorrow."

Officer Peay fired back, "I'd like to work in my garden tomorrow, but tomorrow's court day."

Moon isn't easily riled unless something comes between him and fishing. Officer Peay was unknowingly treading on sacred ground. A standoff ensued with lots of back-and-forth bantering.

"You've got to be in court."

"No, I don't; I told you we're goin' fishin' tomorrow."

Finally, Officer Peay said, "If I remember correctly, Mr. Sunn, you are supposed to be there, too, for the ticket I wrote you for the busted taillight."

Moon gritted his teeth and turned red, the familiar visceral reaction he displayed when his fishing plans were altered in any way.

Next morning, we drove down to the municipal building.

"Now, Shane, our goal is to get out of here as fast as we can. I can just pay the fine for the taillight, and that'll end that right there. I don't know how long that 'talkin' to' is gonna take."

"Okay."

Moon paid the fine, and I noticed him say something to Mayor Glasgow before he sat down beside me. My long-faced friends sat with their parents, scattered about the room. Mayor Glasgow understood the situation and gave a balanced and reasonably short lecture.

"You boys are free to go, but don't let me have to see you in here again."

I was eager to chit-chat with my friends, but I could tell by the expressions of their parents that would have to wait for Monday at school.

"Shane, let's go. It's a perfect day for fishin', and we should've been there three hours ago."

Moon recalled, "Y'all were just bein' boys, and Officer Peay didn't mean no harm. He just did things the way he saw 'em."

I thought, *At least Moon's consistent in his view of authority.*

CHAPTER 21

SOUTHERN LIVING

INTERIOR DESIGN

LINGERING IN THE AIRBNB, I remembered my hesitation to bring friends to Moon's house when I was a kid.

Showing up at Moon's house, you didn't know if you had just arrived at a messy home gym, a hunting camp, a bait and tackle shop, or a used bookstore specializing in antique fishing magazines. "Clean," already near the bottom of the *scout law*, had completely fallen off the list, replaced by the law of "thrifty"—meaning "readily accessible," in a short walking distance. Before Othermother's death, there remained a semblance of discernable décor. But moving forward, MPE and MPPF combined to produce an amusing form of interior design.

Exhibit one, the living room. Southern living rooms, though seldom used, are nevertheless very important, reserved for "special company." Nice furniture conforming to the rules of special company is thoughtfully arranged, not a dust speck visible to the naked eye. Sofa, chairs, draperies, side tables, and lamps are all carefully positioned with special company in mind. Never-read books and magazines all strategically selected, value assessed by their capacity to impress special company. Kids absolutely can't go into the living room, in case they mess something up before you can clean it up, on the outside chance special company might unexpectedly arrive.

In Moon's house, the living room and formal dining room were combined. Entering from the den, to the left, the fine dining table was covered with high stacks of fishing magazines. You could barely see the china cabinet, which had been transformed into a fishing-rod display. Atop the credenza, one could select from a variety of fishing lures and rifle cartridges. Mid-room on the barely visible sofa, an assorted array of hunting and fishing apparel was laid out, including old leaky waders, available for the taking.

Important in the echelon of exercise equipment, a couple of bicycles were leaned against the walls. Side tables were covered with spools of fishing line, dyed feathers, and fly-tying equipment, with an assortment of colorful spinner baits scattered about, creating a sort of mix-and-match appeal. Lampshades were ideal places for hanging whatever might not fit on the tables. If you could negotiate the obstacle course, on display atop a high, narrow table against the wall at the end of the room, was a shrine of sorts. Comparable in importance to the Hope Diamond, the antique brass sword handle discovered while fishing in Whittier, Alaska, oohed and aahed visitors.

Depending on how you looked at it, Moon was either not expecting special company or he entertained a different breed of special company. The special company who showed up at Moon's house arrived to hear hunting and fishing stories; the rest just weren't that special. Besides, they might tempt you to rearrange the décor. He wasn't trying to impress anyone, but like most fine artists, design was simply an extension of the man. Unwittingly, interior design served as stage props arranged to draw you into the story and transform you.

Fishing stories are better told if you must walk around a lure dangling from a light fixture in order to sit down. And then there was the endless array of pictures scattered about. If you picked one up, you were in for a number-one thriller, with every specific detail: where he went, the drive, the weather that day, the song he happened to be listening to on the radio, and finally, how he caught the fish. The pictures themselves served as witnesses to the veracity of the tale.

However, knowing that Moon's house was nothing like my friends' homes, I was hesitant to bring them by. I was afraid of what they might think. I thought I needed a house and daddy that conformed to the rules of "special company." I didn't dare bring a girl, especially if I dreamed there might be any future possibility of a date!

INNER SANCTUM

Moon's bedroom served as the hunting and fishing temple's inner sanctum. It looked like the combination of an American history museum and a Cherokee chief's burial pyre, creating a mystical out-of-body experience.

Tanned white-tailed deer rugs covered the floor, suggesting, "Remove your shoes." Relics consisting of cigar boxes full of arrowheads, spear points, bird tips, grind stones, beads, pottery, and tomahawk blades mesmerized and drew you into another world. On the back wall hung an imposing picture of a Cheyenne warrior, his eyes always probing from wherever you stood in the room. A beaded leather necklace with eagle feathers, turkey beards, and bear teeth dangled from the mirror on the dressing table. A pocked Civil War cannonball alongside an unspent mortar round served as doorstops.

As an imaginative kid, I thought if I somehow transgressed the room's sacredness, the mortar shell might automatically detonate and reduce the temple and me to rubble. The oak dressing table's drawers were filled with varied and sundry items: shark's teeth, old coins, fishhooks, old paper shotgun shells, antique lures, and leather and wooden neckerchief slides. A Winchester Model 12 pump leaned on the wall in the corner, and a Winchester lever action 30-30 lay at an angle in the moose horns on the wall. Over the bed, a beautiful silvery sixty-four-pound king salmon was on display, head facing outward and slightly downward in a delicate right arc, its mouth narrowly agape with the lure he caught it on dangling from its mouth. It still appeared ready to strike. The room was always dimly lit; an unzipped sleeping bag was atop the unmade bed.

I don't remember the first time I brought friends by. I probably needed some fishing gear or camping equipment. I do remember being astounded by their reaction. My friends, at least the boys, loved Moon's house.

Over time, I allowed my friends to venture farther into the temple, even into the inner sanctum, which resembled a tour to the state history museum. To my surprise, they were stricken with awe and admiration. I became their tour guide as I tried to answer their questions, repeating the stories that accompanied every relic. I thought I wanted a dad like theirs with a respectable home and job, but I gradually realized they wanted a dad more like mine.

Melded into the stories I repeated to my friends about the life and legend of the man who happened to be my dad, I, too, was being slowly transformed.

I thought, *This ain't half bad.*

THE YARD

And then there was the yard. Jeff Foxworthy's redneck jokes about Southerners ridiculed for the number of abandoned cars strewn about the yard come to mind. "You might be a redneck if you've ever cut your grass and found a car or you own a home that is mobile and five cars *that aren't*."

Moon's yard was always reasonably neat and the grass cut, if he wasn't in Alaska. The oddity was a large selection of various kinds of watercraft scattered about. If you didn't know him, you might think he was anticipating a flood. It was one of his important sensibilities; after all, you didn't know what sort of boat the day's fishing might require, and you sure the hell weren't going to waste your money on a storage unit. The various kayaks, canoes, and other watercraft were all easily loadable and navigable vessels designed to get you to good "wade fishin."

You never entered Moon's house through the front door. You couldn't, it opened into the living room, which was already cordoned for temple purposes. To visit the temple, you had to walk through an open carport; pass a rock collection from Alaska's rivers and coasts, each rock a relic of some significant adventure; avoid a suspended canoe; and enter through the den.

Though unintentional, the decorative entryway functioned to engage your senses, preparing you for the temple and the stories you were about to hear. Boats, stones, memories, and other bits and pieces spinning, whirling, and colluding, all contributing to a greater literary whole.

Of course, depending on what kind of special company was expected, he might rearrange the set a bit by dragging some of the various and sundry watercraft around to the backyard.

CHAPTER 22

NASH RAMBLER

MISSIN' MOON

IN THE SPRING OF '74, Moon struck out again for Alaska. That summer, my family renovated an old farmhouse in Reform, Mississippi, nine miles from Ackerman. At the time, I didn't fully recognize what was happening, but the move created a growing sense of separation from Moon. My surroundings and activities completely changed. Backyard football and lazy days spent with friends in Ackerman ended. Still too young to legally drive, at least the nine miles to Ackerman on a dangerous highway, my participation in Boy Scouts and pursuit of Eagle Scout also ended. We moved sometime that fall. Before we left Ackerman, I walked down to the old stick fort and found the ruined coonskin cap, bit my quivering lower lip, and stuffed the pain.

Other than my daily farm chores, I poured myself into hunting and fishing. There was nothing else to do! Was I searching for Moon by attempting to be like him? Was the pattern repeating itself?

ALASKA 1975—76

"Whit Hollis went with me in the Nash Rambler in May of '75. That's what the good folk singer Emmylou Harris calls her band, the Nash Ramblers. I was thirty-nine. I turned forty in '76."

This time, Moon stayed through the Alaskan winter. I didn't see him again for a year and a half.

"Whit stayed about three weeks and flew back, but the Rambler didn't make it back."

WORLD RECORD KING

"What I was tryin' to do was catch the world record king salmon. You can't believe how big the kings were in the Kenai back then! I knew more than one world record swam right by me every year. While fishin', I always imagined I was gonna hook the world record the next cast. I think that's one of the things that kept me so motivated. If you can imagine somethin' in your mind, it's a lot more likely to actually happen."

I thought, *Yeah, unless it's not true.*

Moon with a very large king.

"I got there and walked down to the river just above the island and caught a jack that weighed five or six pounds. I threw him back and threw out there again, and man, a big 'un hit it, and I landed him and took him up there to Ken's to have it officially weighed. It weighed eighty-six pounds and four ounces!

"I won the salmon derby again that year on that fish. I marked him on my rod, and I've caught four more that came to that mark, a couple of 'em a little past it. If I'd already kept one, I didn't ever wanna keep another one just to have it weighed, so I'd release 'em. I've caught five or six that'd go well over eighty pounds. The biggest one I ever officially weighed weighed eighty-eight pounds on the dot."

I knew that in May of 1985, Les Anderson caught the world record king on the Kenai. Its official weight? Ninety-seven pounds and four ounces!

Reports indicate the monster king would've weighed more because Anderson didn't have it weighed until after he'd fished all day.

"Not to take a thing away from Les Anderson, but I've always said boats give the angler an unfair advantage."

I believe I detected just a hint of jealousy!

"I believe I've hooked several world records over the years, but the bigger the fish, usually the harder they fight. There may not be any in there that big anymore, but there sure was back then."

What drives a man to fish beyond the ordinary, way beyond? As explained, Moon acknowledges that every fish he's ever caught, Mack was standing somewhere in the ethereal distance, watching.

As I thought about Moon standing for hours in the Kenai, believing on the next cast he was going to hook and land the world record king salmon, the progression seemed logical: "Look, Daddy, I caught the world record king salmon for you."

BEAR HUNTIN' ON THE PIPELINE

Moon continued.

"Since I stayed the whole year, I could buy an Alaska resident hunting license. So, I bought a black bear and moose combination license. Edgar Griffin from Reform, who everyone called "Big Eddy," was stayin' with me in my tent and workin' in the oil fields. He landed a better job on Kodiak Island. He had to take a boat or fly out there, so he left his big Bronco truck and huntin' rifles with me at the campground.

"I worked on the pipeline two months that winter. Not the one that runs from the North Slope to Valdez, the one that runs from Soldotna to Anchorage. It's about thirty miles east of Soldotna before you get to Cooper Landin'. I ran into my boss, Carl Murph, in Soldotna, and he told me, 'If you're ever needin' to go out there, the combination on the gate is three zeroes and a five.' That was easy to remember, and I still remember it.

"It was a warm sunny day about the middle of September. I went to town and bought a box of ammunition, then took Eddy's Remington 7mm-08 and headed out there to the pipeline. I opened the gate and locked it back and drove down the dirt road, which is about twenty miles long. What I had on my mind was killin' a moose or black bear.

"I'd never shot Eddy's rifle before, so I decided I'd better shoot it. I got 'bout a mile down the road and pulled over. I set up a target about a hundred yards out. I set up some cardboard and put a can in the middle. Big Eddy talked rifles all the time, so I thought, *This ain't gonna be no problem. Eddy's a good shot; I should come close to the can.*

"I got me a good rest, aimed at the can, squeezed the trigger, and didn't even hit the cardboard! I shot again and didn't hit nothin', and that left me eighteen cot-treges. I moved closer, fixed a better rest, and tried again. I barely hit the upper right corner of the cardboard. When I fine'lee got where I could hit the can, I looked down and only had one cot-trege left! I said, 'Well I'm out here, I might as well go on with this one cot-trege.' I drove the Nash Rambler on down the road and walked out there on the pipeline.

"The pipeline, like pipelines everywhere else, had mile markers on it. I could see the first mile marker a pretty good ways away—it wouldn't no mile but too far to read the number. So, I looked through the scope. That was in case I got lost. I knew I could remember the number, and that'd keep me straightened out. I didn't want to get lost in the middle of nowhere and not have anybody come lookin' for me.

"I was lookin' through the scope, tryin' to read the number, and saw a hand come up on the orange post! I put the scope down and looked, and there was a big ole' bear, like playin' or somethin' on it. The number was about five or six feet off the ground, and it looked like the bear was tryin' to read it, too, but it was slippin' on the post.

"I moved out a little to get a better look, and it was not one bear but four, and every one of 'em was bigger than I imagined a bear could be! They were all big brown bears or brown grizzlies. The biggest bears in the world live on

Kodiak Island, and I was on the lower side of the Kenai Peninsula. Some say Kenai bears are as big as Kodiak bears.

"I wanted to get a better look, so I walked down the pipeline a little farther. I was still hopin' to see a moose or black bear. The bears seemed to be mindin' their own business, about a quarter mile away. I sat down kinda like you do when you're deer huntin'. The pipeline had a big dip in front of me, and I couldn't see all the way to the bottom. Before I realized what was happenin', those giant brown bears were coming up the pipeline, headed straight for me ... four of 'em! And I only had one cot-trege. I thought, *How'd I get myself into this situation?*

"Then I really got to lookin'! Two were big males, and they were huge. I could tell one bear was the boss. That was the momma. She'd prob'ly kept the males from the time they were born. The other was a female, and she wasn't as big as the momma. But it was easy to see the momma was runnin' the show. I don't know how it happened, but one of the big males got over behind me, and the other one followed it. I was surrounded. The males cut me off from the car, the only place I felt safe! I told myself, *Don't run if you have to try to get there because you ain't gonna outrun 'em.* And I told myself, "*Keep facin' 'em.*

"I knew not to panic and that I needed a plan. I decided if one charged, I was gonna try to shoot the momma in the head with the one cot-trege. Then see if I could bluff the others by making a loud noise or somethin', or maybe the gunshot would give me a chance to get to the car. I remembered you can throw rocks, so I picked up several pretty big ones and put 'em in my pocket. I was scared because I knew I was in a dangerous situation.

"The momma and smaller female were at an angle to my left and started walking straight toward me. One of the big males behind me made a strange noise, and the momma raised up on her hind feet. She fixed her eyes on me, and I could tell she was about to charge. I got the gun ready; my heart was beatin' fast.

"Fine'lee she made a loud noise kinda like a grunt signal. The big males came right to her, right by me, one on one side and one on the other. I took a deep breath and put the gun back on safety. They went on up the pipeline.

"I walked back to the car and didn't go huntin' no more after that. As a matter of fact, I've never been back to that place. I think about it when I drive by that road and wonder if the lock with the combination is still on the gate. And I was in that Nash Rambler."

For me, the Rambler evoked nostalgic memories. I remembered Moon allowing me to drive it all over Ackerman when I was only thirteen!

THIEVERY

"That fall, there wasn't anybody around the campground. I was catchin' lots of fish at first. I set up the green army tent back in the woods on government land. I bought a little ole' sticker for the Rambler, pulled it off one of the dirt roads, as close to the tent as I could, and parked it. I'd fish in the daytime and sleep at night.

Moon with a king and the Nash Rambler in the background.

"Somebody started stealin' stuff off the Rambler, and I couldn't ever catch 'em. They jacked it up and got all my tires, then took my wheels, and then started takin' everything they could. They stole the windshield wipers and anything from inside that looked like it was any good. They busted the radiator tryin' to get it out. I guess fine'lee they got everything they wanted, and the car just sat there.

"One day I was walkin' through the woods to the river and noticed a motorcycle layin' there on the ground. I went over and looked at it, and it looked brand new. I left it there. It made me wonder what those folks were really up to. Several days later, it started rainin' buckets, so I rolled the motorcycle up beside my tent. It was a Suzuki dirt bike. It was yellow, just like the canoe.

"It was gettin' on over in the fall, and I knew I had to fix the Rambler if I wanted to leave for Mississippi. I ran out of money and the fish quit bitin'. It got down to shootin' squirrels and sage hens with my .22 to have something to eat. I started lookin' for any kind of odd job I could find. The motorcycle just sat there in the rain. Someone told me I needed to file a report with the Soldotna police, and so I did. They came out and looked at it and wrote some stuff down and asked a few questions, but they left the motorcycle sittin' right there.

"I fine'lee got some biddlin' jobs from a few people I knew. I painted the ceilin' on the Maverick Bar for Helen Vocho. I cleaned and scrubbed the bar, then cleaned out her chicken houses, then helped her harvest the garden. I did any kinda work she'd give me for days and days and days. Helen told me, 'I own a bar in Sterling, but the roof has a leak, and I can't get it stopped.'

"Sterling is about twelve miles from Soldotna, so she let me use her work truck. I went to town and bought some big metal buckets and two hundred pounds of hard tar in fifty-pound sacks. I built a fire and chopped the tar with an ax and put it in a bucket to get it boilin'. While it was still hot, I'd take the bucket up the ladder, coat a broom, and sweep it on the roof. I did one layer and then another. I bought a bunch of tar paper and put it on and then sealed it again with another layer of tar. It was a messy job, but I fine'lee finished. Helen told me later, 'That's the first time the roof hasn't leaked.'

"Now, I had several hundred-dollar bills in my pocket. I worked for Norman Howe, a well driller, and he paid me fifty dollars every day. But he got behind and owed me about $450, the best I could figure.

"I used the money I was makin' and Helen's truck to start fixin' the Rambler. I found a big junkyard, and I'd go there between jobs. I found a junked Rambler and bought the wheels and radiator and didn't hardly pay nothin' for it all. But I couldn't find no windshield wipers. I fine'lee found some on another junked car and managed to get 'em on, but they didn't fit right. The wiper motor on the Rambler was so weak anyway. So, I just rigged a string I could pull from the inside to get it to work a little.

"I let word get out I was gonna leave for Mississippi, but I couldn't find Norman Howe. I went by the police station and asked about the motorcycle. They said, 'We can't trace it, the serial numbers were rubbed off. It's yours if you want it.' I said, 'I'll take it.'

"I put the Rambler all back together and wanted to see if the radiator worked but hadn't gotten any antifreeze yet. So, I walked down to the river and dipped up a big bucket of water, walked back, and poured it in. The car started right up and ran better than before all the stuff happened to it. I was still keepin' my eyes out in case the thieves showed up again.

"That night, it came an unusual early freeze. I had to drain all the water out of the radiator, but you can't get the water out of the engine block. So, the block got a hairline crack, but that didn't seem to have no big effect on it right then. I packed up all my gear and loaded up. I tied the yellow canoe on top. I'm sure glad they didn't steal that! I'd kept it hidden in the woods out behind the tent. It was hard to get the motorcycle up there, but I fine'lee did and got it tied on too.

Moon beside Kenai and the yellow canoe.

"I was gonna leave the next mornin' but wait 'til it got daylight. So, I drove over to Sourdough Sally's and ordered me somethin' to eat. My plan was to sleep in Sal's that night, or on the car seat if I had to. It was now late fall, and I knew I was takin' a big chance, tryin' to get back at all, but I'd already made up my mind. I was sittin' in Sal's, and in walked ole' Norm Howe. He said, 'I've been huntin' for you. How much do I owe you?' I said, 'Norm, the best I can figure, it's about $450.' He said, 'That's 'bout what I thought. Here's $500.' I took the money and stuck it in my pocket, and that put me over $1,000 when I fine'lee got ready to go."

BORDER CROSSING TROUBLE

Imagine a yellow canoe and motorcycle tied on top of a refurbished Nash Rambler, a crack in the engine block, with 4,500 miles to drive in late October, with only a thousand dollars in your pocket! In 1976, much of the ALCAN was still unimproved. I'm sure you get the picture.

"Early the next mornin', I left for Mississippi. I drove over the mountains, headed up to Anchorage, and I could tell it was gettin' a lot colder. I was worried about the crack in the engine block, but it seemed like the cold weather was keepin' it from overheatin'. I got to Tok, which is about 450 miles from Soldotna.

"The next thing I had to do was cross the Canadian border. The border is about eighty miles from Tok. I got to the border, and they wanted to check all my credentials. I showed 'em my social security card, hoping that'd be enough. My driver's license had expired that year on my birthday, May 19. I'm a citizen of the United States, but I ain't no citizen of Canada. They said, 'Let me see your driver's license.' I handed 'em to them. They handed 'em back and said, 'You can't go across if you don't have a valid driver's license.' I said, 'Well I can't get 'em from here.' I argued with 'em a little bit. They said, 'You'll have to send for 'em before we'll let you cross.'

"I knew that would take a long time. I knew I could go back to Soldotna and stay in the tent, but I was really wantin' to get home. I didn't know quite what to do. The weather was getting worse, and I knew my window was closin' fast for gettin' back at all. I guess they knew that, too, and wondered if my rig was gonna make it through Canada. I was kinda stranded, so the Royal Canadian Mounted Police escorted me back to Tok.

"I don't like drivin' behind nobody; they usually go too fast. But I didn't have no other choices. When we got back to Tok, the weather had gotten a lot worse. In Tok, you are way inland, and when it's twenty-eight degrees in Soldotna, it's prob'ly zero or ten below in Tok.

"It was late in the afternoon when we pulled into the police headquarters. They walked in there with their big hats and long black boots, and I walked in behind 'em. The people in there looked at me like I'd done somethin' wrong. The officers said somethin' to the folks behind the counter and then left.

"I sat there a little bit, tryin' to figure out what my options were. I fine'lee asked to borrow the phone and called the operator in Jackson, Mississippi, and got the number for the State Highway Patrol office. I called 'em and told 'em I was in Alaska and my driver's license had expired, and they put me through to the right people. The driver's license didn't cost but five dollars, but they didn't even take credit cards back then, and I didn't have one no way. They fine'lee said, 'Until we get the money, we ain't gonna send your license.' I knew that would take a lot longer than a week. So, I sat back down, thinkin' I was gonna have to go back to Soldotna. But I'd already spent all that time doin' all them jobs to get the money to fix the car, and I just wouldn't gonna give up too easy.

"I walked over to a motel. The rooms were 'bout a hundred dollars a night. I figured I couldn't do that because that'd use up all my gas money. So, I slept in the car out in front of the police station that night, and it got down way below zero. I started the engine a few times to warm up the inside, but mainly I was still worried about the crack in the block."

Dogged determination is one of Moon's greatest traits. When he sets his mind to do something, he will either accomplish it or die trying. I love him for that.

CHAPTER 23

Knowing When to Hold 'Em and When to Fold 'Em

I REMEMBERED JEAN'S GLANCE the day before as Moon recounted the tale. Her facial expression changed, indicating she was beginning to realize what I'd attempted to explain since the days we first dated. Moon is cut from a different cloth, and nothing can deter him from what he determines to do, whether death or life, angels or rulers, things present or things to come.

TOP OF THE WORLD HIGHWAY

"The next mornin', I went into the police station and got some hot coffee and sat down again. I was thinkin', *If I worry 'em enough, they might help me try to do somethin' about my expired license.*

"A little before noon, I noticed about four or five people walk in wearing uniforms, and I knew they were some kinda law enforcement. They started talking with the people behind the counter, and I could tell they all knew each other by the way they were talkin'. Then I heard one of the uniformed fellas say, 'Ah, we got our winter vacation early this year!' Then I started payin' careful attention. The desk person asked, 'What happened?' The officer said, 'Man, it came the biggest snow up there you've ever seen for this time of year, and we had to close the border and all the roads.' I thought, *Man, I ain't gonna sit right here!*

"I'd already cleaned chicken houses and done a bunch of other stuff I didn't wanna do. Now what I was tryin' to do was get more information. I wanted to know where they'd closed the border. I fine'lee waited until one of the officers kinda separated from the rest, walked over there, and started a conversation with him. He didn't know what I was sittin' in there for, and I sure didn't tell 'em. There was a great big map on the wall, showin' the whole territory. I asked him, 'Where do you guys work?' He said, 'At the border on the Top of the World Highway.' Tryin' not to be too obvious, I said, 'Where's that on the map?' He pointed to a place at the border. I said, 'That looks like a pretty long way. How do y'all get there?' He told me everything!

"He said, 'We usually drive Highway 5 to Chicken and then east straight to the border. We had to close the border this mornin' because of all this snow. It's really bad out there.' I tried to not act too interested. I just nodded a bit and sat back down. I knew because the highway was closed there wouldn't be any custom agents on either side of the border. Most of them roads, when they say they're closed, either have a gate with a padlock or a cable across it. Either way, I was gonna go through it. I got in my mind, *I have my Winchester 30-30 in the car, and I have a hacksaw. If the gate is locked, I'm gonna take the 30-30 and shoot the lock off. If it has a cable across it, I'm gonna take the hacksaw and saw it in two.* I made up my mind right there, 'I'm gonna try to go over the Top of the World Highway.' The border agents left, and I waited 'til the people behind the counter looked busy helpin' others, and I just walked out."

Drastic circumstances call for drastic measures, like shooting locks off gates, hacksawing through cables, and driving hundreds of miles through toe-tingling terrain in three feet of snow in a very suspect Nash Rambler.

"I filled the Rambler up as full of gas as I could in Tok and got five gallons extra. I had a five-gallon can with me. I got my map and looked it over carefully. I'd heard tourists on the Kenai talkin' about the Top of the World Highway, but I'd never seen it. I saw a fella standin' by the pumps and asked, 'Do you think I can make it over the Top of the World Highway?' He said, 'Man, naw, not a chance in your rig! I came through there three days ago with four-wheel drive and barely made it. It's a lot worse now.' I didn't have no other options, so I pulled out of Tok headed north on the Taylor Highway. It started snowin' hard again, and I was pulling the string I'd rigged for the wipers so I could even see. There wasn't another vehicle on the road. I got past Chicken, and the snow was gettin' deeper and deeper.

"I fine'lee made it to some buildings and rubbed the fog off the window. I looked out there and a sign said, 'Top of the World Highway.' The gate wasn't even locked, so I didn't have to do nothin' but drive on through. It was dark and so much snow you couldn't even see the road. I was still pullin' the string to keep the snow off the windshield. I was tryin' to stay out of deep ditches and avoid any dropoffs. I'd be goin' up some of them big mountains, and the speedometer would drop from forty miles an hour down to thirty, down to twenty, and sometimes I wouldn't be goin' but about five miles per hour up them mountains. I thought, *I could walk faster than this car can go up this mountain.* But I'm sure glad I wasn't walkin! Once I'd get to the top of a big mountain, it was completely the opposite. I'd just coast down 'em. It was so dark and hard to see, if I'd wrecked or run off the road, there'd been nobody to help me.

"I fine'lee got to the Canadian border way after dark. I rubbed the frost and fog off the inside of the window and looked, and nobody was there either! The gate was wide open, so I just drove right on through. I kept goin'. On one of them high mountains, I started spinnin' before I got to the top, and the Rambler was just barely movin'. When I got to the top, I got out and let some air out of the tires, and that helped me get a little better traction on the next mountain. The snow was so deep, the Rambler was actually pushin' it like a snowplow. I don't know how the ole' Rambler kept goin', but she did. The crack in the block was doin' just fine as long as it stayed cold.

"I drove and drove and noticed the gas gauge gettin' close to empty, so when I got to the top of the next mountain, I stopped and poured the five gallons from the can in there. It didn't seem like I was gettin' very good gas mileage. I guess the car was havin' to work too hard. The best I could tell, I still had more than fifty miles to go, and I was worried I'd run out of gas, get stuck, or slide off one of them giant cliffs."

CROSSING THE YUKON RIVER

"I fine'lee got down to the Yukon River sometime around midnight, and I could see the Dawson City lights across the river. I drove up there and said to myself, *This ain't right!* So, I backed up, turned around, and tried to pull off at another place, and that's when I realized there wouldn't no bridge there! I thought, *Lord, what am I gonna do now?* The gas gauge was now below empty. I thought, *There ain't but one thing to do.* I got out and untied the canoe and pulled it down to the water.

"It was completely dark, and I couldn't see a thing but the lights over there in Dawson City. I got in and started paddlin' across. I could feel the strong current; big chunks of ice were hittin' the side of the canoe. But I was glad it wasn't frozen over. I guess if it was, I could have tried the motorcycle. I focused on the lights in Dawson City, but the current was so strong it pushed me way further down. I fine'lee got across and paddled up the other side, where I could see the lights. I pulled the canoe up the bank and tried to hide it a little bit. My feet got soaking wet and felt like they were gonna freeze off. I walked up the road toward the lights."

CAPTAIN NELSON

"The only thing open after midnight were bars. I walked into the first one, wet and shaking. It was easy to tell I caught the attention of all the customers. I sat down on the first barstool and ordered a beer. I think I asked for a Schlitz. The bartender said, 'Ah, we don't have any American beers; we only have Canadian.' I said, 'Give me one of them Canadian ones, then.' He said, 'What kind you want, mate?' I looked up there on the sign, and I saw one that said 'Blue.' I said, 'Give me one of them Blues.' He sat it down on the bar, and I reached in my pocket and put an American twenty on the counter. The bartender said, 'I can change that, but it will be in Canadian.' I said, 'That's fine.' He gave me change in bills and coins, and I left the coins sittin' there. What I was really tryin' to do was get information; I didn't even want no beer. But I knew to get the information I was wantin', I needed to look as normal as possible."

I don't think Moon looked very normal!

"I fine'lee said, 'What'd a fella do if he was wantin' to get his car across the Yukon River?' The bartender said, 'I don't know why you'd want over there, there's not a thing but more wilderness, and the road's already impassable.' I said, 'Well I ain't wantin' over there. I'm over here, but my car is over there.' He looked at me kinda funny; I think he thought I'd already had too much to drink. He fine'lee said, 'The only way you gonna be able to do that is see Captain Nelson. He put the ferry up a few days ago. He's been drunk for two or three days, and he's prob'ly in one of these bars around here somewhere.' I said, 'Well, which one does he hang out in mostly?' He said, 'I imagine, the Borealis.' I said, 'Where'd that be?' He said, 'It's right down the street about the third or fourth block on the right. You'll see the sign.'

"I handed him a bill and left the beer sittin' there and walked down the street 'til I saw a sign that said, 'Borealis.' I walked in and said, 'Give me one of them Blues there, neighbor.' He sat it on the counter, and I sipped a little bit and asked, 'Where'd I find a Captain Nelson?' He said, 'That's him back there in the booth with the captain's hat on.' I sipped on the beer and thought.

I asked, 'What's the Captain drinkin'?' He said, 'Lord Calvert.' I handed him some bills and told 'em, 'I wanna buy one for the captain, and while you're at it, get me one too.'

"He took the money, poured me one, sat it on the bar, and then made the captain one and took it back there to him. I was watchin' and saw the bartender pointin' toward me. The captain looked at me and raised his glass. I raised mine toward him. The bartender came back, and I kept glancin' back there at the captain, tryin' not to be too obvious. After I got mine down pretty low, I told the bartender, 'Give the captain another one.' He took it back, and the captain looked and held his glass up again, and I held mine up again. I sat there and finished my drink and then told the bartender, 'Give me another one, give me two of 'em, and I'll take 'em back.'

"I put more money on the bar, walked back, and sat in the booth opposite the captain. I sat the drink down for him, and he looked up and didn't say a thing. I didn't know quite what to say, so I told 'em, 'I'm tryin' to get across the river.' He looked at me and said, 'You don't wanna go over there; you can't go nowhere when you get there.' I said, 'My car is over there.' He looked kinda surprised and said, 'How'd you get over *here*?' I said, 'I paddled my canoe.' I think that impressed him a little bit because he said, 'Okay, we might be able to see about that. I just shut the ferry down a couple of days ago.'

"I told 'em, 'I live in Mississippi, and they wouldn't let me cross at the other place. They told me the snow was too deep on the road.' I sat there a little bit, and he said, 'Do you wanna go down to the ...,' I don't know what he called it, but he was talkin' about another bar. I said, 'Yeah, I'll go.' I really didn't want to go, but at that point, it was kinda like if he wanted me to stand on my head, I'd a tried it. So, we went down there, and I bought him another drink. We sat in there a while, and he wanted to know how I'd made it over the road and across the border in all the snow, and I told him the whole story. He said, 'And ya' drivin' a Nash Rambler, eh?' I said, 'Yep.' He said, 'I'll get you across the river.'

"We walked out and back down the street, and I thought we were heading to the ferry, but he went into another bar. A lot of people in there knew him, and they just stood around laughin' and talkin'. I stood there and acted like I was one of the captain's friends. He talked a while, and by now, I was hopin' he'd hurry up. I looked out the window, and it was just gettin' light. Fine'lee, he said, 'Let's go.' We walked down to the ferry, and he said, 'A couple more days like this, and the river will be solid ice.' The captain fired her up, and we headed across the Yukon. He let down the ramp on the other side, and I walked down and started the Rambler and drove her on. I was worried about runnin' out of gas on the ferry. So, I turned it off soon as I got on. He pulled up the gate, and we headed back across. By now, it was gettin' pretty light outside.

"I drove her off on the other side, but I still had to load the canoe, so I didn't go up the hill. I just pulled over on some gravel beside the road. I helped him tie the ropes back on the ferry. The captain said, 'It was good to meet you. I hope you have good luck on the rest of your trip.' I said, 'Do I need to pay you anything?' He said, 'You already did that.' I said, 'I don't know what I'd done without you. Thank you and I'll see you later.' I knew I never would, but I still think about Captain Nelson sometimes."

In Moon's death-defying adventures, like in his poker-playing prowess, he's learned precisely when to "hold 'em" and when to "call 'em." "Fold 'em" is not part of his vocabulary! Having observed his behavior over the years, it seems to me the more dire the circumstances, the more exhilarated Moon becomes. He's willing to make everything subservient to the task at hand— risk, depravation, even death. Imagine being alone in the dark, on the wrong side of the Yukon, more than a hundred miles from civilization of any sort, in deep snow, on a terrifying road deemed impassable by the authorities, in a suspect Nash Rambler. The prospects of being stranded in a snowbank in subzero temperatures more probable than not.

I recalled, *The stuff you have to have becomes the stuff that weighs you down, and if you let it, will eventually steal all your freedom.*

I'd never considered this might include your life. Your own frozen corpse beside the Top of the World Highway or drowning in the icy Yukon are prices

Moon is willing to pay. I remembered Moon's former comments about Mack's cousin Larry: "I guess we all hope to die doin' what we love."

GERMAN HITCHHIKER

"It took me a lot longer to load the canoe than take it down. By the time I got it tied on, the sun was all the way up. I was still worried about running out of gas, but I knew if I did, I could take the can and get some more. I drove up the hill and somehow managed to get to a station without runnin' out. I filled the Rambler up and aired up the tires. By now it was almost lunchtime, and I was feelin' really sleepy."

This means Moon hasn't slept more than an hour or two for the previous several days. There comes a point when iron determination and Folger's coffee crystals will no longer suffice. He must sleep.

"I pulled out of the station and heard sirens screaming. I looked in my rearview mirror, and two police cars were comin' up fast behind me, their lights flashin'. I thought, *Man they're comin' after me!* That's what you always think when you've done somethin' wrong. I pulled to the side, and they went right on by!

"I headed down to Whitehorse to get back on the ALCAN. I got to Whitehorse 'bout dark. I pulled over, got my sleepin' bag, left my coat on, and went to sleep on the car seat.

"The next mornin' when I got back on the ALCAN, I picked up a German hitchhiker, and he was a big ole' strong fella. He could speak English better than I could, but it was hard to understand his accent. He rode with me all the way down into Montana. My plan that day was to keep drivin' and drive all night. We were drivin' and drivin' and drivin', and just as it was gettin' daylight again, I noticed ahead the cars were all stopped and backed up. I looked up the long hill, and a big eighteen-wheeler had run off on the side and hit a big rock, and the trailer was jackknifed across both lanes. Couldn't no traffic get by in either direction.

"There was a lot of snow, and people were out of their cars beside fires they'd built to stay warm. Some of 'em had been sittin' there all night. I talked to a few people and then walked all the way up the line to the truck. I started lookin' around and noticed pretty steep shoulders on both sides of the road. But down below, it was pretty flat all the way up through there. The snow was a little deep in some places, but patchy in others. The wind had blown most of it up against the road. I walked down the bank to the flat part and then walked all the way back to the car. I knew I could get the car down in there, but I knew the biggest problem would be gettin' it back up on the road.

"The big German fella was leaning on the car, and I said, 'I believe we can make it around the cars and truck by gettin' down in the ditch.' I told 'em, 'I might need you to do a little pushin'.' He said that'd be fine. I let air out of the tires again; that keeps 'em from spinnin' so much. I started the Rambler and pulled down in there, and the German got behind me and started pushin'. The car spun a little goin' through the drifts, but that fella could really push. A lot of folks were lined up watchin'. We made it all the way past the line of cars and the truck, and I kept goin' until I saw a patchy spot. I stopped, left the engine runnin', got out, and told the big German fella, 'Get around on the passenger's side and hold weight against the top to keep me from turnin' over.' He got out and leaned against it, and I picked out the best angle, and we went right up it. We didn't even spin but just a little bit right before we got back on the road. I stopped and let the German in and decided not to pump the tires up right then because the road was still pretty bad. That's another thing that comes in handy on the ALCAN: a bicycle pump.

"I drove on down the ALCAN goin' about thirty-five or forty. I don't ever drive as fast as most people. I got about thirty miles or so, and it wouldn't too long before a car would pass me and then another. Some cars looked familiar, and then I realized they did the same thing we did to get around the jackknifed truck. They all honked and waved as they passed us, and we'd honk and wave back. We stopped in a café I always go to at what they call the 'zero-mile,' close to Dawson Creek. Some of the same people were there, and I guess they recognized my car."

It would have been difficult to not recognize Moon's car and the additional accoutrements!

"When me and the German fella walked in there, the people stood up and started clappin'. I thought, *Man, if you saw what I've already been through, you'd realize goin' up that bank wouldn't nothin'.*

"We crossed the border at Sweetgrass, Montana. They didn't care my driver's license were expired because I'm an American citizen. I told 'em I'd been in Alaska a coupla' years. I let the German fella out somewhere in Montana, I think Billings. I told him, 'Good luck.' He said, 'I hope we'll meet again one day.' I told him, 'Me too.' He was a good pusher."

Rambler Graveyard

"I headed southeast on Interstate 90 toward South Dakota. It was maybe fifty or sixty degrees, and the temperature gauge in the Rambler started goin' way up. I tried slowing down, but the crack in the block just couldn't handle the higher temperatures. It got dark again, and the ole' Rambler fine'lee just played out goin' up a big hill. I pulled her off the road as far as I could and laid down on the seat and went to sleep. A little while after daylight, somebody pecked on the window and woke me up. It was the highway patrolman. I raised up and rolled down the window, and he asked, 'What happened?' I told him most of the story. He smiled and shook his head, 'Do you need a pull across this hill? There's a little town on the other side.' I said, 'Well, thank you.'

"He hooked his patrol car to the Rambler and pulled me up the interstate over the hill and down a ramp, right into a station. A bunch of local rancher types were in there drinkin' coffee and lookin'. I guess they were wonderin' what was goin' on. They didn't say much, but I could tell they were really watchin'. I tried the engine again, and it wouldn't say nothin'. I got out and went in and explained to all of them lookers what I was doin'. I asked a fella who seemed to be the boss, 'Will this car be all right here until I hitchhike down to Sioux Falls to see if I can buy another car?' A large fella in overalls said, 'You don't have to go that far, I'll sell you one.' I asked, 'How much you want for it?' He said, 'All I can get.' I said, 'Yeah, that's what I thought, where is it?' He said, 'Well, it's out on my farm.' I asked the boss fella again, 'Will mine be all right sittin' here?' He said, 'Yeah, ain't nobody gonna bother it.' I got in the farmer's truck, and we drove about ten miles out a dirt road to his farm. He said, 'I'll sell you this one right here.' It was a two-ton Chevy pickup that looked like the ole' Apache I used to own, but with a bigger engine. I asked, 'How much you want for it?' He said, 'I'll take $400.' I said, 'I'll give you $200.' He came down to $300, and I ended up giving him $225. I knew my money was tight, and that truck would burn a lot of gas. I noticed a big fuel tank with five-gallon cans sitting beside it. He sold me eight cans of cheap farm gasoline for fifty cents a gallon! I gave him $2.50 a can and loaded 'em in the back of the truck.

"I still had to go and get all the stuff out of the Rambler and get the canoe and motorcycle loaded in the truck. I went through the papers in the Rambler to make sure I wasn't leavin' nothin' important behind. A fella walked out and offered me thirty dollars for the Rambler. I tried to get fifty, but you can't get nothin' for a car when they know they've got ya'. I took the money and signed the title and handed it to him. I've always wondered whatever happened to the Rambler; I wished I still had it."

Like Mack, Moon is a shrewd trader. He also has a nostalgic relationship with every car or boat he's ever owned. Like the stray dogs, the suspect vehicles required his devoted attention just to keep them running. In his mind, there's an inextricable link between his vehicles and fish. Most of his vehicles smelled like it too!

"From the time I drove the truck off the farm, I never bought no more gas. I poured in the last can in Grenada, Mississippi, and made it on into Ackerman."

CHAPTER 24

REACQUAINTANCE

ACKERMAN — LATE FALL 1976

MOON PULLED UP IN FRONT OF OUR HOUSE in Reform in the Chevy two-ton and honked the horn. I hadn't seen him in almost two years, most of the time battling fear he might no longer be alive. I ran outside. I was surprised; he looked different, like a combination between Chris Christopherson and Charles Manson, long hair and a very long unkempt beard. A strange, ugly emotion swirled in the pit of my gut—*You're going to have to earn the right to reenter my life.*

"Man, you've grown. Ty wrote me a letter and told me you were playin' football."

"Yeah. What happened to the Rambler?"

"It played out in South Dakota, and I had to leave it behind."

"Where'd you get the motorcycle?"

"Somebody stole it and left it in the woods by the Kenai. The police told me I could have it."

"I see the canoe is looking good."

"Yeah, I used it to get across the Yukon River. You know a fella never knows when he might need a boat."

I thought, *Yeah, and a boy never knows when he might need a father too.*

CARROLL COUNTY WATERSHED

In the early spring of '77, we took a fishing trip to a lake in Carroll County, Mississippi. We were esteemed guests because on a previous trip, Moon helped rescue a Charlet bull buried in the mud beside the lake. You don't ignore things like that even if you happen to be trespassing in order to fish.

The bull was in bad shape, completely exhausted from trying to free himself from the deep, sticky mud. Moon walked to the nearby farmhouse and told the rancher he'd found his bull buried in the mud beside the lake. The rancher thanked him and asked Moon if he'd help attempt to free the bull. The rancher drove his tractor as close to the bull as possible without sinking in the mud. Moon dug and strained in the smelly muck until he was able to get two straps underneath the bull's midsection. Once secured, the rancher pulled slowly backward with the tractor. Moon wrapped his arms around the bull's neck, coaxing the exhausted beast to try again. Slowly but surely, they freed the bull from his muddy grave. The rancher told Moon he could fish the lake anytime he wanted.

"That bull was prob'ly worth $3,000."

I was just glad to know we were free to fish without constantly looking over our shoulders. We traveled down a field road and pulled the car underneath a canopy of tall sycamore trees. From the outset, something was perfect about the trip. The hint of honeysuckle aloft, I filled my lungs with the crisp clean air, the hot sun warming my shoulders. Beside the lake, the light green willow leaves danced in the slight breeze. The rippled water lapped gently against the shore, the tingling sticks calling like wind chimes.

After a tin of sardines, we loaded our gas-mask satchels with a variety of lures, mainly spinner baits, and carefully waded into the slightly stained water. I was fifteen and eager to put my lifetime apprenticeship on display. As I waded past the brush, emerging lily pads dotted the shallow gray water, which was cool but not cold. Moon's rod arched, and he landed a nice pre-spawn three-pound bass.

"Man, it looks like they're in here!"

I pulled my green spinner bait high in the water past a small group of lily pads. Whamo! I landed a short, fat two-pounder.

"We keepin' 'em?"

"Well, I don't see why not."

I took nylon cord from my pants pocket and tied the fish to my side. Next cast to the same spot, I landed another one about the same size. I slipped the nylon string through its mouth, pulled it down beside the first bass, and tied the string back to my waist. The fish tugged against my side, surfaced, and splashed; water drops hit my face and dripped off my chin. Several minutes later, I added a third and fourth bass.

Landing the fifth, I reached down to locate the string on my side, it was gone. In my haste to catch another one, I hadn't secured it.

"What happened, Shane?"

"I guess I didn't get the string tight enough on the last fish."

"Don't worry; there's plenty in here. That one's bigger anyway. Get another string and tie him on."

We fished all day, filling our strings with bass and tying them off on bushes in waist-deep water to keep the turtles at bay. As the sun dipped low on the western horizon, we waded back toward the car, stopping at our selected bushes, releasing the smaller ones, and keeping the bigger ones. We put our fish in an old cooler, drove to a country store, bought dinner and a bag of ice, and packed down the day's catch.

That night, we slept in the car beside the lake, swatting the occasional mosquito and listening to owls stalking their nightly prey. The world was right. Moon and I were together and catching fish. I slept like a baby.

Next morning, we awoke to distant caws of crows and blue jays in the thickets, making enough disturbance to raise the dead. Wisps of fog rose from the warm gray water, disappearing into the cooler air above. A warm breeze brushed my face, the lily pads seemed more visible than the previous day, like they'd magically grown in the night.

I selected a green double-bladed spinnerbait, and we waded out into the water. The weather was an exact repeat of the previous day, the fishing even better. In shallow water, we noticed where big bass, preparing to spawn, had fanned out spots in the emerging lily pads. I cast slightly past a spot, turned the pearl white handles of my red Ambassador 5000 a couple of times, and a whirlpool surfaced as the giant bass grabbed the lure. I landed it.

"Shane, that fish will go over eight pounds! Nice job, is that the biggest bass you've ever caught?"

I tried but couldn't hold back a huge smile. I laughed out loud.

"Yeah, yeah it is!"

We fished until midafternoon, collected our fish, and waded toward the car, a good kind of tired. We stopped by the same country store and purchased more ice and a cold sandwich and drove north toward Ackerman. I slept; Moon listened to Tom T. Hall. It was dark when we pulled up the driveway to Moon's house.

"Spend the night, and I'll clean all these in the mornin."

THE CHOCTAW PLAINDEALER

Next morning, Moon laid the fish on the ground in the front yard, and we snapped a few pictures.

Moon and me with Carroll County, Mississippi, bass.

"You can keep as many as you want. I know people who'd really like some; I'll take the rest to them."

I was so proud of two bass in the nine-pound range, I asked, "Daddy, do you mind if I take these two down to the *Plaindealer* office and get a picture taken?"

I suppose I had something to prove.

"Yeah, but don't dare tell anyone where we caught 'em."

"Okay, I know not to do that."

I walked in and told the receptionist I had two big fish in the car and asked if they'd like a picture. Fish pictures, like murder stories, sold papers, at least in Ackerman.

"Sure, let me get the camera."

"Okay, I'll get the fish."

"My lands, those are huge bass! Now Shane, our subscribers are gonna want to know where you caught these."

"Yes, ma'am."

I should've given prior thought to exactly how I'd answer the inevitable question. Akin to tall tales, creative lying is an acceptable high art form among the fishing faithful. However, my usual preferred arsenal, silence and gestures, were off the table unless I wanted to come across like a complete imbecile. From the hierarchy of acceptable lies, I tried to make a swift analysis of my available options.

"I caught 'em in the same place, right in the side of their mouth?"

No, that's horrible! I needed a lie strong enough to convince my inquirer, while maintaining a semblance of reputation, while not revealing the location of our secret fishing hole. Did my slight hesitation betray me?

"Oh, I caught them at the little spillway at Choctaw Lake."

Perfect choice, her face revealing she had swallowed the bait—hook, line, and sinker. Moreover, the serious fishing crowd would skeptically analyze the photo anyway.

When Friday's edition of the paper rolled out, there it was right on the front page of the paper in public print, a bold-faced lie! The caption read, "Shane Sunn caught these two beautiful 9lb. bass while fishing yesterday at Choctaw Lake."

I might have felt a twinge of guilt, but I remembered Moon's former instruction:

"Lyin's a sin, but sometimes bendin' the truth a little is necessary in the fishin' world."

I thought, *At least the sale of park passes might double next week at Choctaw Lake from those gullible enough to believe the tall tale.* For the next several weeks, my popularity grew in Ackerman.

"Shane, did Moon catch those fish?"

"No, I did."

"At Choctaw Lake?"

I answered with only a nod and suggestive smile, leaving them to interpret the truth for themselves.

"I do declare, you're a chip off the old block."

The compliment felt good, right, even strangely mystical, as I sought to discern my place in God's universe. Growing in my confidence and ability to catch big bass, the fish themselves served as trophies of identity.

I'm somebody because I can catch big bass. Or was I somebody because I was Moon Sunn's son? Which was it? What was it?

PAIN AND SHAME

Several weeks later, Moon invited me over for hamburgers. Although he'd always taught me to stay away from alcohol, which I hadn't, he was visibly intoxicated.

As we sat on the patio, waiting for the burgers, Moon said, "Shane, let's see how fast you can run."

Annoyed and with nothing better to do, I accepted the challenge.

"We need a long flat place."

We walked down the driveway to the paved street in front of the house.

"Are you ready, Shane?"

"Yeah, I guess."

"On your mark, get set, go!"

We raced straight down the street. He got the jump, but in ten yards, I passed him. Moon tried to speed up, lost his balance, and fell face down on the pavement. He skinned his hands and chin. I stopped, walked back, and looked down at him. Rather than feeling any sympathy at all, I felt scorn and shame. What do you say? I couldn't say anything. I helped him to his feet. He brushed himself off. His chin and hands were bleeding.

"Man, you're pretty fast."

I didn't want to care what he thought.

"Let's check on the burgers."

We walked slowly up the drive under the canopy of tall pecans. Dark clouds gathered, thunder rumbled in the distance, large intermittent raindrops bounced on the graveled drive ahead of the approaching storm. Somewhere inside, I was attempting to reconcile this moment with two weeks prior.

That time or this time? That man or this man?

From the deep recesses of our childhood memories, we all experience moments that somehow define us. For years, I looked back on this painful moment, and I'm certain as we walked up the drive, I told myself, *You're not a very good daddy.* I internalized the pain still more. *From this day forward, I will be my own daddy, thank you very much.*

As we approached the patio, smoke poured from the grill; the hamburgers were completely torched. Moon decided to take me to a local diner and order dinner. I was reluctant, but we went anyway. We ran to the car in the pouring rain. As we walked into the diner, it was obvious to the local patrons he was drunk; at least it was to me. We ordered, sat down, and waited. Silence.

Moon looked at me, "Shane, are you ashamed of me?"

I hesitated, "No, why'd you ask?"

The truth was, I was. A familiar ugly pattern took root and grew.

In his book, *The Sacred Journey*, Frederick Buechner describes our collective response to pain this way: "To do for yourself the best that you have it in you to do—to grit your teeth and clench your fists in order to survive the world at its harshest and worst—is, by that very act, to be unable to let something else be done for you and in you that is more wonderful still. The trouble with steeling yourself against the harshness of reality is that the same steel that secures your life against being destroyed secures your life also against being opened up and transformed by the holy power that life itself comes from."[11]

At that juncture, I didn't have a clue about what was going on inside.

---

11 Frederick Buechner, *The Sacred Journey: A Memoir of Early Days* (New York: Harper One Publishers, 1991), 167.

AUTUMN FISHIN', GEOLOGY, AND HISTORY LESSONS

A couple of months later, Moon announced, "Shane, it's startin' to cool off. I think we should go to that lake near Walnut; it cools down up there a little sooner. Cooler weather makes the fish turn on, fattin' up for winter."

We loaded up before daylight and drove to Walnut. Walnut, Mississippi, is less than twenty miles from the Tennessee state line. Summer days shortening, the "dog days" loosening their grip, a hint of fall in the air, the very light of the sun seemed different.

Moon is a keen observer of flora and fauna. Around noon, he waded toward me, holding something in his hand. I knew something was up by the way he approached.

He waded up beside me, "Shane, look at this!"

He opened his clenched fist, revealing a handful of sharks' teeth he'd dug from a clay bank beside the lake.

Gesturing with his arms, he said, "Shane, the ocean used to cover all this. I bet Hernando de Soto and his men traveled right along here 450 years ago. This used to be Chickasaw territory. The Chickasaw were more warlike than the Choctaw. American settlers arrived here earlier than other parts of Mississippi, and there were lots of skirmishes with the Chickasaw. Finally, in 1837, at the Treaty of Doaksville, the Chickasaw purchased land from the Choctaws and resettled in Choctaw territory. That was the beginning of their demise, and they were never the same after that. The Chickasaw didn't stay in Choctaw land long. The Indian Removal Act passed, and the Chickasaw Nation walked the Trail of Tears, just like the Choctaw Nation did. When that land greed gets in your blood, there ain't no stoppin' it."

That day beside the lake in Walnut, Mississippi, Moon told the story of the Chickasaw with such elucidation I could visualize a real war party on the shore beside the lake, and in some small way felt the Trail of Tears. But it wasn't only his vivid account; it was the whole experience: the crisp autumn day, the sunlight, the water, the fish, the sharks' teeth, the history, the fishing. The detectable changing of the seasons and the stories summoned a sense that something mysterious, yet real, was coming just over the horizon.

Moon's philosophy of education, of motion combined with history and stories, worked with me. I've never forgotten his descriptions. Late that autumn afternoon, as the orange sun sank in the west and long gray shadows spread across the water, I remember a discernable softening of my protected heart. We loaded our fishing gear, bound for Ackerman.

CHAPTER 25

PURPLE DODGE DART

"IN '79, THE YEAR YOU GRADUATED from high school, I went to Alaska in the purple Dodge Dart I bought from Charles Moody. I was teachin' at the vo-tech and had to wait for my final check before I could leave."

I thought about the year I graduated high school and the couple of years preceding. By this point, I was more independent and busier with my own life and didn't see Moon nearly as often. I had a driver's license and drove to work, football, and baseball practice. Another significant life-changing event had taken place sometime during my junior year. With help from my friends, my dormant faith came to life, grew, and gained fervency. I became more emotionally settled, realizing God was superintending all things, big and small, some exhilarating, others disappointing.

Moon continued, "I knew it was gonna be a challenge to get there in the Dart because it rode so low to the ground. Going, I made it fine, the problem happened on the return trip. I fished 'til the very last day before I had to be back for the first day of class."

This really means Moon fished until the very last minute possible and then some.

Moon with a king in front of his purple Dodge Dart.

HITCHHIKER

"To drive 4,500 miles without stoppin', you gotta pick up a hitchhiker. I picked up a Canadian fella who wanted a ride to Fort Nelson. When I crossed the border headed home, I exchanged nearly all my money for Canadian so I wouldn't get stranded in Canada. I thought I would have time to exchange it back when I got into the United States, but that was a mistake.

"We were drivin' along, and the back left tire blew out. We ended up forty feet down in a rocky canyon. We nearly turned over, and I think we would of, had it not been for the big rocks. Fine'lee, a man in a new pickup with a big powerful winch stopped and pulled us out. I had to fix four flats and pump up the tires with a bicycle pump. After I fixed the flats, I turned the key and the Dart started right up. But it only went about a hundred feet and quit.

"What happened was it only ran on the gas still in the carburetor. I realized the rocks had torn up a bunch of things under the car. At first, I thought it was the fuel line. I worked and worked. I hitchhiked to a junkyard and bought a fuel line. I put on and took off three fuel lines, and nothin' worked. I fine'lee thought, *I ain't gonna get this thing fixed.*

"Then I decided maybe it was the fuel pump. I went back to the junkyard, and this time, I got three fuel pumps so I wouldn't keep havin' to go back and forth. One of the pumps was off a big Chrysler. I put it on, and the Dart started right up.

"By now, I didn't have time to make the entire trip and get back for the first day of class. I took the hitchhiker to Fort Nelson and then had to drive all the way back to Alaska. It took me a whole day and night.

"I knew I couldn't leave the Dart at the airport in Anchorage, so I drove all the way to Soldotna to Charles Calloway's house. It was locked. Just when I was leavin' to go lookin' for Charles, he drove up in his truck. He said, 'Moon, I thought you left here four days ago.' I told him, 'I did, but I'm back. I had a blowout and a bunch of other trouble.' I told him the whole story."

I'm sure he did. Every detail!

I told him, 'My problem is I have to be at school to teach the day after tomorrow. I need to get to the airport as soon as I can.' He said, 'I'll take you; let me make a few calls.' I left the Dart in Charles's yard, and he drove me to Anchorage."

MONEY EXCHANGE PROBLEM

"We got to the airport late that evenin'. I walked in and looked at the board that lists all the flights. The flight I needed from Anchorage left the next mornin' at 7:00 a.m., arrivin' in Jackson, Mississippi, around 10:00 p.m. It had a big layover somewhere.

"I pulled out my money to buy the ticket, and that's the first time I realized I'd forgotten to exchange it. I only had Canadian, and they wouldn't take it. I think the flight was about $600 or somethin'. The lady said, 'The exchange office opens at 8:30 in the mornin'.' I said, 'Yeah, but the flight I need leaves at 7:00.' She said, 'There's another flight that leaves at 11:00 a.m.' I looked at it, but it wouldn't get me to Jackson 'til the next mornin', the same mornin' I was supposed to be teachin'. I said, 'That won't do.' Then she said, 'We're closin' in ten minutes.' I sat down and wondered what I was a gonna do. I noticed a Japanese girl and walked over to her and said, 'I'll give you all my Canadian money if you will give me $600 US.' She said, 'How much ya' got?' I counted it out in front of her, I think about $675. She realized it was a good deal. I walked over and bought the ticket.

"I slept on the floor that night and got on the plane the next mornin', and there was hardly anybody else on there. The stewardess asked me if I wanted to sit in first class. I told her, 'Yeah, I reckon so.' She asked, 'Would you like anything to drink?' I said, 'I know it's pretty early, but I believe I'll have a beer.' I sipped on the beer and fell right to sleep.

"I don't remember where the layover was, but I landed in Jackson about 10:00 p.m. that night. I took a cab to the bus station and rode to Ackerman on the bus and got in about 2:00 a.m. I walked home, took a shower, and tried to find the lesson syllabus. I slept a little bit and took my bike to school and got there at 7:56 a.m."

Who'd even strike out from Mississippi to Alaska in a low-riding Dodge Dart? Like the Rambler, the Dart never returned to Mississippi. It sat in the Calloways' yard for several years. Moon finally sold it for scrap. I'm sure Charles and Alice were elated! The Dart and all Moon's motley vehicles served one purpose: to get you where you were going. For Moon, that's always fishin'.

CHAPTER 26

NORTH TO ALASKA WITH MOON

IN 1982, HAVING SPENT LITTLE TIME with Moon since enrolling at Ole Miss in the fall of '79, I decided to forgo summer work and go with him to Alaska. The adventure was a talking history lesson filled with major life lessons I didn't anticipate. Christia, my sister, was along for the adventure, at least part of it.

I don't know how many times Moon said, "Right along here is where ..." He'd then launch into a thirty-minute lecture. He knew details of every treaty signed and broken with native peoples, including names and dates. I also learned important details about my own life—details you miss when you don't grow up with your dad in the same house.

"Your momma wanted to name you Dudley Patrick. Dudley after your grandma, and she just liked the name Patrick. She wanted to call you Pat. I thought that sounded too much like a sissy. I really wanted to name you Shane. I liked the movie *Shane* so much, with Alan Ladd and ole' Jack Palance. You know at the end of the movie, Brandon deWilde, who played the little boy, says to Alan Ladd [Shane], 'Come back, Shane, come back!' So, I guess we kinda compromised and that's how you got named Dudley Shane."

I listened and silently wondered if more was in play. Why did *this* specific scene appeal to Moon so much? Was Mack Alan Ladd and Moon Brandon deWilde? Or was Moon Alan Ladd and me Brandon deWilde? History has a way of repeating itself. One thing was certain, we both identified with the painful scene. But could either of us see past ourselves to the person sitting beside us on the truck seat now?

We pulled out of Ackerman in the old two-toned, light-blue-on-darker-blue Dodge pickup, bound for Alaska—a truck camper attached, the yellow canoe tied on top. Road distance from Ackerman to Soldotna, Alaska: 4,260 miles. We descended Moon's driveway on Louisville Street as the last light of day turned to darkness.

"I try to stay off interstate highways; them people drive too fast. I try to avoid them big cities too."

We headed west toward Winona and turned due north on US 51.

"I think we will follow the Mississippi River as far as we can and then head for Duluth, Minnesota. When you cross the bridge in Duluth, you can see Lake Superior. We'll cross the border in International Falls, Minnesota, then head west across southern Canada. I think the little town just across the border is called Fort Frances, Ontario. We'll drive through five Canadian provinces before we get to Alaska: Ontario, Manitoba, Saskatchewan, Alberta, British Columbia, and the Yukon. The Yukon isn't really a province, but a territory, so four provinces and one territory."

I guess Moon thought his kids needed to see as much of Canada as possible.

"I've got enough gas money and a little extra for food, if we need any. I've got salami and cheese in the icebox. I told 'em at the school to mail my next check to Soldotna. It oughta' arrive a week or so after we get there."

"Yeah, okay."

I MIGHT BE SLOW BUT I'M AHEAD OF YOU

Twenty years old and full of myself, I felt obliged to challenge Moon's every word. Like a good skeptic, I wondered about the sanity of MPPF and MPE.

Sometime after midnight near Cairo, Illinois, we missed a turn and drove in circles for more than an hour, crossing the various forks of the Mississippi River numerous times.

"Shane, I thought we crossed this bridge already?"

"Yeah, but we were headed the other direction."

"Are you sure?"

"No, but I think so."

"Hand me the damned map!"

We finally figured it out, but I had a growing realization Moon wasn't going to quit driving. The problem was he was going too dang slow. I was itching to get behind the wheel and shorten the trip.

"Shane, it's important on these long trips not to drive too fast but keep a steady pace."

He shared his philosophy freely. A sticker on the truck's back bumper read, "I Might Be Slow but I'm Ahead of You." Frustration building, I decided to challenge his philosophy.

"That stupid bumper sticker doesn't mean a thing! All people have to do is pass you."

Moon countered, "And then they can't read the bumper sticker no more. On these trips, some cars pass me four or five times."

"Whatever."

I knew we were in for a very long trip, much longer than it needed to be. If he'd only speed up. Most of the time, Christia rode in the camper, and I rode shotgun in the passenger's seat. I'd try to sleep a couple of hours, but every slight bump caused my head to rap against the window, waking me up.

"Daddy, want me to drive?"

"No, I'm fine."

Moon's "I might be slow but I'm ahead of you" philosophy entrenched, frustration and exhaustion combined in my head, producing mutinous thoughts.

How in the world does he keep at it day and night?

Feigning sleep, I heard the creak of a jar lid opening. I cracked one eye. I watched Moon open a jar of Folgers coffee crystals, tilt his head backward, shake the jar, and ingest a large portion. Grimacing, he reached over and chased it with water from the milk jug on the front seat. He repeated the process. My eyes wide open, I stared at him with unconcealed disgust.

He noticed and asked, "Shane, want some coffee?" thrusting the still-opened jar toward me with his right arm.

"No, thank you!"

"Them French fur trappers used coffee to help keep 'em goin'. They had to run trap lines before daylight, so they'd eat a little coffee to help wake themselves up."

"Oh."

UNIVERSAL JOINT

Moon drove and drove. I rode shotgun; Christia slept in the camper. We finally reached Edmonton, Alberta, when Moon announced, "We're almost halfway to Alaska!" He thought he was heralding good news. I fell into an instantaneous depression.

"Shane, how'd you like to drive awhile?"

Did he really just say that!? Ascending from the gloom, I said, "Sure!"

We pulled over, grabbed another salami and cheese sandwich, and exchanged places. Heading north out of Edmonton, I seized the opportunity to implement my own philosophy. I waited until Moon fell asleep and pressed the pedal down on the old Dodge to speed her up. The needle hit seventy miles per hour. I glanced over from time to time to make sure he was still asleep; a feeling of calm control quickly supplanted my former emotions.

Suddenly, as if sent by God, a strange vibration begin to rattle the entire truck. Then, *clank!* Something hit the road below.

From dead sleep, Moon startled, "What happened?"

"I don't know!"

"Quick, coast over to the side of the road!"

I managed to get the truck onto the shoulder, most of it.

"Do you know what happened?"

"No, I was just driving along and started feeling a vibration and then heard a loud bang."

"Well, it looks like the drive shaft has fallen out, must be the universal joint. We're gonna have to get a tow."

"Okay." I silently wondered if he knew my secret.

Christia opened the camper door. "Gosh, I thought we were going to turn over. It scared the shit out of me!"

Moon got out and lifted the hood.

I asked, "Why'd you do that?"

"No one will know we've got trouble unless I lift the hood."

"You don't think they already know that!? We're sticking a foot out into the road!"

Finally, a car pulled over.

"Trouble, eh?"

"Yeah, we need a tow."

"You're a long way from home, eh?"

"Yeah, we're from Mississippi."

"Yeah, I noticed your license plate. Where you headed?"

"Alaska."

"Gee, that's a long way, eh?"

I remembered what Moon said about being almost halfway there.

"I live a couple of miles up the road. I'll send for a tow truck."

"Thank you."

"Good luck."

Part of me wanted to offer a confession; the other part wanted to scream profanities. I settled for a question laced with sarcasm, "What do we do, *now?*"

"We wait. Get in the camper and catch up on your sleep."

Moon opened the passenger door and lay down on the front seat. I was annoyed by how calm he seemed. I climbed into the camper and lay down on the bed extending above the truck cab. When I closed my eyes, a weird sensation enveloped my entire body; it felt like the truck was still in motion, headed to Alaska.

DAMN MECHANIC

The airbrakes of a tow truck announcing its arrival startled me from a short and restless sleep. I forced myself to get up and go outside. I watched as the driver first placed a strap under the truck to lift and secure the drive shaft. He hooked to our truck, and we all climbed in beside him on the front seat. We pulled into a mechanic shop somewhere outside of Edmonton. I wondered how reputable the place was because there weren't any other customers. The mechanic seemed overeager and got right to work.

After three days of salami sandwiches, Christia and I were mesmerized by the candy display sitting on the counter. Our mouths watering, we schemed about how we might purchase a Snickers bar without Moon noticing. The mechanic finished his work quickly and handed Moon the bill. I knew we were in trouble when I saw Moon's eyes narrow and his jaw tighten. He clenched his teeth, his lips slightly parted, and although inaudible, I knew I detected the word, "Damn!"

Moon took an envelope from his left front pocket and handed the man several large bills. The mechanic counted out the change in Canadian.

"Thank you, sir. You've got a long trip, eh?"

"Yeah, we are about halfway there."

Ugh. *I might be slow but I'm ahead of you* pecked away inside my head.

A powwow ensued in the parking lot. Moon counted and recounted his money.

"We may barely have enough money to make it, but we can't spend another dime on food or anything else the rest of the way."

We pulled back onto Canadian Highway 2, Moon driving, me relegated again to the passenger's seat. Late that night, somewhere in the vicinity of Lesser Slave Lake, this time I was startled from sleep by a loud bang. Moon repeated his word, this time audibly. The drive shaft had fallen from the opposite end. We limped over to the side of the rock road in the absolute middle of nowhere.

"I knew that damn mechanic didn't know what he was doin'."

There were no discernable lights in any direction.

I asked, "What do we do now?" this time without a hint of sarcasm.

Moon shook his head. "There's nothing to do but catch up on your sleep."

I detected a look of concern on his face.

"Yeah."

Slowly releasing control, I slept like a baby that evening.

GOOD NEIGHBOR

Early the next morning, an Albertan rancher pulled his dually beside us on the road. It was a cold gray morning, a steady wind blowing across the plains.

"Trouble, eh?"

"Yeah."

"I have a welding machine in my barn; let me give you a tow."

The good rancher towed us to his barn. Christia and I stood beside the warm barrel stove inside. He carefully inspected the scratch-pecked drive shaft. I thought about the traveler in Luke's gospel who fell among thieves and was powerless to do anything to help himself, and then a Good Samaritan happened by.

251

"Your shaft is okay. Your universal joint seems to be the wrong size, but I think I can fix it by adding a little length to the other end of the shaft."

He carefully measured and remeasured the shaft. Selecting pieces from a pile of scrap metal in the corner, he cut and welded, designing a part to lengthen the shaft.

"Well, that ought to do it."

"What do we owe you?"

"Not a thing."

Moon insisted we pay something. He took a fifty-dollar bill from the cash drawer in his front pocket and handed it to the rancher. The rancher handed it back. Moon wouldn't take it. I wasn't so sure that was the right decision.

You Cook a Fine Rabbit, Pilgrim

Powwow two convened as we headed north toward Dawson Creek, Christia sitting between us on the front seat. Moon counted and recounted the remaining money for what seemed like the hundredth time, hoping somehow he'd miscounted.

"Shane, get the map and try to add up the distance from here to Soldotna. We don't have any more money for food."

Christia and I exchanged glances. Verbalizing the obvious somehow penetrated the remaining vestiges of my defenses and awakened me to the sobering reality of our situation.

"I hate to ask, but do y'all happen to have any money?" Moon probed.

"Yeah, I have sixty dollars and some change."

Christia hesitated then said, "I have twenty dollars."

"Well, we're gonna prob'ly need every bit of it."

We handed over our money. He stuffed it in the cash drawer.

"We'll need to shoot rabbits the rest of the way in order to have something to eat."

Our choices were: commence a three- to four-day fast, shoot rabbits and eat them raw, or stop and build a fire in order to roast them. The silver lining of sorts: no more salami and cheese sandwiches and nonstop driving! Moon did mention cooking the rabbits on the engine's manifold. For me, our situation was now entering the terrain of the familiar high adventures I'd experienced with Moon from my youth. Christia couldn't hide her obvious disgust.

Late that afternoon, scores of mottled brown-and white snowshoe hares emerged from the firs to nibble the fresh green shoots along the right-of-way.

"Put a cot-trege in the barrel. Open the door quietly; don't shut it."

Standing beside the truck, I aimed the single shot .22 and scored.

"Go get 'em."

I laid him on the floorboard.

"Let's drive a little further and pick out another one."

Later that evening, we chose a nice pulloff somewhere south of Fort Nelson, British Columbia. Our providential money and food crisis slowing us down, the world reestablished equilibrium. I gathered fallen limbs and started a fire while Moon skinned the rabbits. He rinsed them in the stream, patted them dry with a handkerchief, and covered them with salt and pepper. He skewered them on green alder sticks, slowly twirling them above the glowing coals until they turned golden brown. We passed the skewers around the fire, dining caveman-style, pulling off pieces of the tender flesh and stuffing it into our mouths.

The film *Jeremiah Johnson* came to mind, and I declared, "You cook a good rabbit, pilgrim." Moon smiled and nodded. Bellies full, stars aglow, faces reflecting in the campfire against the backdrop of tall dark firs, the world seemed unflawed. We crawled into bed and slept like kings and queens until morning light.

Next morning, Christia confided in tears, "I don't think I can eat another bite of that damned rabbit."

I really didn't know what to say.

I gave her a hug. "Don't worry too much, things will be okay."

A HONEY BUN

A full night of rest under our belts, abundant fresh mountain air, not a cloud in the sky, we hit the road with a renewed sense of vigor. We made good time, reaching Fort Nelson before noon. Scanning signs for the cheapest gas, we pulled in to refuel and pay the restroom a visit. Walking back toward the truck, I noticed Christia standing behind the passenger side of the camper, trying to quickly scarf down a Honey Bun.

"Whatcha' doin?"

"Are you blind?"

"How'd you get that?"

"I didn't give him all my money; he'd bought salami with it!"

"Give me a bite."

"Okay, but don't tell Daddy."

"I won't."

"Not a big bite. I said, not a big bite."

"Thanks, Christia."

"Load up," Moon announced from the other side of the truck.

We quickly hid the evidential wrapper and piled into the front seat. We exchanged glances. Christia smiled.

THE TOAD RIVER

We clipped along nicely in a more westerly direction.

"Look, see those sheep."

"Yeah!"

"Look at the two big rams. Those are stone sheep. When we get on up into the Yukon, we'll start seeing Dall sheep. They'll look like white specks on the sides of the tall mountains."

"How far do we have to go?"

"It's still a long, long way. That's the Toad River. Look at the spots where there's no ice. See how blue-green the water is? French fur trappers worked this river way back in the early 1800s. Many worked for the Hudson Bay Company. The Toad runs northeast and joins the Liard River and then flows into the mighty Mackenzie, which goes all the way to the Arctic Ocean." Moon assumed the role of expert tour guide, covering subjects of natural history and geography. I was thrilled.

"That's Muncho Lake; it's full of giant lake trout. All that ice will be off in the next week or two."

I was astonished by the cobalt color of the water against the ice and emerald mountains. It appeared like someone had mixed watercolor in a giant bucket and poured it into the lake.

Moon said, "I think that color is caused by copper."

We pulled over at a rest stop for a bathroom break. While we waited for Christia, Moon rummaged in the bear-proof green dumpster in the rock parking lot. He pulled out a full box of stale donuts and went to town on them, quickly stuffing one after another into his mouth like a starved animal. I'd never seen Moon eat donuts; it was a violation of everything he'd ever taught me.

I couldn't help saying, "Those things have mold growing on 'em, besides, they're not good for you!"

Moon countered, "Up in Alaska, sometimes, you never know when you're gonna get to eat again."

I retorted, "They could kill you!"

"All that mold is, is penicillin. It's good for you."

I didn't win the argument, but neither did he convince me to try a mold-covered stale donut!

Looking back, at that point, I had a lot to learn about how Moon survived in Alaska. Also, I realized for the first time, MPPF was adaptable, depending on how dire your circumstances might happen to be.

CHAPTER 27

SOMETIMES GAS IS MORE IMPORTANT THAN FOOD

GRIZZLY ATTACKS

Yukon grizzly fishing for salmon.

RATTLING ALONG AT A SNAIL'S PACE, Moon's voice startled me from half-sleep.

"Right along here is where the man got eaten by the bear last year. Yeah, he was biking from somewhere in the states, I think California, and a grizzly ran out of the woods, knocked him off his bike, and ate him."

Travel weariness setting in again, I reverted to challenge mode. "There's no way that happened!"

"Yeah, it did."

I retorted, "Bears don't chase people on bicycles, and I don't think they eat people either."

"We're gonna stop for gas up here in a few miles. Go in there and ask 'em about it?"

"All right."

We pulled our rig beside the outdated pumps. I got out and headed into the store that looked more like a trapper's cabin, intent on setting Moon straight on what really happened. My first mistake was falling prey to a local trick. Entering the store, I noticed a US quarter lying on the planked floor. I reached down to pick it up, thinking we might need it. It was glued to the floor. A deep, almost forced laugh pealed from a burly bearded Canadian sitting in overalls on a stool behind the counter.

"All you Yankees is after is another dime. Ha, ha, ha."

There aren't many forms of amusement in northern British Columbia, so the residents invent their own. Busted, my all-important question stuck in my throat.

"Ah, ah ... did a man get eaten by a bear—"

Before I finished, the man replied, "Oh yeah, some entomologist was counting butterfly larvae at the Liard Hot Springs the other day, and he wouldn't leave the bears alone. One ate 'em."

"Oh, I thought he was on a bicycle?"

"That was last year. If you wanna know more about it, look over there on the board."

I noticed a corkboard on the log wall with various newspaper articles pinned to it. I walked over and zoomed in on a bolded headline, "Cyclist Killed by Bear." The article described what happened the year before almost exactly like Moon had told it. Other gory details included a bear hunt conducted by the park service for a "man-eating" grizzly. Four bears were exterminated; one contained the remains of the victim.

Then I read the story of the entomologist killed two weeks prior while counting butterfly larvae at the Liard Hot Springs. Spellbound, I conceded I might need to pay more careful attention to Moon's stories. Leaving the store, I scanned the dirt parking lot to make sure no bears were around. I climbed in, and we headed out. Still recalcitrant, I didn't mention my discovery, hoping Moon might forget the whole conversation. Moon counted the dwindling supply of money. No one said a word as we trekked west through northeastern British Columbia.

Just when I thought he'd forgotten the bear conversation, Moon asked, "What'd that man tell you back there?"

"I can't believe it, but you were exactly right."

"I told ya."

"Yeah, you did."

LIARD HOT SPRINGS

"How'd y'all like to stop at Liard Hot Springs and get a bath?"

It seemed like a good idea since we hadn't bathed in a week. But from all accounts, it seemed like we had entered "man-eating-grizzly" zone.

I answered, "An article back at the store said a man was killed there by a grizzly two weeks ago."

Moon retorted, "Them bears won't bother you, if you don't bother them."

I remembered the Canadian storekeeper's words describing the ill fate of the entomologist. "He wouldn't leave the bears alone." But something didn't square.

I countered, "The man on the bicycle wasn't bothering the bears."

Pondering my comment, Moon said, "I think some of them bears when they're first coming out of hibernation are just hungry."

That was really comforting. Which was it? They don't bother you unless you bother them, except when they're coming out of hibernation, which means they bother you when you not bothering them at all. I silently visualized the next headline: "Three Mississippians Killed by Grizzly While Bathing at the Liard Hot Springs."

I was bear aware as we walked down the boardwalk toward the hot springs. I read the signs, "Warning — Active Bears in Area!" "Stay in Designated Areas." I noticed a chain across a boardwalk traversing a marshy area. The sign in the middle of the chain read: "DO NOT ENTER! Recent Bear Activity." Hmm, somewhere right out there is exactly where the entomologist met his end. Conspiratorial thoughts entered my skeptical mind. *Why hadn't they closed the park?* Was it the greedy state or the environmentalists who believed a little human blood enhanced the grizzly gene pool? "Recent Bear Activity"? Is that all? Really!? The sign seemed too innocuous, if not intentionally deceptive. I thought of better signs: "DO NOT ENTER — THE FATHER OF THREE YOUNG CHILDREN DIED HERE YESTERDAY" or "DO NOT ENTER — BELOVED ENTOMOLOGIST IS FLOATING WITH THE BUTTERFLIES." Why hadn't they just rubbed a little entomologist blood on the sign to make the real point?

We soaked in the hot steamy pool for twenty minutes or so and then showered in the bathhouse. I felt a bit shaky but relaxed as we made our way back to the parking lot. *Do bears prefer clean or smelly travelers?* Moon rummaged in the dumpster, hoping to score another box of donuts. No luck.

GRAYLING

We pulled back onto the ALCAN headed for Watson Lake, Yukon.

The afternoon sun sinking behind the firs, Moon announced, "Shane, get the .22 ready."

"All right."

Christia rolled her eyes. Like the previous afternoon, we collected another rabbit supply for dinner, this time a couple more. The thought occurred to me: *I could live like this.*

That evening, we selected a campsite just south of the Yukon border. We pulled the truck adjacent to a beautiful stream, its gurgling water flowed over the rocks, circling and eddying in foamy pools. Moon handed me a spincaster with a small Mepps spinner attached.

"There should be lots of grayling in here."

Christia gathered firewood. Moon skinned the rabbits and started a fire. I went fishin', glancing over my shoulders from time to time, checking for any furry visitors.

In a short time, I landed five healthy graylings. I gathered them, and like a member of a Native American hunting party, walked proudly back to camp. Something felt different about providing food we were dependent upon for survival.

Moon looked up, "Those are nice fish!"

"Yeah, thanks!"

Christia let out a "Woo-hoo!" overjoyed our dinner options now expanded beyond rabbits.

Moon designed a cooking rack by laying green alder sticks over flat rocks on opposite sides of the fire. He announced, "I'll clean the fish. Grab some tinfoil out of the camper. While you're at it, I think there's some butter in the icebox."

Moon made a pouch of aluminum foil, salt and peppered the insides and outsides of the fish, and laid them side by side in the pouch. He placed hunks of butter around, between, and on top of the fish, closed the pouch, and placed it beside the rabbits on the sticks above the coals. We sat on logs beside the fire, breathing in our surroundings, listening to the spattering and sputtering of the fish inside the pouch. We flipped the pouch and turned the rabbits and waited on dinner to be done.

"There, that oughta be about right."

We dined stick-and-finger style, stuffing ourselves—Christia on fish, Moon and me on northern BC surf and turf.

I remembered Moon's personal exercise and physiology classes. "That protein is the most important of all them food groups; it gives you that long-term energy."

With plenty of fish and rabbit left over, Moon announced, "We need to keep all these leftovers."

We pulled the remainder from the bones, wrapped it in the aluminum foil, and tossed it in the icebox. We gathered chunks of snow from beneath the trees to replace the melted ice in the box. I remember being amazed that we'd magically gone from next-to-nothing to eat to enough for leftovers. Beyond spiritually zealous at the time, I thought about Jesus feeding the five thousand by the sea and then instructing the disciples to collect the leftovers. I thought, *Two loaves and five fishes, four rabbits and five graylings AND instructions to collect the abundant leftovers!*

GROCERY STORE

With an early morning start, we headed west through the southern Yukon, listening to Johnny Horton's "North to Alaska" for the tenth time on the eight-track player. Bored, Christia pleaded, "Play George Jones," although we'd already listened to George more times than I cared to remember. We stopped somewhere near Whitehorse to refuel. The lever clicked on the handle, announcing another full tank. Moon squinted at the pump register, jotting down the total number of liters.

"Shane, what's the odometer say?"

"Hold on," I grabbed our state-of-the-art calculator, a pen and piece of paper, and calculated the distance since our last fill-up.

Calculations completed, I announced, "I'll sure be glad when we don't have to convert liters to gallons and kilometers to miles. We're gettin' about thirteen miles a gallon."

Moon asked, "How far do we have to go?"

I looked at the map, added and readded each section, and divided the total by thirteen.

"We have about 850 miles to go, and that should take a little over sixty-five gallons if we get the same mileage and price."

Moon asked, "What's the exchange rate again?" He pulled the wrinkled envelope from his left pocket, his counting ritual reduced to two large bills.

"Shane, pull the truck over; I'll be right back."

He walked across the street toward a grocery store. Christia and I watched in amazement.

"Is he really going in there?"

Whether he was aware we were praying for lunch or conceding defeat was hard to determine. As we dreamed of crispy fried chicken, Moon returned with two loaves of bread, a jar of mayonnaise, a stalk of celery, and a yellow onion.

Our hopes of crispy fried chicken dashed, Moon said, "We can make sandwiches out of this; they'll be kinda like tuna sandwiches. Christia, could you get back there in the camper and make 'em?"

"Yes, sir."

I feared that any minute, Christia might explode, but to my surprise, she seemed fine. Maybe a premonition of what awaited us in Alaska was settling in.

"Chip up the cel-re and onion. Chop up the rabbit and fish, and then mix it all up with mayonnaise. Use one bowl to do the rabbit and another to do the fish. Peck on the window when you're done, and we'll pull over so we can all eat up here in the cab. Be sure to put plenty of onion in there."

Rabbit-and-fish-salad sandwiches supplanted the standard salami and cheese for the rest of the trip. They were actually quite yummy.

Beautiful Mountain Girl

Our lunch finished, the bright afternoon sun warmed the truck cab as we neared Haines Junction. In Haines, we stopped for a brief bathroom break. I noticed a T-shirt rack. One T-shirt read, "You might be in the Yukon if you hit a pothole and total your car." I should have filed the humorous information somewhere in my brain's "be careful" category.

Out of Haines Junction, the road turned north. Christia's head nodded back and forth, fighting sleep, finally laying across my lap. Moon opened the coffee jar. I tried to keep my eyes open when Moon pointed out the Dall sheep grazing on the dark lead-colored mountains jutting high into the sky above Kluane Lake. Moon pulled over.

"Christia, get back there in the camper so you can sleep."

I slumped over with a pillow between my head and the door and drifted off, the sound of rock pebbles clicking against the undercarriage.

I awoke, sat up, and rubbed my eyes. "How long did I sleep?"

"A couple hours, I reckon."

"Where are we?"

"We're about fifty miles from Beaver Creek."

We slowed as a caribou herd crossed the road in front of us.

"How many do you think that was?"

"A couple hundred or so, I guess. I used to see giant herds up here. I don't know why there's not as many anymore."

Sometime later, we wound down a mountain incline, and I gazed on the most beautiful site of the entire trip. She was a two-legged creature. She rode down the mountain toward the road on a paint horse, leading a pack horse with a mule deer across its back, her rifle visible in the leather gun scabbard against the saddle. *Am I dreaming?* Her blond hair hung in long braids over her petite shoulders. I was mesmerized by her grace and beauty.

"Slow down!" I really wanted to yell "Stop!"

As we drove past, she pulled back on the reins, touched her hat, nodded, and shyly smiled. I fell in love. I tried to quell my urge to rubberneck.

Moon said, "Man, how'd ya' like to live like that!?"

I was thinking, *I'd like to live like that with a girl like that.*

Thoughts of girls back at Ole Miss quickly faded, as my prospective horizons expanded. I was convinced she was the prettiest girl I had ever seen, although I hadn't seen too many girls recently. My mind entered dreamworld as I imagined riding horses with my new bride, plenteous deer and elk in the meat box, a couple of kids playing in the cabin yard. Problem was the distance between us was increasing with every turn of the truck wheel. I wanted to ask Moon to turn around. I wanted to pray and ask God for a providential flat. Neither happened.

FLAT TIRE

North of Kluane Lake, the potholes increased in size and regularity. We listened to Lester Flatt and Earl Scruggs on the eight-track; our choices were limited unless we wanted to listen to Johnny Horton or George Jones again, which by now we could recite every word of every song.

Moon warned, "Just call them 'Lester and Earl.' Don't ever say the word 'flat.' We might have one."

Along this section, we encountered numerous motorists pulling campers, "Alaska or Bust" proudly inscribed in the rock dust adhering to the back. Every couple of miles, we passed abandoned campers with the "Alaska or" part crossed out and "ED" added to "Bust." They were "BUSTED."

I announced, "I'm sure glad that's not us!"

"Bump, bump, bump."

Moon said, "We're having a flat!"

I thought, *You might be in the Yukon if you hit a pothole and blow out your left back tire. And God, why did you answer my prayer 150 miles too late?*

Moon exclaimed, "Don't worry, Shane, we've got a good spare."

We pulled over on the flattest place we could find.

"Shane, grab the jack and lug wrench from behind the seat. I'll get the spare."

Christia opened the camper door. "What's wrong?"

"We have a flat but don't worry. We have a good spare."

Moon rolled the spare toward the back right wheel. The spare looked, well, reasonably good.

"Shane, start takin' off the lug nuts; I'll get the jack positioned. Don't lose the lug nuts. Christia, grab something out of the camper to put 'em in."

The adhering rock dust made the lug nuts hard to remove. I managed to loosen a couple. The third wouldn't budge. I removed the final two and tried the stuck one again. I pushed, I pulled, I kicked, but nothing.

"Daddy, this lug won't come off."

"Move, let me try it." Nothing.

"Get the WD-40; it's under the front seat."

"Okay."

We sprayed half the can on the frozen lug.

"Try it again."

Nothing.

"Sit down and use your feet to push against both sides of the tire while I try."

Nothing.

"Damn it, I don't know what else to do."

Then he added, "Put the lugs on and let me try pulling forward just a bit."

I replaced the lugs, and we pulled forward. Again, we strained against the frozen lug. Nothing. Stranded again in the middle of nowhere, I thought about the "busted" signs on the abandoned campers. A car passed but didn't slow; the cloud of rock dust choked us like tear gas.

Moon said, "Shane, raise the hood."

I wanted to object but supposed this must be the universal distress signal. Besides, it had worked the previous time. The next truck was pulling a large camper. I heard the engine slow as it approached.

I thought to myself, "It worked again. Daddy's right *again*."

The truck pulled beside us.

"Got trouble?"

"Yeah, we have a flat, but we can't get the blamed tire off, one of the lug nuts is stuck."

"I may have just what you need."

He opened a compartment on the lower side of his camper and pulled out a long piece of metal pipe.

"Try this."

We fit the pipe over the rachet handle and gave a slow steady tug. The lug nut squeaked as it slowly released. Christa let out another, "Woo-hoo!"

"Thank you so much!"

"Glad I could help. Good luck on the rest of your trip."

We hit the road again, bound for Soldotna and the Kenai River.

WELCOME TO ALASKA

The Kenai in striking distance, I don't remember much of the rest of the trip. After more than a week of driving, I couldn't stay awake. I do remember Moon ingesting a double dose of Folgers coffee crystals as we pulled back onto the road. Christia and I were too exhausted to even think about food. I felt like I had taken a narcotic. The truck seat felt like a feather mattress. Moon was now pretty sure we would make it without running out of gas; I even thought I detected an increase in speed. The sound, the truck, the road, the trip all converged, and I fell into deep REM. Moon drove all night.

"Shane, look at that mountain!"

From my slumber, his voice sounded like it was coming from some faraway place.

"We should reach Soldotna before noon!"

After we had come so far, I don't remember if I even acknowledged our approaching triumph. I drifted back into unconscious world.

"Look at that! Wake up, Shane!"

Moon pulled the truck off the highway in front of a marquis on wheels with plastic lettering.

The sign read, "Welcome to Alaska, Shane and Christi Sunn."

I thought, *Wow, someone in Soldotna thinks enough of Moon to take the trouble to rent a sign welcoming his kids to Alaska. I wonder who?*

"Get Christia up. I wanna take a picture with y'all in front of the sign."

Barely awake, Christia asked, "Shane, where are we?"

"We're here!"

Christia responded, "Hallelujah!"

Moon snapped the picture.

Sign welcoming Christia and me to Alaska!

Moon recalls, "When we got to Soldotna, I only had four or five dollars left. On that trip, Christia wouldn't eat rabbits, but she'd eat the graylin's. It was still a week before my check was gonna come in, so I went to the grocery store in Soldotna, hopin' they'd let me buy some groceries on credit. I ran into a woman I knew, Mary Nash. She loaned me ten dollars, and when I fine'lee got the first check, I paid her back. Gas is more important than food in the situation we were in."

Listening to Moon's recollections, I thought, *Yeah, because in Alaska, you never know when you're gonna get to eat again.*

CHAPTER 28

CENTENNIAL CAMPGROUND

IN THE EARLY '80S, Centennial Campground looked like a tribe from Woodstock had hived off and landed in Soldotna, Alaska. Largely drifters and locals, they weren't "Okies from Muskogee"; they were, by and large, the hippie crowd.

There were exceptions. The campground host was a round man from Georgia with a long white beard who most people referred to as Santa Claus. Charles Calloway called him "Moses" to his face. Outsiders were given names based on wherever they happened to be from. Tex, Mississip, Utah.

Two Frenchmen, Denny and DJ, camped in their small tent nearby. They wanted nothing more than to catch a big Kenai king. They spent a lot of time describing to me how the French prepare salmon.

"Wie, how de ye say, we lightle' smoke le' fi'sh and puis slice it very thin, it's a delicace', we have et a' Chrismas."

Touching their hands to their mouths, "Tres, excellente'!"

I couldn't understand much of what they were saying, but their broken English description sure sounded delicious to me.

It took me a bit to adjust to the daily routine. In the land of the midnight sun, you fished all day, most of the evening, and then when faint darkness finally arrived, you sat around a blazing campfire with the hippie crowd and enjoyed a communal feast. Shared goods included more than food. Alcohol and Mary Jane flowed freely. Most girls looked like reincarnations of Janis Joplin. With regularity, I received a personal invitation from some gal twice my age to join her in her tent for the evening. I respectfully declined and dreamed of the mountain girl in the Yukon.

And then there was the communal music making; Moon served as bard. He absolutely loved the pickers and songsters. Leroy, Moon's favorite, referred to Moon as "Jimmy Billy," the man with two first names.

Meal finished, the fire and state of mind right, Leroy broke into an amazing rendition of "East Texas Red" by Arlo Guthrie or "Outlaw Blues" by Bob Dylan. Leroy picked the guitar, played the harmonica, and sang in heavenly fashion. Willie Nelson's "Blue Eyes Crying in the Rain" always made the list.

"Jimmy Billy, let's hear "The Cremation of Sam McGee."

Moon recited the entire poem with perfect intonation without missing a single word. "There are strange things done in the midnight sun, by the men who moil for gold; the Artic trails have their secret tales that would make your blood run cold; the Northern Lights have seen queer sights, but the queerest they ever did see, was the night on the marge of Lake Lebarge, I cremated Sam McGee ..."

His amazing performance induced chills and made my hair stand on end as I headed off to bed. The communal revelries repeated themselves almost exactly the following evening.

Leroy and Moon were good friends but very different and somehow very much the same. Leroy had a compassionate heart but struggled mightily with alcohol addiction.

"Leroy put the sign up out there welcomin' you and Christia to Alaska."

Moon's comment affirmed what seemed obvious to me: Leroy and Moon had a mutual friendship and deep respect for one another.

Years later, Leroy got religion and traveled to Mississippi to share his new faith with his friend Moon. He pulled into Ackerman in his orange Willy's Wagon, a giant blue peace sign spray-painted on the side, with his dog and his common-law wife, Vicki, beside him.

Home from college, I dropped by Moon's house for a visit. Something about Leroy seemed different. He looked different. He seemed calm and at peace. Not many years later, he lost a grueling battle with stomach cancer.

Sitting in Moon's den reminiscing about the trip in '82, a picture of Leroy caught my eye. Staring at his picture, I thought, *Leroy might have lost his battle with cancer, but he won the ultimate battle.*

A LOT TO LEARN

I was overconfident and unteachable, with a lot to learn about salmon fishing the Kenai, but that was hard to admit. The first day out, standing in the river and sporting my thigh-length hip waders, I hooked into a big steelhead. A small crowd gathered.

"That's not a king, it may be a jack, no it's a big steelhead! Would you look at that!"

I got it close, but as my initial trophy slashed about in the current of the shallow water, the lure popped free. The sudden release of tension on the heavy rod surprised me, and the rod slapped me right between the eyes, breaking my thick glasses in half. They fell into the water and washed away in the current. That's not only losing; it's like having the loss rubbed in your face. Fish 45, Shane 0.

"Sorry about that man. How much 'dem glasses cost ya'?"

"I don't know."

I gathered myself, squinted, and headed for the camper to find my contact lenses and massage my bruised pride.

BANK VERSUS BOAT FISHERMEN

Before full light the next morning, Moon tapped on the side of my tent. "Shane, get up, the best fishing is when the first light hits the river."

Most days, Christia slept in and spent the rest of the day powwowing with other campers. She also did more than her share of cooking and cleaning.

Fishing kings "Moon-style," when you hooked one from the bank, the fight was an all-out war. If the fish made a long-determined run downstream, you had to follow so it didn't steal all your line. This required dodging boulders, splashing through mud and muck, and sometimes swimming, if the fish wrapped your line around a rock.

That morning, Moon landed back-to-back monstrous kings. He kept the first—we needed the groceries; he released the second. Nearby boat fishermen noticed his success and pulled in close. A boisterous shouting match ensued. The boat drifted by, trolling their lures behind them, cutting off Moon's ability to cast. Completing their first drift, they motored upstream and repeated the process, completely ignoring Moon as if he weren't there. Moon put down his rod and picked up a handful of hefty rocks. Watching from a distance, I thought to myself, *Oh, no!*

When the boat got close, he launched the rocks one by one toward the boat. He didn't mind hitting the boat. His real goal? Hit one of the fishermen trespassing on his sacred turf. Before lunch that day, still miffed, Moon declared, "Boats give fishermen an unfair advantage; they really don't have to fight the fish. When they hook 'em, all they have to do is keep tension on the line and follow the fish downstream in the boat. Besides they've got the whole damn river, but they see you catch one and think the whole river belongs to them."

For the first time, I thought, *Moon's ire for boat fishermen isn't only about his respect for the raw power of the king; it's also about the tendencies of some boat fishermen to ignore and disrespect the rights of bank fishermen.*

On the Kenai, civil war broke out between the bank fishermen and boat fishermen as they battled over exclusive rights to the river. On many occasions, the Soldotna police showed up, attempting to intervene before blood was shed. Like the Hatfields and McCoys, the bitter feud lasted years. Finally, the City of Soldotna hosted a public hearing. Moon testified. The eventual outcome: Centennial Campground from the Sterling Highway Bridge to below the big island downstream was declared, "Bank Fishing Only."

Greg Calloway remembers, "Finally the police just got tired of having to show up at the campground every day. Moon was so determined and unrelenting, I think they got tired of dealing with him too!"

THE MIGHTY KENAI KING

The raw power of a Kenai king can jerk grown men to their knees. Like Hemingway's marlin in *The Old Man and the Sea*, the mighty king can "bust" your gear, bruise your ego, and break your heart. Unless you've hooked and landed one, you can't imagine the ecstatic thrill these powerful and exquisitely beautiful fish provide their committed pursuers. Not to mention the delectable table fare. Once you land just one, you realize the mantra is true—"You didn't hook the fish, the fish hooked you." After I finally landed my first king, I knew I, too, was hooked for life.

Moon explained, "Kings are so strong because they've stored up enough energy to travel up rivers against the current to spawn. On some rivers, like the Yukon, they travel almost two thousand miles inland!"

In Centennial Campground, an old rusty white scale hung from a board lashed between two fir trees. Scales don't lie, but maybe this one did just a bit, as well as those who are still alive to tell the tales.

That summer, once I ate enough humble pie to vomit my pride and apprentice under the expert, I managed to land sixteen kings. Moon? Three times as many—forty-eight! My largest, according to rusty scales, sixty-two pounds; Moon's: eighty-three. We released most. The ones we kept we ate or canned, affirming the mysterious cycle between man's sustenance and nature's abundant provision.

Me with a king on the rusty white scale
in Centennial Campground.

Like an epic episode of *Meat Eater,* sometimes while cleaning a big salmon, Moon would carve off a big juicy slice of flesh and scarf it down.

"Shane, want some?"

"Sure."

"How you like it? Salmon is best just like that."

"Yeah, it's good."

It was tasty, but "best" might have been stretching the truth a bit. I liked it best grilled and slightly smoked over a campfire of green alder wood.

We set up a canning operation on the picnic table in our campsite. An uncompromising opponent of waste of any kind, Moon always keeps a couple of cases of canned salmon and canned venison in the shell camper of his truck. MPE and MPPF in play, the preserved healthy protein not only serves as sustenance but also as currency to keep you fishing.

That summer, Moon's eighty-three-pound king won first place in the local salmon derby, and he used his winnings to purchase gifts for Christia and me. Today, forty years later, I still have the Case hunting knife he gave me. Sometimes, I take it out and look at it, and my memory travels back to Centennial Campground and the summer of '82.

FAITH AND PERSEVERANCE

The fisherman's greatest assets are faith and perseverance. In order to make the first cast, you must believe the fish are there and at least some are hungry or curious enough to coax a strike. The initial step of faith is harder than some pretend because usually you can't see the dang things. Then, if no evidence presents itself, you must believe enough to keep casting.

"Most people give up too quickly. You can't catch one if your hook's not in the water."

That summer, I watched the interaction of faith and perseverance repeat itself over and over. After someone yelled, "Moon's got one on!" like gates suddenly opening at a bargain clearance, folks grabbed their gear and rushed to the riverside, to cast and cast away. Very often this produced tangled messes and near fights as everyone tried to cast at once. Then slowly, one by one, they'd give up and meander back to camp. Until, once again, there was only Moon stealthily moving along the bank, eyes squinted, concentrating on every cast. And then, whamo, a giant king would grab his lure.

The peanut gallery watching from the riverbank repeated their yell, "Moon's got one on!" and the news spread through the campground like wind-driven wildfire. The whole process repeated itself almost exactly as before. Sometimes in exasperation, people lost faith and gave up altogether. Others stood around, waiting to interview the expert to get the magic tip so they, too, could tie into a big Kenai king.

"Moon's got one on!"

GUIDE

Depending on how forlorn and desperate a particular inquirer happened to be, Moon might take special interest. Moon has a propensity for the weak, and he likes challenges. So, if you happened to catch him in the right mood, you might score a personal salmon fishing tutorial from the expert. Some of his understudies donned fishing lures that wouldn't catch a fish this millennium. Their weird contraptions appeared better designed to warn the fish a novice was in hot pursuit. Others had fishing line so old and weak it wouldn't have mattered if they managed to hook a fish or not.

Moon selected a few of these folks and taught them how to fish. The more desperate you appeared, the better your chances of garnering his time and attention. Pretty women were the only exceptions; they received preferential treatment. Lessons began with the critical importance of the right gear. Horrendous lures were closely rivaled by archaic rods and reels, some of which looked like they'd been in the garage since the previous decade. Some gear so bad, it was judged hopeless. Where you ranked on the "desperation scale" determined what happened next. Moon accomplished this by looking you over and sizing you up. If Moon decided his potential client possessed the means to buy the proper gear, he provided detailed instructions on what was needed and where to purchase it. Lesson two was dependent on completing lesson one.

"When you get all your gear, come back, and I'll help you rig it up and show you how to fish it."

If you ranked high on the desperation scale, meaning poor and almost hopeless, it usually meant he let you use his extra gear. Proper gear in hand, next up, casting instructions. At this point, Moon put his gear aside and first demonstrated the cast using their gear, which by now, might be his own. I think he did this to prove a fundamental lesson: "The gear won't cast itself." Many times, his understudies made awful casts and then looked disgustingly at their gear as if somehow the gear was the problem, which by now, wasn't the case. Building on instructions from lesson one, Moon first cast their gear two or three times, demonstrating every detail of the cast.

"Don't try to throw it halfway across the river. Shorten your motion. First, get comfortable with the basic technique and then gradually increase your distance. There, that's better. Try to release the lure a little sooner."

Once they were able to make reasonable casts, he'd launch into explanations of where to cast and how to retrieve.

"You wanna cast the lure at a ninety-degree angle from the bank. You might increase the angle just a bit to give the lure a chance to get close to the bottom. When your lure gets about twenty-five degrees from the bank, reel it in and throw it again. Big kings are usually deep, and you want your lure in the strike zone for the maximum amount of time. Sometimes they're in close, but it's more important to keep the odds in your favor."

Like the movie *Moneyball* and batting averages, Moon's fishing brain calculated how to maximize the potential of every single cast.

"You don't want to retrieve too much. Let the current do the work. You wanna feel the vibration of the lure. You can tell ya' got it right by watchin' the wobble at the tip of your rod."

Reasonably satisfied his trainee was finally fishing, Moon picked up his gear, waded a short distance into the water, and cast away, continuing to demonstrate, encourage, correct.

"Repetition is how people learn."

DISCIPLES

Now that they were his disciple, Moon was "all in," ardently devoted to their success. If they scored and hooked a king, Moon let out a loud "whoop," put his gear aside, and enthusiastically coached the fight.

"Pound for pound, kings are the strongest fish in the world; they've stored up enough energy to swim a thousand miles against the current in order to spawn!"

The powerful fish often snatched an unsuspecting disciple to their knees, and if they didn't hold on, took their rod. In the chaos, Moon grabbed their rod, gave them time to sturdy themselves, and handed it back.

"Put the butt of the rod on your stomach and keep pressure on the fish. You gotta follow 'em; they can go wherever they want."

Kings are prone to make powerful runs and then, like a bottle rocket, quickly reverse course.

"Reel your slack, reel your slack, you've got to try to keep up with 'em!"

Sometimes all the coaching wasn't enough, and the fish wrapped the disciple's line around a boulder in the river. That's when Moon went swimming in his standard wetsuit: cutoff blue jean shorts and tennis shoes. His goal: help his new disciple succeed. The strong current and frigid water temperature were intimidating but never phased Moon. If it did, he never acted like it.

"You can do a lot of things when your adrenlin' is pumpin'."

First, Moon grabbed the rod to make sure the fish was still on. If so, "kabloosh," he hit the water Greg Louganis-style from the platform.

"When you're swimmin' a river, the most important thing is to get a good jump."

Neck and right shoulder visible, Moon somehow managed to swim otter-style, keeping two hands on the rod while retrieving slack line as he pushed forward. Sometimes he swam around the boulder, and sometimes he'd swim to it, slide beaver-style onto the boulder, stand on top, and fight the fish. "Still on, still fightin'." "Kabloosh," Greg Louganis off the boulder, swimming toward shore. Wading out, he handed the rod to his disciple to the cheers of the peanut gallery gathered on the banks to watch the show. Moon's disciples became ardent missionaries of the "Moon-Sunn-bank-fishin' method." As converts spread their newly discovered fishing gospel, curious new people showed up in Centennial Campground, just to meet their famous leader.

Moon with a Kenai disciple.

MARKETING

The campground host, Moses from Georgia, helped facilitate Moon's popularity. The early '80s were the heyday of the CB radio craze. Moses didn't like to fish, but he loved CB radios.

"He owned a radio with a powerful booster, and he could talk to people all the way to Anchorage. He loved talking with people on the military bases."

Hoping to fill the campground on weekends, Moses used his CB as a state-of-the-art marketing device.

"Mississippi landed a sixty-pounder around lunchtime."

"Comeback?"

"Yeah, I'm looking at him right now, and as a matter of fact, he's got another one on!"

"How will we be able to recognize him?"

"You can't miss him. He wears cutoff jeans, tennis shoes, and a felt cowboy hat with a turkey feather sticking out the side."

That weekend and every weekend until the king run ended, the campground filled up, Moon the *accueillant le pratiquant*.

Moon became such a legend among the "bank fishermen" on the Kenai the very patterns of salmon migration were attributed to him.

"Why aren't the salmon in here yet?"

"They must be waitin' on Moon to get here from Mississippi."

Moon didn't want to let the fans or the fish down, so every spring in Ackerman, he prepared for his annual trek to the Kenai. Sometimes, trying to figure out how to transport local converts he had proselytized that winter with stories of the mighty Kenai king.

BEAR ENCOUNTER

As energetic teenagers and young men are prone to do, one afternoon, Greg Calloway and I thought it'd be great fun to put the yellow canoe in the Kenai at Centennial Campground and paddle downstream to the Calloway residence. We eagerly made plans for the following day.

Midmorning, we pushed off from shore, the air crisp and clean, hardly a cloud in the sky, a great day for a scenic canoe trip down the Kenai. Greg in front, me in back, we paddled toward our destination. We really didn't have to do much paddling; the current was sufficiently strong to push us to our planned terminus.

Several days before, while fishing below the campground, I'd observed groups of moose swimming to the big island, then resting before they swam the remainder of the river. Paddling and mostly drifting about five hundred yards above the island, we spotted what we initially thought was a moose.

"Greg, look at the moose on the island about to cross. Let's see if we can get close enough to get a good look."

Above the island, the river splits and the current only increases. By the time we realized the moose was a giant grizzly, we couldn't stop our rapid momentum. We tried to backstroke, but to no avail. The strong current pushed us directly toward the ferocious beast.

I recalled Moon's words: "Them bears won't bother you, if you don't bother them."

A rapid conversation ensued in my head: "Well, we're bothering one, a really big one! We're doing exactly what you shouldn't do!"

Anticipating our rapidly approaching unavoidable encounter, Greg boated his paddle and lay prostrate in the front of the canoe. I hyperventilated. Like cornering an angry T. rex, we drifted within five feet of the threatening beast. His giant clawed paws slapped the water. He snarled, his mouth agape, revealing his terrible white fangs. Armed with only a paddle, stories of King David killing a lion and a bear offered absolutely no solace. Completely vulnerable, sheer panic engulfed my entire being. Nearing cardiac arrest, I closed my eyes and waited for the inevitable mauling, already anticipating my bloody watery grave below.

Quietness. Nothing! *Am I in heaven?*

I opened my eyes. Greg sat up. Somehow, we'd managed to drift past the terrible creature. We watched the bear exit the water, shake himself dry, and climb the steep hill beside the river. A huge hump protruded from his wide shoulders. I felt shaky and weak. We paddled to shore and relieved ourselves.

"Them bears won't bother you, if you don't bother them."

"Yeah, easy to say, but sometimes not so easy to do!"

JAIL TIME

Johnny Cash spent time in the Starkville City Jail. Moon spent time in the Kenai City Jail.

One afternoon, I decided to go into Soldotna to refurbish our diminishing grocery essentials. Backing the old Dodge, I felt a jolt and heard glass break. I'd hit a fir tree, shattering the right back taillight.

"Shane, you need to get that taillight fixed."

"Okay, I will."

Several days later, "Shane, you need to get that taillight fixed."

"Okay, I will."

Several more days, "Shane, you need to get that taillight fixed."

Late afternoon, Moon started the blue Dodge, bound for the Maverick Saloon to drink beer with the local crowd. On his return trip, he was pulled over by a local policeman.

"Sir, one of your taillights is out. Have you been drinking?"

"Yeah, I've had a few."

"Sir, I'm going to need you to blow into this machine. I'll be right back."

"Sir, this is your second offense. You will have to see the judge and likely have to pay a big fine or serve jail time."

Moon's not about to use his fishing money to pay fines, so he opted for jail time. The king run almost over, the campground had thinned substantially, but the hippie crowd was still around. The week before, Christia—having stomached all the rustic living she could endure—left with a nice family from Oklahoma. We planned to pick her up on our return trip.

Roles reversed, with me driving and Moon riding shotgun, we left the campground and headed for the Kenai City jail. The silence was awkward. Belying the fact he'd experienced jail time before, Moon broke the silence. "Most of them people in jail just sit around and drink coffee all day, and then they can't sleep. All I do is catch up on my sleepin' and read a lot. They usually feed ya' pretty good in there too."

"Oh."

We arrived. Moon opened the truck door and reached for a stack of books and fishing magazines on the seat between us. What do you say at a moment like this? "Have a nice day"? "Hope you have fun in jail, while I'm fishing"?

Moon said, "See ya' later."

"Okay, see ya' later."

I pulled the column shifter into drive and headed back to the campground. An instant palpable loneliness gurgled up from somewhere deep within my very being. Low foggy clouds rolled in; the roadside firs resembled tall gray ghosts; raindrops spattered against the windshield.

I arrived at the muddy rain-soaked campground. As if frozen in time, I sat in the truck and stared trancelike in the rearview mirror. Fog formed on all the windows, enclosing me in darkness like a cocoon. Christia gone, Moon in jail, I was twenty years old and all alone in Alaska—the fact not lost on Janis Joplin.

I opened the truck door and sprinted for the cover of the camper. I slipped into my raincoat and mindlessly began cleaning and putting things away inside and out. I scrubbed the countertops in the camper while scanning my meager dinner options. I heard a truck pull up outside. I stuck my head out the creaky door. Charles Calloway rolled down his truck window.

"Shane, you seen Moses around?"

"No, he left about a week ago, headed back to Georgia."

"Why don't you come stay with us until Moon gets out of jail?"

Charles knew the persuasive power of loneliness.

"I don't know, Charles, somebody's got to watch all this stuff."

"You sure you don't want to come stay with us? Alice is a really good cook."

I remembered Moon's advice: "In Alaska, you never know when you're gonna get to eat again."

"Okay, I reckon I will."

Although in Alaska, I was more concerned about the bears, I've always wondered if Charles knew he was actually saving me from the *cougars*.

OUT OF JAIL

Moon showed up at the Calloway residence less than a week later, books and magazines under his arm in a paper grocery sack. He'd hitchhiked the twelve miles from Kenai back to Soldotna.

"They didn't make me serve the entire sentence. They let me out on good behavior. Are the silvers showin' up yet?"

I gathered my belongings. As we drove to the campground, the warm sun appeared, burning away the suspended whiffs of fog. The fir-ghosts disappeared, replaced by brilliant colors of emerald and gold.

"What did you do in jail?"

"I read and slept."

We changed our heavy king gear to standard bass fishing tackle and got after the silvers. The run just beginning, the silver fishing was slow. We managed to land a couple each day.

"Shane, when do you have to be back at Ole Miss?"

"I have to register for classes a week from today."

"Well, we better start packin' all this stuff; we've got to pick up Christia down there in Oklahoma. So we can make better time, I'm gonna take the camper and leave it in Leroy's yard."

Our fishing days together on the Kenai were numbered. The morning of our last day, we loaded the remainder of our gear into the back of the truck and covered it with a green canvas tarp.

Packing finished, preparing for a long journey, Moon said, "Let's go down to the boat ramp beside the lagoon and make some final casts."

On my second cast, I hooked and landed a nice silver. Two casts later, I hooked and landed a beautiful red.

"Man, those fish look like twins. Hold 'em up and let me snap a quick picture."

He snapped the picture; it seemed like the perfect ending. We left midmorning, Moon driving, me riding shotgun, heading north for Anchorage.

Me with a silver and red salmon on our
last day on the Kenai in 1982.

CHAPTER 29

THE NORTHERN LIGHTS

MOON DEVISED, what seemed like at the time, a clever driving plan.

"Shane, once we get through Anchorage, I'll let you drive so I can catch up on a little rest. We've got a long way to go!"

"Yeah, I remember."

"I'll drive all afternoon and as long as I can tonight, kinda like drivin' the first leg. When I get sleepy, I'll pull over and let you drive the second leg. If we can do it like that, we can keep this truck rollin' all the way to Mississippi."

"All right."

Late that evening, somewhere on the Glennallen Highway east of Anchorage, he pulled over and we switched sides. The weight of the camper gone, I put the pedal to the metal, and we headed northeast toward Tok. Moon asleep in the passenger's seat, me trying to stretch the "second leg" as far as possible. Sometime around midnight in the Yukon darkness, I noticed an intense white glow just above a shadowy eastern mountain.

I thought, *Oh, the moon must be rising.*

But then I saw through the right corner of the windshield, high in the sky, the moon. Something was obviously happening rapidly in the heavens, and

I couldn't think of any plausible explanations other than a nuclear attack or the Second Coming of the Christ. Either way, it was probably a good idea to at least wake up Moon. No thought of the Aurora Borealis ever entered my mind. Searching for an explanation, I deduced, *If the Second Coming is real, it must have to happen sometime. I don't know why it has to happen right now while I'm busy driving the "second leg," though.*

I quickly scanned my brain, trying to remember the little theology I knew. I'd heard Jesus was to return from the eastern sky, descending on the clouds. Goosebumps formed between my shoulder blades, tingled up the back of my neck through the collar of my shirt, and roosted on my head. I recollected parts of the Nicene Creed, "He shall come again with glory to judge the living and the dead, his Kingdom shall have no end." From my scant experience of "reformed worship," I remembered reciting, "Christ has died, Christ has risen, *Christ will come again.*"

What began as intense white light over a distant eastern mountain was now beginning to change colors and move toward us, the *"will come again"* part was quickly approaching in real time. I had no other explanation. *This is it! What do I do?* Time seemed frozen and compressed. I might have a minute or maybe just a few seconds. As pressure mounted, eternity in the balance, the prospect of eternal guilt for saying absolutely nothing to Moon a real possibility, I quickly devised a "drive-up, five-second, say-some-words, and get right with God" plan of salvation.

I pulled the truck over to the side of the road. My immediate plan? Wake Moon and blurt out, "Daddy, you need to pray the 'sinner's prayer' quickly, as fast as you can, as in, right now! Repeat after me ..."

My heart and mind betrayed me. His son who'd not mentioned one word of God all summer, who had rather over and over hinted my disgust at some of his uncouth ways, now all of a sudden had the zeal of a Mormon missionary? I nudged him, words lodged in my throat, and Moon leaned forward and rubbed his eyes. "Man, look at the Northern Lights!"

I was instantly relieved to be off the hook and downright elated I hadn't blurted out some unintelligible words and come off looking like a complete idiot and the hypocrite I was ... am. As we stood outside the truck, just the two of us in the middle of nowhere, underneath the astounding brilliance and glory of the Aurora Borealis flashing every color of the prism, a warm sensation came over me. "God's got this."

Sitting in Moon's den, continuing to reminisce, Moon said it best, "I've seen the Northern Lights lots of times, but I don't think I've ever seen 'em like we did that night. It was like we were standin' in 'em."

HITCHHIKERS

If you've been one, you have more compassion for those who are one. For Moon, hitchhikers are the only lot able to disrupt the normal patterns of MPE. Of course, hitchhikers were sometimes enlisted to help him carry out MPE!

Somewhere south of Calgary, Alberta, on Canadian Highway 2, we picked up two college-age hitchhikers. Asleep on the front seat, I heard Moon pull the truck onto the side of the road, make a "u-ey," and pull over. Awaking from my slumber, I heard Moon ask, "Where ya' headed?"

"We're headed down to tour Glacier National Park."

"Get in, I'll take you."

Sometimes, Moon doesn't think before he speaks. How were four persons going to fit on the front seat of the truck?

Finally, the couple said, "We'll just throw our packs in the back and ride back there. Thanks for the lift."

The couple looked happy, donning designer gear, leather hiking boots, and colorful new packs. It appeared like a page from L. L. Bean had suddenly materialized on Canadian Highway 2. The girl was beautiful, like the Yukon girl on the horse with the mule deer. I didn't know whether that was because I'd been in the wilderness entirely too long or due to my recent experience with the homely cougars. I tried not to look too obvious as I turned my head and peered through the back glass, attempting to get a second look at the beautiful girl now riding in our truck! Moon noticed.

"Shane, everything ridin' okay back there?"

"Real good!"

Assisting the hitchhikers required a departure from the usual and easier route. Rather than crossing the border at Sweetgrass, Montana, we stayed south on Canadian Highway 2, entering Montana at the Piegan-Carway border crossing. We let our guests out in St. Mary, Montana, the eastern gateway to Glacier National Park. The now-not-just-pretty-but-gorgeous girl strapped her camera around her neck. Moon gave the hikers several cans of salmon from our recent exploits. They loaded them into their colorful packs.

"Thanks so much for the ride and the salmon."

"You're welcome; enjoy the rest of your adventure."

I was glad we could now focus on the most direct route to Oklahoma!

WE INTERRUPT THIS BROADCAST

We headed south toward Kiowa and turned almost due east through the heart of the Blackfeet Indian Reservation. Moon repeated what I'd heard him say many times before: "When that land greed gets in ya' blood, they ain't no stoppin' it.

Ole' 'Yellow Hair' got what was comin' to him. That's what the Lakota Sioux and northern Cheyenne called General George Armstrong Custer." Moon launched, "The way this country has treated native peoples and blacks is the darkest scars on our history. This country has never acknowledged her sins in a whole lot of areas."

I listened to the man, the history teacher. I recalled former days, my experience telling me I was in for another long description. But now, maybe for the first time, I completely trusted he knew exactly what he was talking about. After a reasonably short twenty-minute lecture, weariness setting in, I reached over and tuned the radio to a local station. Instantly, we heard the familiar screeching blare preceding a public service announcement. We listened.

"We interrupt this broadcast to bring you a special announcement. A female hiker has fallen to her death in Glacier National Park. Details are sketchy at this point, but it appears she slipped and fell from a road culvert while attempting to take a photograph. At this hour, her male companion is being held for questioning. Sources say the couple was traveling together from Canada and dropped off by a motorist in St. Mary around 1:00 p.m. this afternoon. Anyone with any information should contact the park service."

Moon pulled the truck to the side of the highway. We both knew what we didn't want to know. We were the motorists, and the referenced couple had been happily riding in the back of our truck two hours prior, not a care in the world. The radio screeched again; the unbelievably sickening announcement repeated. It seemed surreal, hard to accept and get our minds around. How could such a tragic event happen so quickly?

I asked, "What should we do?"

Moon thought a moment and said, "Well, I guess we need to go back."

We turned around and headed back to St. Mary.

"Shane, them big road culverts always have a little water tricklin' through 'em, and algae grows on there and makes it real slicky. They probably walked in there to take a picture, and the girl slipped on that; it was like a death trap. The more I think about it, there's not anything we can do once we get there. Besides, that questioning could take a long time, and we have a long way to go. I don't want you to be late for college. From what I can tell from the announcement, the young fella is gonna be okay. Sometimes, them accidents just happen, and they ain't a thing you can do about 'em. When it's your time to go, it's your time to go."

"Okay, I guess you're right." I thought, *I'm sure glad it's not my time to go!*

After five or six miles, we turned around again and set our sights on Oklahoma to pick up Christia.

Home Again

Moon kept the truck rolling. The "taking a leg plan," which seemed like a good idea the day before, quickly faded into the background. When awake, I dined on smoked salmon and saltines. Moon dined on smoked salmon and Folgers coffee crystals. Outside temperatures rose into the nineties. Rather than sleeping in the truck cab, I climbed into the back of the truck. I stared at indentations in the canvas tarp where the boy and girl had sat the day before. It was still difficult to get my mind around and accept. I fell into a two-day slumbery trance and felt but didn't see much of the rest of the trip—the hum of the tires against the pavement, the hot days and warm evenings, my sun- and wind-burned face. I floated on a puffy cloud toward Mississippi. I vaguely remember picking up Christia in Oklahoma.

Sitting together on the front seat of the truck, we cheered when we crossed the Mississippi state line and again when we pulled into Ackerman. As we ascended Moon's drive, August light filtered through the tall pecans. Unpacking our gear, I thought to myself, *You're a pretty good daddy, at least a one-of-a-kind.*

When I showed up at Ole Miss two days later, my friends said, "You don't look the same!"

I said, "I don't feel the same." Looking back, I wasn't the same.

Moon recalls, "I remember we had to go to Oklahoma to pick up Christia, who was stayin' with them nice folks she left Soldotna with. I also remember listenin' to bluegrass music and sayin', 'Don't say Lester Flatt, we might have one!' I guess we shoulda' said 'another one' because we'd already had one."

*

CHAPTER 30

ALASKA—THE
LATER YEARS

TEACHIN' MPE

CHRISTIA FINISHED COLLEGE in '86. Moon's teaching career ended on May 18 the same year, and he turned fifty the next day.

"I got credit for teachin' ten years. I taught one year and then stayed in Alaska two years and then taught nine more. Teaching ten years helps you draw teachin' retirement from the state. You can't draw it until you're fifty-nine. I draw about $1,200 a month, or somethin' like that, which ain't no whole lot of money to some people, but it's more than it takes me to live on. I save money out of that. I just want to be sure I have enough to bury me when it's my time to go."

Once retired, Moon was free to go wherever he wanted whenever he wanted and fish as much as he wanted. Of course, for the first nine years before he "drew" teaching retirement, he had to determine how to make ends meet. But this never worried him one bit. He had minimal bills; all he needed was gas money. The rest, like for the biblical prophet Elijah, was provided by the ravens!

He felt as free as he did when he first owned the '38 Plymouth. Fish from Florida, Alabama, Louisiana, Maine, Minnesota, Montana, Colorado, Nebraska, Texas, the Mexico border, Canada, Alaska, and everywhere in between beckoned, and Moon obliged. He'd read a fishing article, plan a trip, and strike out. He never had to do much packing because his small truck was always in "go-mode," boat permanently attached. It became even more difficult to keep tabs on Moon. He refused to own a telephone; he didn't want to pay for it or be interrupted. Ty Cobb, who drove to Moon's house after work a couple of days a week to check on him, became my informant on his general whereabouts.

VALDEZ OIL SPILL

The Exxon Valdez oil spill became a sobering sad reality on March 24, 1989. A captain error resulted in eleven million gallons of crude spilled into Prince William Sound. The spill afforded Moon the opportunity to display his wading skills and practice MPE.

"They had a lot of technology, but nobody knew how to get around in that water. In Valdez, them rocks are slicker than ice. I knew how to move around without fallin'. At first, I moved pipe around they used to suck oil out of the water and off the rocks. In the saltwater, the oil would clump together and make big gooey blobs. Birds' feathers got all slicked over until they couldn't fly. You'd see dead birds and fish floatin' around everywhere. I don't know how many birds I saved by cleaning them off with fresh water.

"One day, the props on a skimmer got tangled in an old fishing net. No one knew what to do; they just stood around. They fine'lee decided to call in an expert dive team from Anchorage."

"I told 'em, 'Man, I can fix this in about ten minutes, and it won't cost you a dime.'

"They issued us wetsuits, but them things just made it harder to get around, so I didn't wear one. I got a sharp knife and held it in my teeth so

I could swim with both hands. I took a deep breath and dove under to the first prop. It was a bigger mess than I expected, and it took me a couple of dives to get it all cut loose. Then I dove under and did the same thing on the other prop.

"Before they fine'lee ended cleanup operations, I was runnin' the skimmer. Sometimes, I still had to stop and get off to help move pipes around. Them people couldn't ever figure out how to wade in them slick rocks.

"We shut down operations when 'ice-up' came every year and started again early the next summer. I knew whenever I got back, I'd have a job. I think that's why I liked it so much. I could do the work and still get in a little fishin'. But the main thing, I was able to save a lot of money. I think I still have some of that money I earned workin' on the Valdez oil spill."

I thought, *I'm sure you do!*

GRAND MARSHAL

I suppose there are numerous ways stories, at least parts of them, become fabricated and take on a life of their own. I'd heard for years Moon was the Grand Marshal of the Soldotna Progress Parade. But something didn't add up.

First and foremost, the Moon I knew would never accept such an invitation. For Moon, parades and other similar things are to be avoided like the Black Plague.

Second, let's just say, Moon isn't the kind of individual any city would invite to be Grand Marshal of their esteemed parade. Either Soldotna was different, very different, or Moon's fame on the Kenai had increased to epic proportions.

It turns out the source of the cock-and-bull story happened quite innocently. Moon's second cousin, Alaskan state trooper Webb O'Bryant, called the police chief in Soldotna on a business matter. While Webb had the chief on the phone, he took the opportunity to inquire about how Moon was getting along.

The chief responded, "He must be doing pretty good; he was the grand marshal of the parade last week!"

Webb said, "No joke!"

"No, he was leading the parade in his old truck with the windows rolled down, waving at all the spectators."

Of course, Webb talked regularly with his family living in Ackerman, who also inquired about how Moon was getting along in Alaska. Webb repeated what he was told, and the story spread like tabloid drama throughout Ackerman and beyond.

So, I took the opportunity to ask, "Is it true you were the grand marshal of the Soldotna Parade?"

The real story, as always, begins with fishing.

Moon chuckled and recalled, "I was down there on the Kenai, and on my first cast, I hooked and landed a beautiful king in the seventy-pound range. Someone came to the riverbank and yelled, 'Moon, you're havin' a flat!' But I wouldn't gonna worry about that right then. A couple of casts later, I hooked another one, and it was much bigger."

Remember, at this point, Moon's goal is to catch the world record king from the banks of the Kenai.

"I fought it hard for ten minutes, and then it broke my line. The first fish must have nicked my line or somethin'. That don't ever happen to me too much, but I think that fish was just that big. I think it was in the ninety-pound category. I didn't have the same lure with me so I could offer the exact presentation, so I ran back to camp. I could hear air goin' out of the left front tire. The other problem was my spare didn't have no air in it either."

The circumstances presented a real-life dilemma for Moon. He could get the lure he needed and hurry back to the river to catch the world record king or deal with the flat. MPE kicked into gear as he carefully analyzed his available options. If he didn't do something quickly before the tire completely deflated, it'd mean a lot more work later. The MPE handbook says, "Time spent working equals time away from fishing."

"The big kings were hot, but I realized if I didn't do somethin' quickly about the flat, it was gonna cost me a lot more time later. I decided I might be able to get to town and get the tire fixed pretty quick and get back to the river before the hot streak ended. So, I got in the truck and drove to town as fast as I could on the low tire."

Soldotna proper is only a half mile from Centennial Campground. Moon's philosophy of time and speed change in harmony with fish activity. He thinks differently than most men. It's always about the next cast, the next fish.

"I crossed the Kenai River Bridge into Soldotna and noticed a roadblock ahead. I said to myself, 'I'll be damned, every time the big kings are bitin', somethin' like this happins.' Luckily, I was first in the line forming behind the barricade. I pulled up and asked the deputy, 'What's goin' on?' He looked at me kinda funny and said, 'Don't you know, we are about to start the parade any minute?' I told him, 'I'm havin' a flat!' He said, 'Oh,' and came closer to have a look. You could hear the air comin' out of the tire. He bent down and listened. I said, 'I'm gonna be stranded right here if you don't let me through.'"

In Alaska, there are different sensibilities about what's important that sometimes take precedence over parades and things like that.

"The deputy told the other officers standin' around, 'Move the barricade and let this man through.' I rolled through the barricade, and the parade pulled out on the main drag right behind me. That's how I got in front of the parade. There was nothin' to do but go slow 'cause people were crowdin' the whole street. So, I rolled down my window and started wavin' at every-body. I think they thought I was gonna throw 'em some candy or somethin'. Everybody thought I was leadin' the parade. I got up there a little ways and the crowd thinned a bit, so I darted off into a fillin' station. That parade kept me from gettin' back to the river as fast as I wanted to. I don't think I've ever seen the big kings as hot as they were that afternoon. I wish I'd never even thought about gettin' that flat fixed."

I thought, *Now everything adds up and makes perfect sense.*

"The big ones were in thick that day."

CROSSIN' THAT BORDER

Sometime during the late '80s or early '90s, on one of his annual trips to Alaska, Moon was turned back at the Canadian border. The struggle lasted three years.

"Did you hear them Canadians won't let Moon go to Alaska?"

Like the interruption of a natural process, the news created a general stir in Ackerman.

"I don't know how I got sideways with the border crossin' people. I think the first time I got detained was because they found my .22 rifle behind the seat. I never go anywhere without a .22 because you never know when you might need it. Matter of fact, I'd forgotten the gun was back there. I guess I should have taken the time to fill out the papers so I could have carried it across legally. But the rigmarole you gotta go through these days just to get a gun across the border ain't worth it. Especially for the purposes I use it. There had been some recent gun smugglin', and they thought I was intentionally bringing the gun across.

"I told 'em, 'This is the only gun I have, and I always keep it in this truck. I don't even remember the last time I took it out.' They tore everything apart lookin' for more guns. They took the seats out and went through ever piece of my gear. I had to sit for hours, and then they sent me home. I thought that was gonna be a one-time thing, so I went back the next year with John Pugh. When we pulled up to crossin', I saw some kinda light start flashin', and they made us pull over to the side.

"It turned into an interrogation, and they thought they were expert interrogators. They acted like detectives or somethin'. They put John in one room and me in another. They'd ask ever kinda question imaginable. Then they'd switch people. You'd see 'em whisperin' and tellin' what they found out from one of us, hopin' our answers would cross. Then they'd send somebody else in there and do it again. I told 'em, 'I'm damned ready to go. I'm tired of sittin' in here.' I told 'em the same thing about fifty times, but they kept at it. One woman marched in there clickin' her boot heels against the floor. It seemed like she wanted me to say, 'Attention,' and salute her or somethin'. I fine'lee got so disgusted, I didn't pay her any attention. I'd listen a little bit and then just look at the floor. I guess that didn't help matters too much, but I'd run out of anything else to explain.

"What's really happenin' is the people at the border crossins' have put in for higher positions. But they have to stay a long time before they ever get it. So, they act like professional interrogators, but they ain't.

"Once I got on their bad list, I couldn't cross the border with a tooth-brush. I tried gettin' a letter from the Choctaw County Sheriff's Office, but that didn't work. I tried everything I could and got turned back every time. I think I got turned back three years in a row."

Listening, I knew for Moon this was no small matter! It kept him from doing exactly what he wanted to do and ended his twenty-year pattern of salmon fishing every summer in Alaska. The silver lining of sorts: the ordeal only served to expand his fishing horizons.

ST. CROIX RIVER

"I fine'lee got it straightened out up in Minnesota when I was fishing the St. Croix River. One day I drove up to the Minnesota-Canadian border. The traffic was light, so I struck up a conversation with a fella at the crossin' who looked like the head honcho. I told him how much I liked to fish, and he said, 'I like to fish too.' We started talkin' about fly-fishin' for smallmouths. He said, 'I like catchin' smallmouths on the fly too.' I told him, 'I do a lot of fishin' in Alaska,' and I showed him some salmon pictures. He really got interested in that and told me, 'Sit down.' I told him, 'I haven't been able to go for several years because I can't cross the border, and I'd like to find out why.' He asked, 'Do you have your papers with you?' I handed them to him, and he looked 'em over. He started tappin' around on the computer and put my name in there. I told him, 'I've never done anything wrong.' But that's what everybody says that's done somethin' wrong, so I was kinda caught up in that situation. I told him the places where I'd been stopped. He tapped around on the computer a minute or so and said, 'You ain't done anything that it shows on here. I can understand how you can't get across sometimes. Once you get flagged, they look at you more carefully.'

"He said, 'The next time you go, you should drive to Seattle and ask for the Canadian Consulate.' He wrote me a little note on a piece of paper and said, 'Come back tomorrow, and I might be able to get 'em on the radio.' I said, 'I've spent a lot of time on this already, and I've driven all the way from Mississippi to fish the smallmouths.' He gave me his card and the note and told me to go to Seattle and see the consulate. Ty got all stirred up about it and managed to get a letter from Senator Roger Wicker's office.

"The next year, I went to Seattle to the consulate. I took the man's note and the letter from Senator Wicker. The consulate looked at all that and printed me an official document. I ain't never had a problem since. I still don't ever go through that big crossin' north of Seattle they call the Peace Arch, where they have all that equipment."

Moon's explanation sounded true to form. I thought, *Yeah, and you try to avoid big cities and as many interstate highways as possible and drive as slow as a turtle!*

MPE AND MPPF PERFECTED

Listening, I imagined Moon in his truck, camper shell attached, driving back roads on his way to Alaska. It occurred to me, *Not only has his equipment improved over the years, a perfected version of MPE and MPPF has also evolved.* Like his fishing reels, rods, and lures, Moon is always thinking about how to perfect anything related to fishing to gain the slightest edge.

Over the years, I'd observed, scattered about his truck, various and sundry old cans of store-bought stuff, so ancient the labels had worn off; in more recent years, cases of salmon and venison neatly stacked and reasonably organized. Don't get the wrong picture—the more organized jars and cans still appear antique ... with no shelf-life dates affixed!

I thought, *Like a turtle shell, Moon's food rides on his back.* No need to waste valuable fishing time driving to a store or spend extra money on unhealthy food. When you get hungry, just open a can and dig in—as close to the water's edge as possible!

Ten years ago, while crappie fishing a lake in the Mississippi delta, we took a break for lunch. Moon opened a container of canned venison and made sandwiches. Yes, he's slowing down in old age and occasionally stops long enough for lunch.

"Shane, these things will keep as long as you're alive."

I thought, but never said, *Yeah, that's because they will end your life the minute you decide to take a bite. And if they don't kill you, they will make you wish you were dead.*

I was so hungry I risked my life and ventured a cautious bite. My hesitation wasn't because I don't like canned venison. The can looked like leftover "C-rations" from WWII!

The venison tasted better than Grade A canned beef, *and* I have lived to tell about it!

TRAILBLAZER

Moon is a fading legend among the bank fishermen on the mighty Kenai. The world is composed of trailblazers, pioneers, and settlers. The trailblazers don't like the pioneers, and the pioneers don't like the settlers. The settlers don't tolerate either. Trailblazers and pioneers believe settlers make the surroundings too crowded and tip the balance between man and environment. When the pioneers move in, the trailblazers move on. When the settlers move in, the pioneers move on.

Moon is a trailblazer. He has a hard time imagining change. He wanted the pristine Kenai to remain just like it was the day he first set foot on its hallowed ground in 1968.

"When I first went up there, there were hardly any boats on that river. Now you can't hardly fish for all the boats runnin' up and down it."

As I listened to Moon, the trailblazer's detectable ire, I recalled again, "That boat gives the angler an unfair advantage."

The changes on the Kenai were inevitable, but Moon couldn't bring himself to reconcile her new future. However, today the spirit of the original bank fishermen lives on in Greg Calloway and his son, River. If you want guides who understand the river, its history, and its spirit, there are no better guides than Greg and River. Greg can tell you stories few people know. And if you go, ask about Moon, Charles, and Alice.

FLY-FISHIN'

"After the Kenai changed so much, I knew my chances of catchin' the world record were over. I'd rather catch one on a fly rod anyway. So, I started fishin' salmon with the fly. That's the reason I bought the little boat I can carry on my back."

Remember, Moon's telling me this in his eighties!

"Really, I'd druther fly-fish than any other way. It's a truer sport."

Moon could open a used fly shop with the sheer number of fly rods, reels, and fly-tying material he owns.

"I guess I got into rod-and-reel fishin' because that's what Daddy liked to do. When I first started fishin' at Choctaw Lake, it was fly-fishin'. But I found out in that muddy water at Grenada you have to cover lots and lots of water. It's hard to do that with a fly rod. The best way to do that was with a baitcaster. That's what got me usin' a rod and reel. I prefer the fly rod, but if I'm crappie fishin', I use a jig pole. I never fish kings with a rod and reel anymore.

"It got so busy on the Kenai I started fishin' the Kasilof a lot more. I can cross the Kasilof in that little boat and be the only one on the other side. Most kings in the Kasilof don't get as big as the ones in the Kenai. But I think some kings that eventually go up the Kenai come into the Kasilof on the high tide and then go back out. They're gonna end up Kenai kings, but they'll go in both them rivers. Can't nobody prove that; that's just what I think. But there's been lots of big kings caught on the Kasilof.

"I caught two on my fly rod the same day, and I had to do like this." He gestured with his arms in a way that meant the fish were so big he had to place his arms around their midsection to pick them up. "One of 'em was a big male and the other was a big female. Some people want to keep every fish they catch. I'm the opposite: I wanna throw every one back. I don't ever keep 'em anymore. That's what I call promotin' 'em. But I realize some people are hungry and can use 'em. Me too, sometimes."

I knew Moon never kept fish unless he or someone else needed them for sustenance. Furthermore, I knew he didn't believe in wasting anything—not only a fish, not even a single dime.

As Moon aged, he finally learned to wear waders.

WELCOME TO ACKERMAN

I am convinced Moon has driven more miles to and from fishing destinations than any man alive, every single journey laced with meaning. Lake Washington with Mack and back again, Grenada and back again, Alaska and back again—a pattern emerged that continues today. The sheer driving distances, the countless trips, the years, the endless coming and going is hard to get your mind around. At the intersection of Highway 12 and Main Street in Ackerman, a red brick sign reads, "Welcome to Ackerman, the Home of Governors J. P. Coleman and Ray Mabus."

Curious, I asked, "Why didn't you permanently leave Ackerman and move to Alaska?"

"Over all these years, I've never lost the sense Ackerman is my home."

"Hmm," I wondered but failed to ask.

I thought maybe it's because it's where he knew Mack—where Mack lived, died, and is buried. If you're looking for your daddy in Alaska, but his memory still haunts the streets of Ackerman, you can never completely leave one for the other. Plus, all Moon's surrogate parents live in Ackerman—their lives and memories part of his collective consciousness. Having recently binged on folk singer John Prine, after learning of his death attributed to COVID-19, I thought about his song, "My Darlin' Hometown." I thought, *Not only do all our journeys begin at home, but there's also something about the natural order that suggests they should end there too.*

Ackerman to Soldotna, Soldotna to Ackerman, both places call to Moon—they deeply call. The trips, the places, the people, the fish, and the stories all merge and become one man, one journey, one life.

Of course, until the final curtain closes, he doesn't want to keep the salmon from coming up the Kenai and disappoint the bank fishermen.

Welcome to Ackerman.

CHAPTER 31

WHAT HAPPENED
AND WHY

IT WAS NOW ALMOST NOON. We were supposed to take Moon to lunch, but I was still sitting at the dining room table in the Airbnb. Jean sat on the sofa across the room, buried in the novel she was reading. Again, I contemplated her previous question, "Where were you, and what were you doing when this or that happened?" I recognized that over my lifetime, no matter where I was or what I happened to be doing at the time, Moon's stories and lessons were always there, swirling around in my head. Broad-sweeping stories and lessons covering history, politics, possessions, race relations, the poor—life, death, and the future. I also knew for years, like a good skeptic, I had tested and retested his lessons and hypotheses against my own experiences.

I remembered a paragraph from *A River Runs Through It*, when Norman said that after Paul's death, he and his father didn't talk about it. I also recalled Norman's father told him to make up a story and the people who go with it, and "only then will you understand what happened and why."[12]

---

12   Norman Maclean, *A River Runs Through It* (Chicago: University of Chicago Press, 2017), 118.

I knew my story wasn't fiction, but sitting there, the imperfect man, the imperfect son, the pain and the glories all converged, and I understood with more clarity *what happened and why*.

It's a curious thing how a father's traits are passed down almost imperceptibly. Most of us are fulfilling a script already set in motion by our parents that's hard to admit in our younger days. We can add to the script and press it forward but only so much. The best father-son relationships are nevertheless broken. Dads want to impart lessons sons aren't yet interested in, and sons want something dads can never completely provide. What happens on the journey? *Why does it happen?*

I thought of Dostoevsky's words in *The Brothers Karamazov*: "I believe like a child that suffering will be healed and made up for, that all the humiliating absurdity of human contradictions will vanish like a pitiful mirage ... at the moment of eternal harmony, something so precious will come to pass that it will suffice for all hearts, for the comforting of all resentments, for the atonement of all the crimes of humanity, for all the blood that they've shed; that it will make it not only possible to forgive but to justify all that has happened."[13]

What happened? Why? My life unfolded the way it has so I could tell the stories, the pain and glories, and the lessons learned from a flawed but amazing man who happens to be my dad. Sitting there, I thought, *Some of Moon's lessons are profound, others heartwarming, and others downright controversial and may not be readily accepted.* I thought, *So what?* Put on your waders, and let's wade through a few lakes. Warning: some are deep!

ALLIGATORS AND GRIZZLY BEARS

All my life, for some reason, the local crowd felt compelled to make sure I knew, "Moon ain't afraid of nothin'!"

---

13 Fyodor Dostoyevsky, *The Brothers Karamazov*, Translated by Constance Garnett (New York: Modern Library Edition, 1996), 261–62.

I was always a bit annoyed by their freely distributed observation, knowing that I was afraid of lots of things, most of them intangible, hard to look at and admit to. So, I filed the locals' comment in my "male-role-model" folder.

In the childhood world of *Captain Kangaroo* and *Mr. Rogers*, male role models were in short supply. It seemed unmanly to wear a cardigan in the beautiful neighborhood and teach children how to feed Mr. Hamster. Nonsensical in Ackerman, most local kids had been feeding some farm animal since they could walk that didn't live in a cage in an apartment in New York.

I settled on *Daniel Boone*. "Daniel Boone was a man. Yes, a big man. He was brave; he was fearless and as tough as a mighty oak tree."

So, every afternoon after school, I watched Fess Parker throw knives and hatchets and shoot muskets. The problem inside the Ackerman city limits was there weren't many good reasons to throw knives and hatchets or shoot muskets. So, I practiced on the oak tree in the backyard, with mom's kitchen knives and our dull camping hatchet. Fortunately, I didn't own a musket!

Daniel *was* brave, fearless, and as tough as a mighty oak tree. But I liked something else about ole' Dan. He was fair, caring, and gentle, often defending other pioneer families at the risk of his own life. Most tough guys I knew weren't very caring or gentle. At least, not that I could tell. Most "gentle" men didn't seem very tough.

Over the years, I've had to reopen my male-role-model folder more than just a time or two! Enamored with Samuel Clemens from youth, in 2018, I purchased both volumes of his autobiography. I waded through the enormous volumes that describe the backstory of his works. Numerous comments caught my eye, but two stuck out. *Roughing It,* written in 1872, describes his experience in Western mining camps. Clemens said he learned that gold in its native state is but dull unornamental stuff. It's only low-born metals that excite the admiration of the ignorant with an ostentatious glitter. But, like the rest of the world, I still go on underrating men of gold and glorifying men of mica.

I knew my real role model was always Moon. He resembled Daniel Boone, or did Daniel Boone resemble him? Don't mishear me. Moon is flawed, very flawed. But I first had to see and admit my own flaws before I could ignore the mica and see the gold.

In 1894, Clemens says that "courage is resistance to fear, not the absence of fear." When I read it, I thought, *That makes perfect sense.*

So, finally on our way to lunch, curious, I decided to test the "not-afraid-of-anything" hypothesis and asked, "Daddy, are you afraid of anything?"

Moon cleared his throat followed by a long silent pause, indicating he was deep in thought. I could tell I'd asked a significant question in the hierarchy of Moon's perceived values.

Finally, he said, "Yeah, yeah I am."

"What?"

"Well," he paused before continuing, "alligators and grizzly bears."

"Why?"

"I reckon it's because they've both stalked me and tried to eat me."

After he thought a bit more, he said, "I guess I wouldn't mind gettin' eaten 'cause that happens real fast; it's that stalkin' I don't like."

He then launched into a story about crappie fishing in Loakfoma Lake in the Noxubee County Refuge.

"I was down there crappie fishin', and I paddled my kayak out to an island and tied it off and got out and started wadin' with my jig pole. I noticed a few big alligators paddlin' in."

Note 1: Big alligators at Loakfoma is a gross understatement. It's more like a bunch of T. rexes in a bathtub making hungry grunts, lying around in the shade and mud of the cypresses, waiting to devour someone.

Note 2: A boat's purpose is to get to good wade-fishing, away from areas easily accessible from nearby roads that have usually been overfished.

"I landed a few nice crappie, findin' a couple here and there in four to five feet of water."

Which means he was wading in moderately deep water.

"Wading along, I noticed a group of button bushes extending out about fifty yards off an island. I thought, *Those should be 'bout the right depth.* I got farther and farther from the shore, and I noticed out of the corner of my eye in the open water what I thought was a log driftin' in the waves. Before I realized it was a huge gator, it had cut me off from the island."

This is when most people panic, pee themselves, flail the water, and disappear forever unless there happens to be a gator hunt. Then relics like rings, watches, necklaces, bones, and teeth are found.

"What did you do?"

"When I realized it was stalkin' me, I knew not to panic."

Easy to say, harder to do.

"Then what?"

"I was at least fifty yards from the island, so I figured out the best angle to keep some distance between me and the gator."

Note 3: Angles take on significant importance when Moon's being stalked.

"I slowly turned around, careful not to make any commotion, and picked out the best *angle.* I stayed on that angle one slow step at a time. I kept my eyes on the gator, realizin' that at any second, he might submerge and attack me."

Gators first grab their prey with their powerful jaws and drown them, then drag them somewhere and store them for a future dinner.

"I felt into my right pocket and made sure my knife was handy in case I was gonna have to fight it. But I don't think I'd stood a chance. Alligators have tough hides. I sped up a little bit when I got to shallower water, now focusin' more on the safety of the shore. When I looked back, that gator had disappeared. I decided not to go back out there."

I thought, *What kind of crazy person even takes the time to consider such a decision? More crappie or death? Hmm.*

"I walked along the bank of the island back toward the kayak, thinkin' I'd try another place."

Fishing would've already ended for most people, while they checked into the local hospital for an electrocardiogram.

"I spotted my kayak floatin' in the distance. I left the island and waded toward it."

Moon's kayak has a homemade anchor system consisting of rope and cinder block.

"I'll be damned; the same gator was floatin' in the waves twenty yards from my kayak, just waitin' on me. He knew exactly what I was doin'; those things are smart and know just how to stalk you and get ya'. I slowly waded backwards to the island. I picked up some big sticks and started throwin' 'em at the gator. It fine'lee moved on. I waited a little bit and waded back to my kayak and went to another place. That's why I'm afraid of alligators."

"Yeah, me too! What about grizzly bears?"

"One time I was fishin' on the Kenai, and it had rained four or five days straight, and the river had silted up. I knew a creek with clearer water that runs into the river. I thought I'd give it a try, so I hiked in the rain to try it out. When I walked down the trail to the creek, I noticed fresh grizzly tracks in the mud. The rain let up a little bit, so I fished about an hour but didn't get any strikes. I decided to head back to the campground. Walking back up the trail, I noticed a broken green saplin' leanin' across the trail. It dawned on me, *That wasn't here when I came down the trail*. What the bear was tryin' to get me to do was leave the trail and walk around the saplin' into the brush. Remembrin' the tracks, I hesitated and started lookin' in all the brush beside the trail. It was late and gettin' dark. Then I saw a big clump of brown hair. I squinted and looked closer; it was a giant grizzly just waitin' on me. If I'd taken one step off the trail, he'd have eaten me alive."

"What did you do!?"

"I froze and stood real still for a moment and took in a couple deep breaths and let 'em out real slow, tryin' not to get too afraid. Them bears can smell fear. I took one slow backwards step at a time. I thought, *If I can get the proper angle toward the water, it might decide to leave me alone. I knew not to turn my back*."

Remember, in Moon's head, proper angles are important if you ever find yourself being stalked by alligators, grizzlies, or anything else!

"I cleared the brush and kept walkin' backwards one slow step at a time. I got to the rocks and got another angle, tryin' to increase the distance between me and the bear. About twenty yards from the river, I slowly turned around, tryin' not to move my arms or head too quickly. I kept my eyes focused on the trail. You never wanna turn your eyes on somethin' like that because that's when they charge because they know they can get ya."

"What were you going to do if it charged?"

"You can't outrun no grizzly bear! By then, I was hopin' I'd made enough distance to swim for it. I changed my angle again and started walkin' faster along the riverbank. I stopped every now and then and looked back to make sure it wasn't followin' me. I don't mind bein' the hunter, but I don't like bein' the hunted; it's just somethin' disturbin' about that. That's why I'm afraid of grizzly bears."

"Me too!"

When your role model can admit fear, it makes him or her real—flesh and blood, vulnerable, human. It also helps you admit and face your own fear. Courage is resistance to fear, not the absence of fear—and that's not mica, that's gold!

CATCH-AND-RELEASE AND FISHING PHARISEES

I thought about Moon's former comment concerning catch-and-release: "That's what I call promotin' 'em. But I realize some people are hungry and can use 'em. Me too, sometimes."

I realized something considerable: something more than popular views of catch-and-release was in play. Moon's view of catch-and-release is nuanced, depending on his circumstances and the circumstances of others around him, some of whom might be hungry.

Moon has always admired and respected every fish caught, a prize to be utilized in the best way possible. Over the years, the poor and elderly have received Moon's "fish gifts" like packages from St. Nick on Christmas morning. The gifts have spread general good cheer and helped hungry people eat. Moon's fileted fish always comes special delivery, wrapped in a story about generally where and how they were caught.

I attribute my view of *catch-and-release* to Moon's lessons and example over the years. Early on, Moon taught me the importance of conservation. When we fished smaller ponds or lakes and happened to be doing particularly well, he always said, "Shane, we need to leave some of these fish for seed." If he wasn't going to eat the fish himself or give them to someone, he put them back. Moon has released more fish than most fishermen have caught. Many more.

When I was little, and before I could understand, I strongly objected to releasing any. Why would anyone go to all the trouble, experience the mystery and thrill of pulling a fish from the water, only to put it back? Throwing any back seemed nonsensical, a violation of basic common sense. No amount of reasoning, explanations, or conventional wisdom worked with me about why we should release a single one.

"We need to put some back so they can make babies so there will always be lots of fish."

Wailing, crying, and stomping to strengthen my argument ("There are already lots of fish. Let the ones we haven't caught make the babies"), Moon consoled me by personifying the fish and giving it a name. "This here is George. Shane, say hello to George. See, he's a boy; this is how you can tell. We are going to clip a little bit of George's pectoral fin so we will recognize him the next time we catch him. Then we can congratulate George on how big he's grown. Say goodbye to George."

"Bye, George."

"Let's see if we can catch another one and name it Fred or Susan."

"Okay!"

So, sometimes we kept a few, sometimes we kept more than a few, and sometimes we didn't keep any at all. As a result, at an early age, I developed a healthy skepticism for catch-and-release purists. Maybe a bit harsh, but I refer to them as fishing Pharisees. Tighten your waders, the water is about to get deep and murky!

Howell Raines, former executive director of *The New York Times,* is a passionate advocate of *total* catch-and-release. I love his book *Fly Fishing Through the Midlife Crisis,* but in it, he speaks of "fish-hauls," "fish killers," and "the redneck way."[14] According to Howell's description, Moon is a *fish killer,* a hopeless disciple of *the redneck way.* But I call Moon's philosophy of catch-and-release, "the modified redneck way." Moon has always provided fish for the many poor and elderly living in and around Ackerman who could not otherwise provide the tasty morsels for themselves. It can be argued that fish and other forms of wild game still hold important significance as primary food sources for the nation's rural poor. It's easy to toss them back and chalk it up to conservation if you know that evening you will be dining on whatever you please.

Howell also explores the relationship between "fish killing" and social class. In 1986, *The New York Times* sent him to London to do a story on fly-fishing. Howell says that deeply rooted in the British class system is the difference between the "remorseless fish killer," actually referred to as "redneck," and the affluent, who he refers to as "Tweedy Gents." Raines was shocked when he watched a Tweedy Gent kill a fish. For him, a class inversion had taken place right before his eyes.

To be fair, Howell Raines remains staunchly consistent in his advocacy of total catch-and-release and the denunciation of the redneck way. I like people who stick to their convictions. However, according to his description, keeping just one fish puts you on the stringer with all advocates of the redneck way. The spiritually enlightened throw 'em back—every single one.

The Tweedy Gents should know better; the doubly predestined poachers, hopeless. With a little more catch-and-release gospel, it should be possible

---

14   Howell Raines, *Fly Fishing Through the Midlife Crisis* (New York: Harper Perennial, 2006), p. 35-36, 98-99.

for the Tweedy Gent to climb Jacob's ladder to the heaven of the spiritually enlightened. Like a nuclear winter, if we turn the poachers loose, we'd have no more fish. The enlightened need to preserve as much habitat and fish as possible to protect fish populations from the unwashed hordes of barbaric poachers.

I have to say, if keeping just one fish places me in the social caste with the poachers of the British Isles, so be it. My choices are limited. Should good sport fishing only be available to the privileged and spiritually enlightened with the finest gear who control access to private streams and lakes? Do they own all God's water and all God's fish? By what right do they? Is North America truly the home of the free and the brave or the land of freedom and posted signs for the privileged? Are the privileged really preserving the land and fish for future generations or hording both for themselves? I do know one thing: total catch-and-release isn't all it's cracked up to be.

THE WHITE PELICAN

The white pelican is a magnificent, protected bird. A mature adult stands four feet tall with a nine-foot wingspan! Like manmade gliders, the beautiful white birds soar in formation on warm wind currents as high as ten thousand feet above the earth. Magnificent, beautiful, and awe-inspiring, the White Pelican consumes an average of four pounds of fish per day during a lifespan that can reach thirty years. If a pelican's fishing remains consistent, one pelican consumes 43,800 pounds, or twenty-two tons, of fish in a lifetime!

Put another way, if every fish averages a half pound, a pelican ingests 87,600 fish before they go the way of all the earth—and they absolutely love to eat trout! White pelicans go fishing every single day, and there are many more pelicans than anglers. Suppose the average angler keeps twenty two-pound fish per year. Over the same thirty years, the *fish killer* would harvest and consume 1,200 pounds of fish, slightly more than a half ton.

Who are the advocates of total catch-and-release kidding: themselves or the pelicans? Who's more important, people or the damned pelicans? We better all get out there before the pelicans get all the fish and there's none left to release.

Is there another way? A way between fish killing and thoughtful conservation? Might there be "redneck" conservationists in the world who abide by limits and care for public lands and healthy fish populations, a determined medium between private land ownership and public land access for the common man? And what about Lige Weaver who just needed something to eat?

THE MIRACLE MILE

Several years ago, I went fly-fishing with a good friend to the famed Miracle Mile on the North Platte River in Wyoming. We left Denver early, stopped off at the West Laramie Fly Shop to get licenses and the latest fishing report, a bacon and egg biscuit, and to add a few hot patterns to our arsenal.

That day, the fish were big and hungry. We landed fish after fish—rainbows, cutthroats, and browns. Finally, I pulled an evil stringer from a pocket in my fly vest and tied a healthy specimen to my side. My fishing friend looked at me like I'd just brazenly broken one of the fishing ten commandments. When I kept the second one, he looked at me like I'd murdered his mother. I wanted to preach a fiery sermon, but I knew it'd be pointless, so I reluctantly joined the ranks of the "catch-and-don't release-all-of-them" outcasts. I carefully packed my two beautiful trout on ice in my small zip-topped cooler.

Hungry, headed back to Denver, we stopped off at a good restaurant. We scanned the menu. My Tweedy-Gent friend ordered the cedar plank grilled salmon as my two hefty trout slumbered in their cold graves in the trunk of the car. When the waiter placed the steaming salmon in front of him, I thought, *Someone somewhere had to kill this fish, and it was probably raised in a pen and fed tainted feed, laced with hormones.* It made me wonder if growing numbers of people don't even realize where food comes from in the first place. Even vegans eat plants that must die for the vegan to live. I told you it was deep murky water we were entering!

As I munched on my mushroom and swiss burger, my poor friend, proud as a peacock to be a card-carrying member of the catch-and-release crowd, oohed and aahed about how tasty his store-purchased salmon was. The dining experience was nice, but I wondered if my friend would even know what to do if he ever decided to "kill" a fish. Maybe with available technology, one day, we might figure out how to mix up some chemicals with the essential amino acids, vacuum seal the mixture, and scarf it down on the run. I suppose we could save trees because we'd no longer need dining tables or china cabinets.

How many people would spend time planning an exquisite meal—carefully placing their best tableware, considering appropriate beverages, creating the perfect mood—seat their guests, and then just sit there and stare at the food? Not one guest even considers a sip of wine or bite of the delectable food. Then the host announces, "Let's go out for dinner." That'd be grossly unnatural, halting a natural sacramental process meant for consummation.

I had plans for my fish. I was going to honor God's fish, and them me, by participating with others in what they were designed to do in the first place.

FISH-HAULS

Furthermore, "fish-hauls" are always seasonal. No matter how hard you work to catch fish, there are cyclical days of feast and famine built into the very patterns of the moon.

In *Braiding Sweetgrass*, Robin Wall Kimmerer eloquently describes the production cycle of pecans and hickory nuts. An accomplished forest and environmental biologist, Kimmerer understands the boom-and-bust cycle of pecans and hickories known as mast fruiting. Robin's native forebearers learned the cyclical pattern, gained the wisdom, and stored the nuts that sustained them for generations through boom and bust.

Nature, food shortages, and hunger have ways of teaching lessons that abundance can't provide. "Fish-hauls" are seasonal, and we have the technology—it's called refrigeration—to preserve some of the catch for winter days when no man "fisheth," except Minnesotans.

I tend to have a more epiphanic experience dining on a fish in January that I pulled from the water in July than one I bought in the frozen food section at the local grocery store. Why? I'm closer to the actual living and dying of the fish I caught, touched, admired, and sacrificed than the one I purchased from the shelf at Kroger. I'm many steps removed from the living and dying of the Kroger fish. One fish is cloaked in mystery and helps me better understand my hallowed place in God's universe. The other, not so much.

In case you're wondering, I do sometimes buy tilapia, raised somewhere in a pen in Indonesia, from a frosty bin at the local Safeway, and it tastes good—but it's not the same. Something feels right about acknowledging I'm a dependent creature of the fertile earth, the sacramental nature of all things, the large-scale dying in order to live. From where does my bread originate in the first place?

CHAPTER 32

MOON'S MORAL
PHILOSOPHY

REDNECK LIVES MATTER

AT THIS POINT, you may want to swap your waders for scuba gear.

Four years ago, Jean and I fished the legendary coho run in Valdez, Alaska. It was early September, the initial height of the Black Lives Matter movement.

That day, big bruisers were in close, and fishermen of all types lined the jagged rocks, casting away like there was no tomorrow, dreams of joining the ranks of the successful. The rhythmic swells rose and splashed between the big rocks, creating foam and whirlpools as the turbulent water returned to the ocean.

Jean and I and a couple of other fisherpersons stood on the only small section of beach between the giant rocks. Trying to remain inconspicuous, Jean walked close and tapped me on the shoulder. "Read that guy's T-shirt!" I slowly turned my head. On top of a big rock not fifteen yards away stood a man wearing a dirty trucker's hat and knee-length white rubber boots, visibly missing several front teeth, chunking his heavy spoon into the brine.

His T-shirt read, "Redneck Lives Matter." Not a better living stereotype, and I couldn't help laughing out loud.

Minutes later, I hooked a giant coho. The fish made numerous powerful runs, getting into my backing several times. The fish finally tired, but I couldn't manage to beach it. He made another run, entering the surging torrent between the rocks, tangling my leader and my hopes of landing it. Risking life and limb, the redneck went airborne off his high perch and pounced on top of the big fish. He grabbed it and held it up.

"That's a giant 'un, nice job!"

We exchanged high fives.

Jean asked, "Do you mind if we get a picture with you and the fish?"

"Of 'cos not."

"Thanks for the help!"

"I'd do 'dat for anybody."

Thinking back on the humorous event, I wondered, *Would I have done that for him?* Hmm. I certainly didn't offer him the fish. The redneck exposed the classism of my dark heart. I thought about Moon and all his motley friends.

Redneck lives matter, all lives matter: red, yellow, black, and white, poachers and Tweedy Gents.

THE PRESIDENT'S INITIATIVE ON RACE

I remembered Moon's comment from the previous day, "Black people deserved what they were strivin' for, and the only way they could do that was to bring it into the light. So, I switched around and got for them."

I thought about his lessons from childhood and how radical his stance must have been, especially in Mississippi in the 1960s. I considered my own journey related to race.

In 1998, I had the privilege of participating in President Bill Clinton's "The President's Initiative on Race."

President Clinton's stated purpose: "I want this panel to help educate Americans about the facts surrounding issues of race, to promote a dialogue in every community of the land to confront and work through these issues, to recruit and encourage leadership at all levels to help breach racial divides, and to find, develop and recommend how to implement concrete solutions to our problems—solutions that will involve all of us in government, business, communities, and as individual citizens."

I heard John Hope Franklin and Governor William Winter speak at the Gertrude C. Ford Center for the Performing Arts on the campus of Ole Miss. Leading up to the event, leaders from local government, businesses, education entities, and religious institutions were paired with individuals of a different race in their respective fields of work. My dialogue partner was the Reverend Doctor LeRoy Wadlington, pastor of Second Missionary Baptist Church in Oxford, a traditional black congregation.

We met weekly for six weeks for dialogue. I will always be indebted to Dr. Wadlington for his candor, honesty, and vulnerability regarding his experiences of race. For me, the impact was life-changing and continues to bear fruit in old age. The most poignant session was when we were asked to describe our experiences related to the following questions, "What are your first memories of learning that there was something called race? Have you ever felt different because of your race? If so, what was your first experience of feeling different?"

I listened to Dr. Wadlington describe his childhood experience living with his family in a farmhouse on Highway 6 outside Oxford during the Ole Miss Race Riot of '62.

"I lived with my family in an old farmhouse on Highway 6, west of Oxford. The night of the riots, bullets were fired through our house. We were terrified, and my father instructed us to hide on the floor under the beds. After it was over, he had to explain to me that some people hate you simply because of the color of your skin. That's the first time I remember realizing I was different because I was black."

It was clear to me Dr. Wadlington was reliving the horrible events. He wept. I wept. It was emotionally painful to go back with him to the time and place, but it was enlightening and deeply impactful. I didn't know what to say, but one thing I knew: growing up as a white kid, I didn't have a clue what it meant to struggle with race like he had.

It was my turn. "Have you ever felt different because of your race?" My different was a bad kind of different: a privileged difference, a sheltered difference demarcated by societal racial sensibilities—"separate and not equal" sensibilities. I had never explored how race had impacted me, but it had. I thought about Mrs. Jackson and Charles Thomas and their weighty influence in my life. I also wondered why all the black friends I'd known as a kid just one day disappeared from my life, vanishing like smoke. I thought about Titus. What happened to Titus?

Titus had a team of mules, and every spring, he tilled local gardens in and around Ackerman. Afternoons, Titus drove his mules down the street in front of our house on his way home after a tiring day's work. I sat on the front porch and watched, fascinated with Titus and his mules. I figured out his routine and sat on the steps every afternoon, anticipating Titus's arrival like Santa's sleigh. Not able to contain my excitement, I jumped and waved accordingly. Titus always removed his hat and waved.

Finally, one day he pulled his team up to the curb and motioned for me to come over. He got down out of the wagon and held me up and let me rub the mules' noses. He pulled me up into the wagon and let me hold the reins. He pulled a candy bar from his overall pockets, broke it in half, and we sat in the wagon and enjoyed a communal meal together. After that day, on many occasions, Titus stopped, and we repeated our ritual. I liked candy bars, but I really liked Titus.

What kind of separate world had I assumed when I don't even know what happened to Titus, a man who shared his time, kindness, and candy bars with a curious white kid?

And then there was Gladys. Gladys was my black momma who kept me while Farrah tried to make ends meet at the local shirt factory. Gladys loved me, and I loved her. One day, these dear people just vanished, erased by the assumptions of separate societies.

Pastor Wadlington nodded, "You're on the right track."

I remembered Moon's words on our return trip from Alaska in 1982: "The way this country has treated native peoples and blacks is the darkest scars on our history. This country has never acknowledged her sins in a whole lot of areas."

I wondered, *Would I be on the right track if not for Moon's immeasurable influence in my life?*

IZOLA DOTSON JACKSON

The following spring, on one of my annual visits to Ackerman, I dropped by Mrs. Jackson's dilapidated trailer on a rural road in Choctaw County to see if she was still alive and still lived there. She answered the door and looked to be in her nineties. It took her a bit to remember me. First, she remembered my sister, Christia, and then me.

"Shane, oh yeah, Shane! What do you do now?"

I told her.

"You made a preacher?! My, my, I do declare, let me pray for you."

She did. I remembered her words the day she paddled me in the hallway in 1970, and on this day, I whispered under my breath, "Mrs. Jackson, God bless your sweet cherry pie soul."

CHARLES THOMAS

Sitting in the restaurant having lunch, I thought again about how rare Moon's impartial treatment of others has always been. Remembering the previous evening's obsession, I thought, *I should try to go see Charles Thomas while I'm still in town.* I Googled his name on my iPhone. Jean gave me the look, which I knew meant, *Put your phone down.* I rolled my eyes and slightly crinkled the left side of my mouth, which was my defiant reply: *I know I should, but I'm not going to.* I looked at the screen, and the first thing I saw was his obituary. "Charles Thomas died at home on Friday, October 31, 2008."

I felt grief and instant shame that I didn't even know. I remembered the man's simple kindness. Feigning attention to the conversation at the table, I allowed my memory to travel back, and I was momentarily driving Mr. Thomas's purple truck. I Googled and continued to read.

Finally, after more than a decade of relinquished benefits afforded white principals, substandard pay, denied promotions, and a nasty demotion for no other reason than the color of his skin, Mr. Thomas had endured enough.

On August 3, 1984, Charles L. Thomas filed a motion in US District Court, alleging violations of Singleton provisions and racial discrimination in violation of United Supreme Court rulings, 1981, 1983, and The Civil Rights Act of 1964. The honorable Neal Brooks Biggers, Jr. presiding, the court ruled in Mr. Thomas's favor. He was awarded back pay and recovery for utilities and the fair rental market value of the house occupied by the white principal of Ackerman High School from school year 1970 through 1985. Mr. Thomas used some of the retributive money to begin a nonprofit serving the youth of Choctaw County.

I was pleased to learn justice was served, but then I wondered, *Was it really?* What about the goodness of the man, the pain he and his family endured, the forfeited social good the community could have enjoyed if they could have only seen past skin color? I thought, *What a crying shame!*

Since that afternoon in the restaurant, I've had time to read and further reflect on Moon's invaluable influence in my life, as well as the racial assumptions of the post-desegregation 1970s South. I've read several enlightening books, but a critical essay in *The Southern State of Mind,* by Charles Reagan Wilson, former director of Ole Miss's Center for the Study of Southern Culture, entitled "The Myth of the Biracial South" made the most sense and helped me better understand the racial assumptions that affected my childhood experience.

Wilson states the biracial myth can be traced to the conservative idea of the South as a hierarchical society working smoothly where everyone understands his and her place. Yes, there's been the occasional wild racial radical whose frenzied rhetoric and violence has come to force. But the conservative understanding of the region's economic need for African Americans suggests an ideological awareness of the need to keep blacks at the supper table, even if their table is separate and in the kitchen.

I recalled Moon's words, "that had to be a gradual thing." I thought, *Yeah, maybe too gradual.* During my youth, although Dixieland was slowly changing, small-town Mississippi couldn't accept a society where blacks and whites lived and worked side by side as brothers and sisters—equal pay, equal opportunities, equal.

Reflecting again on Charles Thomas's influence in my life, I want to tell him posthumously, "Thank you! Thank you, Mr. Thomas, for 'giving answers within your wisdom, leaving space between truth and lies' (as Dwight Yoakam sang about in 'V's of Birds'), for a white kid to discern years later. Mr. Thomas, one day we will ride together again in your purple truck. This time we won't need money for gas, and I'll be ridin' shotgun."

In the previous essay, Charles R. Wilson refers to a 1957 article in the *New Republic* by Charles L. Black, a white Southerner who taught at Yale Law School. Although living in Connecticut, Charles Black had a dream born of the common agrarian affinities he observed between Southern blacks and whites. In 1957, he believed desegregation could lead to something beautiful. His dream was that one day, sight would clear and blacks and whites would recognize one another. He believed if that happened, something unique and beautiful would transpire, and the South, which has always felt itself reserved for high destiny, would have found it and come to flower at last.

Utopian? Maybe, but I believe Charles Black's dream is still the hope. Reflecting again on Moon's immeasurable influence in my life, I thought, *The apple never falls too far from the tree.* I realize I'm only carrying forward, in some small way, something very important Moon taught me years before.

LIGE WEAVER

After lunch on the last day of the interview, still trying to bring some degree of closure to the stories swirling around in my head, I asked, "Daddy, what happened to Lige?"

"He died and was buried while I was in Alaska."

I recalled our brief morning visit the day before with my uncle Ronny Wood, who lives in an assisted living facility near our Airbnb. Already engrossed in this story, I asked him about Lige Weaver. His answer surprised and saddened me. "Me and Jim Miles dug Lige's grave. There wasn't anybody there to say anything at his graveside."

I asserted, "If Moon hadn't been in Alaska, he'd have been there, and he'd have said something too." Now, only a day later, I was more convinced of my assertion.

Sometimes, if not most of the time, social outcasts own the greatest ability to teach life's most important lessons, revealing our cold, insensitive hearts. I recalled a past sermon when I'd rather casually quoted a couple of lines I'd read in Charles Haddon Spurgeon's devotional *Morning and Evening*.

After an admonition to the poor not to despise the rich, Spurgeon flips the script. Allow me to translate; the English is a bit archaic:

On the other, maybe you are rich and beside you reside the poor. Do not scorn to call them your neighbor. Own your responsibility to love them. The world calls them your inferiors. I ask, in what way are they inferior. They are more your equals than your inferiors. Hasn't God made of one blood everyone that dwells on the face of the earth? It's your coat which is better than theirs, but you are by no means better. They are human and what more are you than that?

Remembering Moon's interactions with Lige taught me lessons I've not always emulated but would've never realized otherwise. I realized Lige's life mattered to me. Every life has worth, eternal worth. If avoidable, nobody should die or be buried alone; it's a failure of our common humanity.

TY COBB

In late July 2014, Moon brought Ty to fish with my family in British Columbia. Ty was suffering from an aggressive form of dementia. He was no longer the bright curious intellect of former days. We mainly fly-fished for salmon from the beach, but some afternoons, I fished for halibut from my boat.

Ty said, "Shane, I really want to catch a lingcod on a rod and reel."

"All right."

The next day was stormy, with three- to four-foot swells. I thought better of taking Ty out in such conditions. But I already told him I would, and he was eager to give it a try.

We launched and moved to a point across the bay arched with bull kelp in about forty feet of water. It was hard for Ty to balance himself to even stand up in the front of the boat. I kept the stern forward with the engine slightly in gear and told him to drop his jig. He did, and when the white curly tail jig hit the bottom, it was instantly seized by a ten-pound ling. I let the boat drift in the swells, netted the ling, and tossed it in the live well. Ty smiled, and I turned the boat for the dock.

Moon recalls, "That was the last trip Ty ever went on. I didn't know he was that bad off when we started. By the time we got home, he didn't have any more good days."

Ty died on September 14, 2015. I presume with a name like Ty Cobb, his daddy wanted him to be a baseball player, but God wanted him to be the superintendent of education of the Choctaw County school system, at which he excelled. Today in Ackerman, the Ty A. Cobb Sports Complex proudly honors the man and his memory.

Ty's widow, Carol, called Moon and asked him to recite "Annabel Lee" at the funeral. Of course, Moon obliged.

"I was a little nervous when I stood up in front of all those people, but after I said a line or two, I was fine. Ty was a close friend; he'd always do anything in the world he could to help others in any situation. I really miss those days when he'd come by the house and we'd argue and then go fishin'."

As Moon reflected, although it'd been five years since Ty's death, I somehow still expected him to be standing in the driveway when we returned from lunch. I suppose it's part of the expense of living in Colorado, away from the people I've known and loved. I told Moon, "I miss him too."

GEORGE EARL GRIFFIN

"What happened to George Earl?"

"George Earl got bad on the alcohol and pills. I went by to see him while he was in jail. He was always kinda lazy, and I guess he thought he deserved stuff without workin' for it. He never got nothin' paid for, and he had two different FHA homes and never made a payment on one of 'em. One day, he decided he wanted a new truck, and they made him a price on one, and he tried it out and said he'd take it. They needed a co-signer, and his momma wouldn't sign. She said, 'Everything I've ever signed for you, I end up payin' for myself.' This time she refused, and George Earl got to drinkin' and got madder and madder and got a shotgun, and before he thought, aimed it at her, pulled the trigger, and blew her head off. He was sorry for that, but it had already happened; it couldn't be changed.

"The last trip we took together was to the St. Croix River in Minnesota, and he camped with me on the island. He caught a giant walleye and cooked it. Man, George Earl was one of the best cooks I ever saw. Before he died, he'd married another woman and was livin' in an FHA home somewhere near Jackson. He died in 2005 of a heart attack, watchin' TV during Hurricane Katrina. I think he was fifty-one or fifty-two years old."

Listening, I already knew Moon loved George Earl, but I did wonder, *how?*

JOHN PUGH

I continued my quest for closure. "Is John Pugh still alive?"

"What John liked to do in Alaska was go halibut fishin'. He's still livin', but all he can do is lay on the bed. He's in the VA rest home in Kosciusko. Sometimes they put him in a wheelchair so he can sit in the sun. But basically, he'll never get out of that care facility. I've been down there to see him a few times. You have to sign your name and put your age on there too. I'm ten years older than most of the people in there. I just wanna stay out of them kinda places if I can. Other than ole' John, there ain't any of my friends left who went with me on all them trips to Alaska." [Note: John died in November 2021, after I completed this manuscript. Moon regrets he couldn't visit John due to COVID restrictions.]

GRADIE ERVIN

Before taking Moon home, we stopped by one of Ackerman's "gas and grill" establishments to gas up for our trip to the airport. The credit card reader malfunctioned, so I had to go inside. Jean and Moon stayed in the car. Inside, someone recognized me because I resemble a taller version of Moon.

"You must be Moon Sunn's boy, you're the spittin' image. What do you do now?"

"I'm a pastor in Denver, Colorado."

"Well, I'll be damned, Moon Sunn's boy a preacher, well I be damned, who'd ever figard'd?"

I recognized Gradie Ervin, my sixth-grade science teacher, sitting at one of the booths drinking coffee. I walked over and told him who I was. I thanked him for his influence in my life, and we talked about baseball. I knew he'd ask me about Moon.

"How's Moon gettin' along?"

"He's getting older but doing well, still fishing. He's in his eighties now and still drove to Alaska last summer too. He's out there in the car if you want to speak with him."

"I don't want to bother him; tell him to bring me some fish."

I did. Moon obliged. I checked to make sure a couple of months later.

Moral Philosophy

Driving Moon home, still curious, I asked him how he apparently managed to treat everyone the same. I was really asking him to explain his moral philosophy related to mankind. I regret, I forgot to engage the recorder, but he said something like this, "People are gonna be who they're gonna be, and they're gonna do what they're gonna do. Life itself is the great teacher. You either learn the hard lessons or you don't. My job is to be a friend to whoever might happen to come across my path."

And I knew he meant everybody!

Life's Journey

For Moon, fishing has always been more than the actual fishing; it's about the entire trip—the planning, the anticipation, the preparation, the drive, the music, the weather, the place, the fishing, the reward, the trip home again, the memories, the fileted fish gifts, the stories told and retold, the entire adventure. The entire *journey* is permeated with potentially transformative power.

The Bear by William Faulkner describes how the repetitive hunt for 'Ole Ben', a wily old black bear, transformed young Isaac McCaslin. Like life's journey, trips, you might even say "quests," are imbued with the capacity to change the pilgrim. First you must conceive a fish, a goal, a place, a celestial city enough to set out and cast your bait on the water. Pilgrims who persevere to the end receive the reward.

Over the years, I've thought about Moon's, "I might be slow, but I'm ahead of you" philosophy. Those who know me well will tell you slowing down hasn't been one of my fortes. But as I age, I'm getting a little better, and when I happen to slow down enough to live in the moment, I feel unruffled, more attentive to others, better able to take in the wonder and mystery of my surroundings and loved ones.

"I might be slow but I'm ahead of you."

"Yeah, you are."

CHAPTER 33

LOOK, DADDY!

"The earth was formless and empty, darkness was over the surface of the deep, and the *Spirit of God* was hovering over the waters."
— Genesis 1:2[15]

WRITING THIS STORY began like this: Initially, it was like a single oak leaf falling and gently brushing my shoulder. Pretty soon, another and another. Before long, I was standing in a windstorm of swirling oak leaves lifting me off my feet and carrying me to some landing place far away, known only to the Almighty. The initial leaf? All the people who over the years repeated, "You've got to write a book about Moon!"

I mostly shrugged it off with, "Yeah, maybe one day I'll do that."

SILVER ALERT

The storm gathered unexpected intensity in the summer of 2012. Jean and I planned our biennial trip to Vancouver Island to read, relax with our children, fly-fish for salmon, and gather big Dungeness crabs from the eelgrass in the Cluxewe estuary.

---

15   Genesis 1:2, NIV.

I departed ten days early to spend an entire week fishing with Moon. I was giddy with excitement. After packing my gear and hooking up the boat, I left Denver around noon for Port McNeill, British Columbia, Moon's DNA of "never stop driving" coursing through my veins.

I stopped around 2:00 a.m. at a rest area west of Missoula, Montana, beside the Clark Fork River and slept in the back seat of the truck. At 4:00 a.m., I jumped out of my skin when a semi pulled up beside me and released the airbrakes, which, with my windows cracked, sounded like a 747 taking off three inches from my eardrum. Drake, my chocolate lab, jumped feet-first into my lap. I got up, poured the remaining cold coffee from my Stanley thermos, and hit the road.

I made the 6:00 p.m. New Westminster ferry at Tsawwassen, British Columbia, and slept with Drake in the back seat as the ferry crossed The Strait of Georgia, landing at the Duke Point terminal in Nanaimo. I pulled into Cluxewe sometime after midnight and slowly drove through the campground, scanning all the sites for a white Ford Ranger with a camper shell and Mississippi license plates. Not here, yet.

On long trips, Moon arrives a day or two early, no exceptions. I climbed into the back seat again and caught up on much-needed sleep. The cry of a bald eagle, sitting atop a towering cedar beside my truck, awakened me early the next morning. I thought, *Much better than the semi's airbrakes yesterday.* I sat up, rubbed my eyes, and wondered why my back felt like it had been beaten with a baseball bat. I rubbed a spot off the fog that had formed on the inside of the pickup windows and scanned the calm gray ocean. I noticed a group of gulls having breakfast on baitfish. I slipped into my waders while tearing the top off a packet of Starbucks Via, carefully tamping it into my water bottle.

I thought about my '82 Alaska trip with Moon. "Here, Shane, want some coffee?" I expected to see his white Ford Ranger pull up any minute. The cold coffee working its magic, I hurriedly pieced together my Sage, running the line and tippet through the eyes. I selected my preferred fly, a pink-and-chartreuse deer hair streamer, the product of the previous year's buck I dyed and tied in preparation for the trip. I walked over the rocks and shells across the beach and waded knee-deep into the gray water, which now had a slight roll. I stripped the fly in a slow, rhythmic motion, and bam! The rod arched; the silver-sided "pink" did a couple of acrobatic somersaults. I played the fish until it tired and pulled it beside my wet waders and carefully released it back into the ocean, thinking, *The pink run is already beginning; this is going to be a good year!* The thought of keeping it for breakfast crossed my mind, but I still had to set up camp. I still expected to see Moon pull up any minute. I couldn't wait to tell him the salmon were already in.

TELEPHONES

"I despise cellphones. I knew how to use telephones when they hung on the wall, but I ain't never got used to punchin' them buttons on cellphones. I fine'lee got rid of every kind of phone. People don't think you can live with-out 'em, but you can. Every time I got back from Alaska, the phone company had turned off my phone and I'd had to pay an extra fee just to get it turned on. Fine'lee, I just told 'em to take the damn thing out. Them cellphones ever body uses these days are just too complicated. I've always thought if anybody really needed to find me, they'd be able to."

I spent the day setting up camp and waiting on Moon. I had an eerie feeling something wasn't right. I cooked and ate dinner alone that evening. Friends in the ministry trade from Seattle, Jason and Jenny Dorsey, arrived with their family and brother Jed and his wife, Renae. I shared my concern with Jason.

"Moon never arrives late. In fact, all my life he's always arrived a day or two early, especially if it has anything to do with fishing."

Jason reassured me. "He's probably having some sort of car trouble."

"Yeah, you're probably right."

"Why doesn't he have a cellphone?"

"Good question. He says he hates the things."

"That Moon's something."

"Yeah, he is."

I crawled into my sleeping bag on the cot inside my Cabela's outfitter tent. At Cluxewe, cellphone reception is sketchy. But that evening, my cellphone buzzed repeatedly.

I noticed a text from Jean. "There's been an awful shooting at a theatre in Aurora. I don't know all the details yet, but many are dead and wounded. Is Moon there yet? Love you."

I texted back, "Keep me posted on anything you hear about the shooting. No, Moon isn't here yet. Love you, too."

Next, I received a text from a former parishioner in Clinton, Louisiana. "Can you go to the Medical Center of Aurora; Bonnie Kate Pourciau was badly wounded in the shooting and she's in surgery and there's nobody with her except the friend she was with. She was traveling through Denver and decided to stop off and see the midnight screening of *The Dark Knight Rises.*"

I texted, "I'm so sorry but I'm in Canada. I will call Jean and let her know. I'm sure she will go to the hospital."

That evening, as bits and pieces of the horrific details of the Aurora Theatre shooting lit up media outlets, my concern for Moon increasing, I didn't sleep a wink.

Jason and Jed dropped by the next morning on their way to the water.

"Any word on Moon?"

"No, nothing."

I asked, "Did you hear about what happened in Aurora?"

"No, what?"

I described as much of the ghastly event as I knew.

Jason asked, "Can I pray for the victims and for Jean and Moon?"

"Sure. Thank you, Jason."

There was nothing to do but wait for more news from Denver and hope Moon would show up. I went fishing, but my heart wasn't in it. I found myself scanning the road, hoping to witness the arrival of Moon's truck. Nothing. My initial excitement of life's increasingly rare opportunities to spend an entire week fishing with Moon decreasing with every passing minute.

Three days passed. Christia called.

"Is Daddy there yet?"

"No."

"He should be, he left Ackerman a week ago. I went by his house the day before he left, and he said he'd been having chest pains. Something's wrong."

"Yeah, he should've been here five days ago."

I don't know why in these circumstances you begin to imagine the worst. I imagined Moon at a roadside rest area, the victim of a heart attack, dead, rotting in the heat inside his camper. Or maybe he fell asleep at the wheel and drove off the side of a mountain. In the ravine below, his decaying remains will be discovered in a week or two. The depth of my emotional struggle caught me off guard. I felt afraid, weird, off balance.

"Christia, I will call tonight and before then if he happens to show up."

The forecast called for fog and light drizzle the following day, excellent conditions to troll in close for big kings and silver salmon. I invited the Dorsey brothers to join me. The fishing was excellent, but in the dark, wet fog, I found myself planning Moon's funeral.

"What will I say; how will I say it?"

It was only then I slowly realized Moon's profound and indescribable influence in my life. The wind swirled, the trees shook, more leaves fell.

We docked, trailered the boat, and cleaned the beautiful fish. I called Christia.

In tears, Christia said, "I'm going to the Choctaw County Sheriff's Office tomorrow to file a missing person's report."

"That's a good idea. Call back and let me know any details."

That evening, I floated on a semi-conscious cloud, half of me awake, the other half experiencing vivid dreams of fishing with Moon.

Christia called the next morning at 8:00 a.m. "The Sheriff's Department is putting out a national Silver Alert sometime in the next few hours!"

"Okay, good."

"I'll let you know if I hear anything."

"Okay."

"Shane, I think he's dead."

I attempted to reassure Christia. "Yeah, he could be, but he's magically appeared from bigger scrapes before and come out smelling like a rose."

Really, I felt lost, unmoored, dread and palpable loneliness reverberated in the pit of my stomach. Within an hour, I began receiving calls and texts from different parts of the US and all over the state of Mississippi.

"We heard Moon's missing, we're praying, hang in there."

I was humbled and astonished. "Hell, the whole world is looking for Moon. I didn't know he mattered so much to so many people."

Less than an hour later, Christia called. "They found him, they found him. He's on a ferry out of Port Angeles, Washington!"

I was stunned. My voice quivered as I tried to say something.

"Hallelujah! I love you, Christia."

"I love you too. Y'all have fun fishing."

"I'm sure we will, after I kill him."

Just before dark, Moon rolled into the Cluxewe campground. I wanted to kill him and hug him at the same time. I opted for the hug.

"What in the world happened?"

"I didn't only have one major breakdown, I had two. The second was in the middle of nowhere in Oregon. It was last Thursday afternoon. I had to get towed to the Ford dealership, which was sixty miles away. I got there, and they couldn't get the parts they needed 'til Monday. The parts didn't come in 'til Tuesday.

"What did you do?"

"I just slept in the truck and read."

"Why didn't you call? I was worried sick!"

"There were no pay phones around there."

"Why didn't you use a phone in the dealership?"

"I wouldn't sure I had your right number."

"I told you, I'll buy you a cellphone and pay the monthly fee."

"There ain't no need to do that. I can't work the dang things anyway."

"Daddy, it's been more than a week since you were supposed to be here. We thought you were dead."

"Well, there wouldn't been anything you coulda' done about that anyway."

"Yeah, I guess you're right. Christia was so worried she put out a Silver Alert."

"I know. That got me held up when I got off the ferry in Canada. They said I was on the missing persons list and made me pull over until they notified the proper authorities. Don't you worry about me. When it's my time to go, there ain't nothin' you can do about it."

"Yeah, but I don't think you understand how the people who care about you feel."

"Are the fish a bitin'?"

"Yeah, they're in pretty thick."

"Well, let me get some sleep and set up for tomorrow."

"Okay. Did you bring, Barker?"

"Yeah, but he's calmed down a little bit in his old age."

"Okay."

That fall, Christia gave me a copy of the Silver Alert that originated in Ackerman. It read, "Seventy-six-year-old male last seen in blue jeans, cowboy boots, and a sleeveless flannel shirt. Left Ackerman, Mississippi, in a white Ford Ranger with Mississippi license plates sometime around July 12, driving north and west to Vancouver, British Columbia. He is believed to be of Indian descent."

All my life, I'd heard locals say, "That Moon Sunn must be part Indian." I couldn't believe the folk myth made the official Silver Alert! I laughed.

The whole incident awakened me to the coming inevitable reality that somehow I had never considered, except maybe in a general sort of way.

Moon seemed to me invincible. It also set in motion an arduous process of awakening me to myself. I've officiated lots of funerals. I know conducting my dad's would present an entirely different level of difficulty. But something else was happening inside I thought I'd dealt with years before. I had buried parts of my pain under deep layers of self-protective granite. My encounter with the prospects of Moon's death awakened me and revealed my deception. Like a silent drippy wet November day in the South, leaves poured down.

Moon and me fly-fishing at Cluxewe
Campground, British Columbia.

SABBATICAL

Five years later, spent from thirty years of beginning new churches and pastoring the flock, I applied to The Lilly Foundation for a sabbatical grant.

The purpose of the grant is to provide space for rest, reflection, and renewal away from the normal torrid pace of ministry. Jean and I needed it.

The arduous application required deep reflection about my life of ministry—triumphs, difficulties, and unhealthy patterns. Congregational input and agreement were requisites. A reading list focused on renewal was suggested. It's amusing how perceptive parishioners can see what you can't see or admit in yourself. The grant requires extended periods of travel away from your normal setting and routine, budgeting accordingly. Jean and I dreamed of where we might go and what we might do. Should we travel to Europe, Africa, Mexico, or South America? We unwittingly settled on Canada and Alaska. We dreamed of an unhurried pace with absolutely no obligations to do anything or see anything other than what the day unfolded. We wanted the journey itself to work its magic. We wanted "to be," not do. I was naïve for what awaited.

The application process itself was enlightening. Jean and I both agreed that even if we weren't selected, the process had been worth it. Really, we were attempting to protect ourselves from disappointment. As the date for award announcements approached, we bounced around somewhere between anxiety and dared hopefulness.

I was surprised when Mitch Groothuis, my administrative assistant, walked into the office and handed me a letter from The Clergy Renewal Grant, Lilly Foundation, a full week prior to the posted award announcement date.

"Look what came in the mail!"

"It's a week early, so it's probably a rejection letter."

I took a deep breath, trying to downplay my apprehension, feigning the possibility of real disappointment. I slowly opened the letter, office staff glued to my every movement and expression. I unfolded the letter.

"Dear Pastor Sunn, Congratulations ..."

"What!!!!?"

"... it is our pleasure to inform you that you have been selected to receive our Clergy Renewal Grant."

Trying to appear at least a little calm, I could hardly wait to call Jean. After a few high fives and hugs, I excused myself and pressed her number.

"Guess what!?"

"I don't know, but I can tell by your voice that it's something good."

"We were awarded the grant!"

"What!? I can't believe it. Really?"

"Really!"

After a celebratory send-off party on Sunday, July 23, 2017, we left Denver in our Ford F-150 and Hallmark truck camper, bound for northwest Canada and Alaska. I felt like Bilbo Baggins leaving the shire on an exciting, yet mysterious journey. No deadlines, no interruptions!

We drove, this time at a more reasonable pace, to Cluxewe Campground, British Columbia, Archie, our year-old yellow lab, in for the adventure of his young life. Our children and other family members joined us for a couple of weeks. I was different, better able to enjoy lingering conversations and simply be with my family.

We fly-fished the pink run and dined on delectable fire-roasted salmon and copious amounts of merlot. I caught a small lingcod in the estuary, and I thought about Ty. We purchased a propane firepit in Port MacNeill, due to a fire ban in the campground. What's a camping trip without a campfire? We sat around the firepit, told stories, and laughed until it hurt. The following day, the same.

After two memorable weeks of long days and conversations, we said goodbye and drove our truck camper onto a BC Ferry in Port Hardy, bound for Prince Rupert, British Columbia, and Alaska. We enjoyed a private cabin on the eighteen-hour cruise north. We slowly unwound, mesmerized by the picturesque beauty of the inland passage. We fly-fished the Skeena and Kitimat in northern British Columbia. Jean outfished me on the Kitimat, which, I'm sorry to admit, was irritating. We read, she painted, I wrote, we hiked, we existed.

Jean with a pink salmon on the Kitimat River, British Columbia.

We trekked north along the Cassiar Highway, hoping to catch an early glimpse of the Northern Lights. We turned north and west onto the ALCAN and marveled at the tundra swans, sandhill cranes, buffalo, caribou herds, and black and brown bears. Thoughts of my trip with Moon and Christia in 1982 swirled inside my head. Nights, reading for as long as we wanted and sleeping in until the morning sun warmed the inside of our camper, we cooked late breakfasts. After the second or third cup of coffee, bits and pieces of this story bubbled to the surface. Free with no time constraints, I began writing them in my journal. I simply wrote a stream of consciousness wherever it took me. I realized painful stories were attempting to rise. But I pushed them down, not yet ready or able to completely explore their meaning.

It would take more time for me to realize that confronting personal pain is something we'd rather not do. In fact, most of us would prefer a root canal without anesthesia than embark on the grueling process of self-discovery that is required. At this juncture, I thought I'd safely hidden my pain under the thick concrete of religious performance and achievement. I would need a muse.

VALDEZ, ALASKA

We turned south in Tok and headed for Valdez to fish the historic silver run. The purple snowcapped mountains of the Coastal Range towered above us, and we marveled. Scanning the clouds and pale blue bay below, I visualized Moon out in the cold water, helping to clean the shores from an eleven-million-gallon oil spill.

Next morning, standing on the rocks, casting away with my baitcaster and a #5 blue-and-silver Vibrax spinner, feeling a bit guilty I had put my fly rod aside for the moment, I managed to hook and land a couple of nice silvers.

From behind, I detected a very discernable Southern accent. "Any silvers in here yet?"

I realized, *That's not just a Southern accent, that's a central Mississippi accent!*

For years, Moon had told me about Bobby Dale and June Martin from nearby Weir, Mississippi.

"Bobby Dale Martin is an excellent fisherman. He and June fish the Kenai every year, and they usually fish the silver run in Valdez."

I took a chance, turned around, and said, "Bobby Dale Martin!"

Bobby Dale looked surprised and confused.

"I'm Shane Sunn, Moon Sunn's son, from Colorado."

Try that for a confusing tongue twister. Bobby Dale did a double-take as his mind caught up with my risky presumptive introduction. Jean was standing beside me, so I introduced them.

"This is my wife, Jean."

"Good to meet you."

"Good to meet you, too, Bobby Dale! I've heard a lot about you."

We fished together the following morning.

When I met June, she laughed out loud and said, "Let me tell you what happened last night."

"What?"

"Yesterday evenin', Bobby Dale came into the camper all excited and said, 'Guess who I just met!?' I said, 'I have no earthly idea.' Bobby Dale said, 'I just met Moon's son and his wife.'"

June confided, "I thought he meant, 'I just met Moon Sunn and his wife!' I said to Bobby Dale, 'Moon got married? I'd never thought that'd happen in a thousand years!' Bobby Dale looked at me kinda funny and said, 'No, Moon's son's wife.' I said, 'Who?' Still confused, I asked Bobby Dale again, 'Who did you meet?' He answered, 'I met Moon's son, and he introduced me to his wife.' Finally figuring it out, I said, "Oh."

June then turned to me and, seemingly without changing the subject, said, "You've got to write a book about Moon!"

"Yeah, yeah, I know."

Bobby Dale, June Martin, and me in Valdez, Alaska.

June's words drilled through another crusty layer of my heart that I knew by now I was attempting to resist. As we cast away, in the thin line between the gray ocean and sky, my mind's eye could see Moon there in the distance doing the same.

"Oh, by the way, here's Greg Calloway's number. He said he'd like to see y'all when you're in Soldotna."

McCarthy, Alaska

After a wonderful but rainy time in Valdez, we said goodbye to the Martins and headed north to an airstrip near Chitina, Alaska.

The plane bounced as it landed, turned around, and taxied toward us. We were bound for McCarthy, Alaska, to meet our friends Austin and Shannon Robel, former parishioners from St. Patrick Presbyterian Church in Greeley, Colorado. During Alaskan summers, Shannon runs a gift shop near the abandoned Kennecott Copper Mines. Austin is a tour pilot and part-owner of Wrangell Mountain Air, offering daily tour flights of the Wrangell-St. Elias Mountain National Park and Preserve. Austin and Shannon are fun-loving, wonderful folks.

Austin, Shannon, and Linde Robel in McCarthy, Alaska.

Exploring the Kennecott Copper Mines, we were transformed into history buffs and rockhounds. We hiked to a nearby glacier field and checked out the ice caves, the Robles' adorable daughter, Linde, riding atop Austin's shoulders. The iridescent light, filtered by layers of compressed ice, glimmered cobalt blue, eliciting a surreal sensation. We stood there in awe, attempting to avoid a cold shower from the water drops falling from the top of the ice cave. The drops splattered against the rocky floor, joined the small stream, and began their long journey to the ocean—drops from the layers of my icy heart continued to melt and join them.

Jean and me in a glacier cave.

After a yummy burrito from a food truck, Austin took us up in his plane. We flew over glacier fields; you could see downward into giant dark-split crevasses plummeting hundreds of feet into the glacier. We flew right beside towering cliffs. I felt like I could reach out and touch the granite mountains with my hand. I was mildly terrified.

Austin, part daredevil, banked the plane, straightened out, and then pulled back on the sticks. We climbed up and over a high peak. The plane rattled and shook, buffeted by the strong wind currents bending over the peak. The distinct possibility of death entered my mind as I twitched from one butt cheek to the other. I was a bit annoyed that Jean seemed just fine.

"Austin, what happens if you run into engine trouble up here?"

Austin smiled, "See that river down there in the valley?"

I looked across the plane out the left window, and far below, a serpentine river, cut by millions of years of glacier melt, wound through the valley as far as the eye could see.

View from the Robels' airplane.

"Yeah, I see it."

"If the engine quit, I'd glide the plane on the currents and land on the flat ground beside the river."

Not the least bit comforting, I mumbled, "Yeah, well good."

Continuing to stare at the river below, partly to avoid looking ahead, I thought about the timeless salmon. I thought about Moon.

SOLDOTNA, ALASKA

We waved goodbyes. Shannon, Austin, and Linde taxied on the runway, gained velocity, and lifted into the Alaskan sky. Lingering until the plane's wings became tiny white specks against the distant towering mountains, we headed for Centennial Campground and the Kenai River.

Turning right on Centennial Park Road, we bounced along over numerous jarring potholes. I was momentarily ridin' shotgun in the old blue-on-blue Dodge. We picked a site in the almost-empty campground; the rain poured down.

Next morning, I pulled on my waders and zipped my raincoat and headed for the river. The campground was much different, a widened paved parking lot and boat ramp, bathhouses, restrooms, and a fish-cleaning facility, metal boardwalks providing access for bank fishermen and habitat protection for spawning salmon.

The fish can wait. As if propelled by the wind, I journeyed back in time to 1982. I slowly meandered to the area that would have been the original campground. I expected to hear Moses jabbering away on his CB radio. But the old rusty white scale and the hippies were all gone. I remembered the evening campfires, the revelry, Leroy, and the Bard.

GREG CALLOWAY

I called Greg.

He asked, "Wanna go fishing tomorrow morning in my boat?"

"Sure!"

"Okay, I'll be down there before daylight. Meet me at the boat ramp; dress warm."

"Okay, see you in the morning."

Greg hadn't changed much in thirty-five years. Reacquaintance was easy; we shared a common story. Between Greg's scheduled guide trips, we fished together every day for five consecutive days. We motored past the big island, remembering the canoe trip and the bear. The Kenai was different, lined with homes, docks, and outfitters.

Greg anchored the boat across the river from the house Charles built. I asked questions. Greg told me about the day they decided to sell the house and move back to Mississippi. As we landed silver after silver, he told me about Charles and Alice's divorce and their eventual deaths. I ached a familiar ache for Greg. I listened somewhere between the pain of the story and the elation of the catch.

Greg Calloway and me after a day of fishing.

Greg said, "After those years in Mississippi, I decided to move back up here because this is where I grew up. I guess I could never quite get this river out of my blood."

THE NORTHERN LIGHTS

After a week on the Kenai, we journeyed north to Denali National Park and Preserve, still hoping to catch a glimpse of the Northern Lights. The first evening, I was greeted by a personal visit from the stomach bug. So, we camped well south of our planned destination and turned in early. Next morning, feeling much better but ravenous, we decided to enjoy a breakfast of sourdough pancakes and maple syrup at a local roadside establishment.

On one of the tables, I zeroed in on the headlines of a local newspaper: "Brilliant Early Display of the Aurora Last Evening—high probability of repeat occurrences the next several evenings."

"Dang it, look at this, Jean! If I hadn't been sick, we would have seen the Northern Lights."

I downloaded the "Live thirty-minute Aurora forecast," from NOAA on my cellphone. The nifty app provides real-time probability of seeing the Aurora, based on current location. We were hopeful.

After our delicious breakfast, we toured the park, enjoying its history, especially petting the sled dogs. After an early dinner, we drove north toward Fairbanks. Like a man possessed, I constantly monitored cell reception so we could receive live Aurora updates.

"Watch the road!"

"I'm watching the road!"

I wasn't.

We searched for the perfect campsite without trees so we could maximize our view of the eagerly anticipated experience. Just before dark, we discovered the perfect place. We pulled in, and while Jean fixed dinner, I built a campfire and positioned our camp chairs. We ate by the fire and waited. I constantly monitored the live updates—probability still good.

"Clouds, dang it."

Jean grew skeptical; I grew more determined to wait it out, hoping the clouds would clear.

At midnight, Jean announced, "I'm sleepy," and headed for bed.

I said, "I'll join you in just a bit."

I lied. I gathered more firewood and dozed on and off in the camp chair until 3:00 a.m.

After a shortened night of sleep, the next morning, Jean asked, "Did you ever see anything?"

"Well, I thought I got just a glimpse around 2:00 a.m., but I couldn't really see through the clouds."

We left around noon, and the scenario repeated itself almost exactly the next evening, except this time, we didn't have cell coverage. At least I could watch the road and not obsess on my cellphone app. Another cloudy evening.

Next day, progressing down the ALCAN and into the Yukon, we arrived at Kluane Lake late in the afternoon. Jean checked *The Milepost* for the best suggested campground. We pulled in. The almost-full campground only had a few available sites, all under a thick canopy of trees. We decided to move on. Near the south end of the lake, we discovered an obscure winding road and followed it. It ended on a flat rocky shelf beside the water, overlooking the enormous lake. Alone together beside the mysterious lake, breathtaking mountain vistas in every direction, a bright starry night, the heavens unobscured, I announced, "Ideal!" I surmised, *No wonder we've not seen the Aurora yet. God has been saving this exact spot just for us.*

It was cold. I gathered arms of dry driftwood and built a warm fire, and we sat down and waited. We observed amazing meteor showers, but the Northern Lights hid themselves. Jean went to bed; I repeated the 3:00 a.m. routine. Frustrated and sleepy, I slowly conceded.

Next morning, I told Jean, "The farther south we drive, the less our chances of seeing the Northern Lights."

"You should give up."

"Yeah, maybe."

NORTHERN BRITISH COLUMBIA

Early October, crisp blue autumn skies, yellow and golden birches and aspens aglow, we continued our slow journey down the ALCAN. In the late afternoons, snowshoe hares nibbled on the grass beside the road. I remembered. We pulled over beside the cobalt and green Toad River. Jean read, wrote, and painted. I fly-fished for graylings. I kept a couple for dinner.

That evening, we located an "off-the-grid" secluded campground, six miles off the ALCAN, at the end of a scary dark road. We weren't surprised we were the only ones there. I poached the graylings in an iron skillet and prepared a rich white wine cream sauce topping. Dinner finished, I let Archie out to do his business before bedtime.

"Jean, come here!"

As we stood in silent awe under a dazzling display of the Northern Lights, my last vestiges of resistance melted and joined the river of stories that must be told. I leaned close. "Sweetie, I have to write the book."

MID-OCTOBER 2017, BERKELEY, CALIFORNIA

Hearts full, we increased our pace, arriving in Denver two days later. I spent several days unpacking camping gear, washing and waxing our bug-splattered camper, and preparing for the next leg of our sabbatical, which focused on time alone to reflect and write. Two days later, I flew to San Francisco and drove to a private retreat center in Berkeley for four full days of reflection. In the mornings, I read, and on sunny afternoons, I hung out in cool coffee shops and continued the process of writing these stories, some of which had already begun a month prior on our journey through Alaska. Sitting outside a coffee shop on the second afternoon, I noticed a small independent bookstore next door. I've never seen a bookstore I didn't like, so I sacked up my journals and ventured in. Perusing the shelves, a new edition of *A River Runs Through It* caught my eye. I purchased it, and the next morning read the entire story in one sitting.

This time, Norman's elegant and poetic description of the story's origin penetrated my soul. I paused, read, and reread it three times. His comment that "stories of life are more like rivers than books" haunted me, and the acknowledgment that his story had begun years before Paul's death "near the sound of water" nudged me forward, and I knew "up ahead there would be sharp turns, deep circles, a deposit, and quietness."[16] That afternoon at the coffee shop, the bones of this story came together from somewhere deep within, and I wrote furiously.

LEO ROSTEN

Upon further reflection, although I didn't know what was happening at the time, this story had begun years before, when I was a bit bored. It was around the holidays, and we were visiting Jean's parents. I pulled a volume of *Reader's Digest Condensed Books* from the bookshelf and thumbed through it. A story by Leo Rosten (best known for his popularization of Yiddish) caught my eye, "People I Have Loved, Known, or Admired."[17]

Rosten's opening lines sucked me in, "We buried my father not long ago, and wayward memories of him—a laugh, a sigh, a smile—keep washing over my mind in unexpected wavelets. He was a simple man, without a shred of pretentiousness or self-righteousness. His tastes were innocent, his desires easily satisfied."

I kept reading. "He made no demands on anyone, he paid the highest respect to plain character. His greatest praise was to say of someone, 'There is a prince.' I think he meant to say, 'a prince of a fellow.' But he only said, 'a prince.' He loved the water and spent a thousand happy hours on its shores, in Michigan, California, and Florida."

Of course, Rosten's description reminded me of Moon. I pulled the ball cap I was wearing down to cover my eyes, slumped in the sofa, and continued, "The last time I saw him, he was in a hospital again, in Chicago, under the canopy of an oxygen tent, propped up dozing. My wife and I said good-bye to

---

16 Norman Maclean, *A River Runs Through It* (Chicago: University of Chicago Press, 2017), 73.

17 Leo Rosten, "People I Have Loved, Known, or Admired," *Reader's Digest Condensed Books*, Volume 87, Autumn 1971.

him, but he could not hear us. I blew him a kiss. I did not think he saw it. But he had. He nodded and made a wry, wrinkled up grimace—the face he always made when he said, 'Don't worry about me,' 'Don't wait,' or 'Go home now.' Then he managed to raise 2 fingers to his lips and blew me a kiss in return."

By now, I felt tears forming in my eyes, so I excused myself to the bathroom and continued to read. "He was a dear kind gentleman and I loved him. After he was dead, I swam a lot, every day. You weep in the water, and when you come out red-eyed, people attribute it to the swimming. The sea my father loved is a fine place for crying and so is the indoor pool in which I swim in the winter. And now, as I write this, adding to what I wrote before, it is over 4 years since my father died, and I still ache when I think of him. I never knew how much you can miss someone. I miss him more than anyone I have ever known. It pleased him to be with me, and it was so simple and happy for me to be with him. How very much of him lives on in my mind—so vividly; and portions of him rush into unexpected recollection at the oddest moments. And then I hear myself crying, 'Oh Papa, Papa, you were a prince.'"

Locked inside the safety of the bathroom, a flood of tears streamed down my face. Since that day, I've always wondered what I will do and how I will react when I receive the news of Moon's passing to the fishing grounds above. Today, as I already hesitantly anticipate the coming inevitability, my mind sees Moon in his distinct stealthlike movements on his quest for the next fish. I could easily pick him out of a crowd of a hundred anglers. Leo swam; I know I will go fishin'. And I know if I happen to hook and land a nice fish, my heart will say to him like Moon said over and over to Mack, "Look, Daddy, I caught this one for you."

However, he's eighty-five and slowing down in some ways, but in others, still going strong. I guess it must be the cod-liver oil! He wore out his right shoulder from too many overhand casts over the years. For almost a year, he could barely lift his right arm. But like his wrist injury many years before, he improvised and learned and perfected the two-handed method of casting. Heck, he drove himself from Mississippi to Alaska last year to fish the silver run and see his granddaughter, Mary, and her husband, Kyle. So today, all I can say is, "Look, Daddy, I wrote this one for you."

"That rod and reel enables you to feel the fight and power of the fish."

Frank Sinatra did it his way. You did it your way. Daddy, you don't need anybody to tell you this, but you are the best there ever was at what you did and how you did it. You are truly the king of the Kenai.

Moon fly-fishing in the fog with a salmon on.

EPILOGUE

WE ASCENDED MOON'S DRIVEWAY on Louisville Street in our rental car. Spring had not fully arrived. There were no buds on the pecans; their branches resembled dark ink sketches against the gray sky. But there were signs of spring: blotchy patches of green grass and brilliant daffodils. We walked through the garage past the yellow canoe and entered the fishing temple. We sat around awhile and looked at old pictures. It got quiet, Moon was tired, and Jean and I were too.

Then, Moon broke the silence. "Last summer when I went up there to find Mary and Kyle in Homer, I didn't do too much plannin'. I just thought about it one day and left the next. I was doin' just fine, but when I got 'bout ninety miles from Tok, the truck started runnin' rough and losin' power. It sounded like 'plump, plump, plump,' and maybe would only go about twenty-five miles per hour. I kept goin', and when I fine'lee got to Tok, I saw a garage and pulled in.

"Tok's a pretty good-sized town, and they had two or three garages, so I just picked one out. A man walked out and listened to the truck runnin' for a minute and said, 'You've got some kind of trouble.'

"What they said the main trouble was, wouldn't the spark plugs, but the wires that transferred the power. The wires were cooked; they are down in a hole, and it's the worse design I've ever seen.

"This was a Monday, and they said, 'We might be able to get to it Friday.' So, I just sat around and didn't do much of nothin'. I bought my fishin' licenses to save a little time. I sat around the fishin' shop and talked. But mainly, what I did in Tok was just wait. They put me in four new spark plugs and tried to patch the wires, and they fine'lee got it runnin'.

"When I left there, it was runnin' pretty good. I didn't do too good this year on the silvers. I fished on the Homer Spit. I pulled the truck right in there behind the sign that says 'No Campin'.' Didn't nobody ever say a word to me 'bout that. I caught 'em real good the first couple of days. The trouble with the fishin' up there this year was it was too sunny. The fish knew I was out there. I could see them, but the problem was they could see me too. If it had been cloudy, I could have tricked 'em. I caught most of 'em when the tide started goin' out.

"When I started this year, I said, 'This will be my last trip,' but since I didn't do so good, I think I'm goin' back next year."

"Daddy, Jean and I plan on going to Alaska this summer to see Mary and Kyle. We're planning on flying, but if you will drive out to Denver, we'll drive, and you can ride with us. We have plenty of room."

"What that'd do would make me have to depend on y'all, and I couldn't quite do that. I'd be better off not dependin' on nobody."

Moon quickly changed the conversation in his non-subtle fashion.

"If you gonna fish the kings, the cheapest place to buy fishin' tackle is that Trustworthy Hardware right up there above the bridge on the main drag in Soldotna. That's where I bought this rod, and it's just like the rods I used to make. This rod is supposed to be about ten and a half foot long. And you need a reel about like this, and I like mine to reel back'ards. I got used to takin' the brakes out, and I can't fish any other way. I don't fish much like that anymore; I like to catch 'em on the fly rod. If you can wait a little bit, and if you're ever up there in September, they'll have more stuff on sale for cheaper than any other place you could ever buy it.

"I like to read them old fishin' magazines. I was readin' one the other day about brackish water fishin' on the Spain River that borders between Louisiana and Texas. It might all be in Texas; I'm not sure. The article talked about fly-fishin', and the writer caught largemouth, redfish, grinnell, speckled trout, and sheepshead, all on the fly rod. One day, I think I'm gonna go down there and try it out. I carried some of them crappie I caught the other day by Maury's and gave some to Webb O'Bryant."

I see blue skies and lots of mysterious edible fish up ahead—Mack, Moon, and the bank fishermen glistening in the sun beside the water.

ACKNOWLEDGMENTS

UNTIL A MUCH-NEEDED SABBATICAL in 2017, I filled most of my "space" with endless activity. Thanks to the Lilly Endowment for Clergy Renewal and to perceptive parishioners—Cindy Day, Laura Grouthius, and Jared Wallen—who took time out of their busy schedules to help write and perfect the sabbatical application, I was granted leave. They knew I needed quiet space. I was naïve for what awaited.

Writers need space, quiet space, to listen, reflect, and write. A slow pace through northwestern Canada and southeastern Alaska, the path of my 1982 trip with Moon and Christia, provided the space I needed to listen and reflect. Jean, my amazing wife, was by my side, encouraging and nudging me forward. The astounding beauty surrounding us and the rhythmic motion of my fly rod worked their magic, and bits and pieces of this story bubbled to the surface.

A subsequent trip to Berkeley and a sit-down with *A River Runs Through It* propelled the writing forward. But then, I reentered busy space and all but parked the pen. When a worldwide pandemic began in late 2019 and COVID-19 emerged, I was reluctantly again forced to reenter the space of quiet and the not-too-busy. Maybe COVID afforded too much space! The

Sunn clan's proclivity for history, my inexperience with memoir, and with writing, for that matter, combined to produce a very large and unwieldy manuscript. I wrote one hundred and seventy thousand words; thirty thousand of those were endnotes!

Bobby Haas, my initial developmental editor, commented, "What you have here is an encyclopedia. In the future, if anyone wants to write a story about your dad, your book will be the primary source!" After all the work, that was hard to hear, but undoubtedly true. Patience is a virtue, but it isn't one of mine. I'm much better at busy and stubborn. Thanks goes to friends Joe Maxwell and Jim Wood for their encouragement and constructive criticism during this time as I sought to rearrange and trim the encyclopedia. And then, I was provided an angel in the form of my current editor, Donna Mazzitelli. Her undying patience, encouragement, and expertise were truly a Godsend.

This past year, I posted some initial book excerpts, and like the epiphany I experienced during Moon's Silver Alert in 2012, I was again amazed at how much Moon means to so many. People, encouragements to keep writing, and new "Moon-stories" literally came out of the woodwork. I'm indebted to past and present citizens of Ackerman and Choctaw County, Mississippi, for their influence in my life and for sharing their stories.

Thanks to John David and Martha Adams, Larry Prewitt, Ed Sallis, Pam Watson, Jerry Sanders, John Robinson, Bobby Dale and June Martin, Robin McMinn, and to Moon's former history students and school bus riders. Thanks to Kelly Swick for her research on the Arkansas "Son" family. And thanks to Catherine Retzlaff for her encouragement throughout the process. Thanks to Greg Calloway and my sister, Christia, who've walked parts of this exhilarating and sometimes painful journey with me. And lastly, thanks to Norman Maclean for sharing his story of pain against a backdrop so familiar and with such lyrical power that it opened me to mine.

ABOUT THE AUTHOR

THE REVEREND SHANE SUNN resides in Denver, Colorado, with his wife, Jean, and their yellow Labrador, Archie. The Sunns have four grown children. In his spare time, the reverend guides elk hunters and fly fishers. To learn more about Shane Sunn, be sure to visit ShaneSunnAuthor.com.